The Social Development of the Intellect

INTERNATIONAL SERIES IN EXPERIMENTAL SOCIAL PSYCHOLOGY

Series Editor: Michael Argyle, University of Oxford

NOTICE TO READERS

Dear Reader

An Invitation to Publish in and Recommend the Placing of a Standing Order to Volumes Published in this Valuable Series.

If your library is not already a standing/continuation order customer to this series, may we recommend that you place a standing/continuation order to receive immediately upon publication all new volumes. Should you find that these volumes no longer serve your needs, your order can be cancelled at any time without notice.

The Editors and the Publisher will be glad to receive suggestions or outlines of suitable titles, reviews or symposia for editorial consideration: if found acceptable, rapid publication is guaranteed.

ROBERT MAXWELL
Publisher at Pergamon Press

The Social Development of the Intellect

by

WILLEM DOISE and **GABRIEL MUGNY**
University of Geneva

Translated by

Angela St. James-Emler and Nicholas Emler
University of Dundee

with the collaboration of
Diane Mackie
University of Princeton

PERGAMON PRESS
OXFORD · NEW YORK · TORONTO · SYDNEY · PARIS · FRANKFURT

U.K.	Pergamon Press Ltd., Headington Hill Hall, Oxford OX3 0BW, England
U.S.A.	Pergamon Press Inc., Maxwell House, Fairview Park, Elmsford, New York 10523, U.S.A.
CANADA	Pergamon Press Canada Ltd., Suite 104, 150 Consumers Road, Willowdale, Ontario M2J 1P9, Canada
AUSTRALIA	Pergamon Press (Aust.) Pty. Ltd., P.O. Box 544, Potts Point, N.S.W. 2011, Australia
FRANCE	Pergamon Press SARL, 24 rue des Ecoles, 75240 Paris, Cedex 05, France
FEDERAL REPUBLIC OF GERMANY	Pergamon Press GmbH, Hammerweg 6, D-6242 Kronberg-Taunus, Federal Republic of Germany

First edition 1984

Library of Congress Cataloging in Publication Data
Doise, Willem, 1935–
The social development of the intellect.
(International series in experimental social psychology; v. 9)
Translation of: L'développement social de l'intelligence.
Bibliography: p.
Includes index.
1. Intellect—Social aspects.   2. Cognition in children.
3. Social interaction in children.   I. Mugny, Gabriel.
II. Title.   III. Series.
BF431.D5413   1984   155.4'13   84-9227

British Library Cataloguing in Publication Data
Doise, Willem
The social development of the intellect.—(International series in experimental social psychology; v. 10)
1. Intellect—Social aspects
I. Title   II. Mugny, Gabriel   III. Series
153.9'2   BF431
ISBN 0-08-030209-2 Hardcover
ISBN 0-08-030215-7 Flexicover

First published in France under the title 'Le Développe-ment Social de l'Intelligence' by Willem Doise & Gabriel Mugny © 1981 InterEditions, Paris.

A. Wheaton & Co. Ltd., Exeter

Foreword

In the field of intelligence, as in other areas in the human sciences, there are several possible approaches to the same phenomenon, each one generating its own explanation. Psychologists and sociologists, for example, resort to numerous analytic frameworks to grasp the various aspects of a complex reality. Thus psychologists are interested in the cognitive organisation that underlies the individual's behaviour, whilst sociologists are more likely to study the dynamics of differentiation which allow some social environments to produce more 'intelligent' children than others. It is not disputed that each of these approaches is legitimate; intelligence is clearly both an organisation of individual behaviour and an institutionalised social characteristic. But if we speak about intelligence in several 'tongues', it still does not seem possible to 'translate' one into the other. It remains for us to interrelate analyses of individual dynamics with those of social dynamics. This is the principal aim of the present work.

The first chapter will consider the limits of different explanatory systems of intelligence. Advancing beyond these limitations will, in the second chapter, call for a social definition of cognitive development. The following chapters will develop and illustrate this social definition of intelligence experimentally. In fact, there are more than twenty experiments to show how social interaction, not only between children, but also between child and adult, can be an especially important context for cognitive development.

This book is intended not only for psychologists and social psychologists, but for all those interested in the cognitive development of individuals. Readers who are unfamiliar with experimentation and with statistical language should not be put off. This book presupposes no profound knowledge of experimental procedures. With regard to statistics, it is sufficient to understand that the normal statistical thresholds (indicated by $P<0.05$ or 0.01, for example) refer to a probability of obtaining purely by chance the observed differences between experimental conditions of less than 5% or 1%, when these differences are in the direction hypothesised. In other words, the lower the probability indicated, the greater the certainty with which the differences obtained can be considered as actually resulting from the influence of the experimentally introduced variations between the different conditions.[1]

---

[1] All the statistical calculations and subject classifications were redone for this book. We have in some cases adopted new criteria to ensure that the analyses of the different experiments would be comparable. For further information on the statistical tests used, one may refer to Leach (1979). Unless otherwise indicated, the significance levels are for one-tailed tests.

To elaborate a theory of cognitive development is itself, according to the central thesis of this book, a social activity. This work has in fact resulted from a genuine collaboration between the two authors, who have co-ordinated their efforts with those of A. N. Perret-Clermont (1980a). Le Fonds Suisse de la Recherche Scientifique has made possible much of the research described here, while the published reports have been co-authored with various collaborators (see Table at the end of Chapter 2). They must all be thanked, as must our colleagues at the universities of Auckland (New Zealand), Barcelona (Spain), Bologna (Italy) and Tilburg (Holland), who have suggested variations in our paradigms and have enriched the social conception of intelligence presented here.[2]

W.D. and G.M.

[2]We would also like to acknowledge here our thanks to the Department of Public Instruction in Geneva who gave permission for much of the research reported here, to the teachers who allowed us into their classes, and to the pupils who participated in our research.

Preface

One tends to feel almost confused by the richness and diversity of the studies on the psychology of the child that have been and are still being carried out. Some, under the impetus of psychoanalysis, are primarily devoted to the blossoming of the child's affective life as it develops against a background of family relationships. Other studies, extending the work of Piaget, attempt to provide better descriptions, if not explanations, of the mental and moral development of individuals. For the sake of completeness, one may also define a third trend, of mixed origins, which describes in detail the beginnings of the child's principal competencies, its recognition of a face or an object, attachment to the mother or other person and so on. Such studies show marked traces of ethology. However, in spite of the reverses, attacks and critiques to which they have been subjected, the ideas of Piaget still predominate. And at present there is not even a remote sign of their being replaced. But, as in many other current ideas in psychology, there is a gap between declared principles and achievements – or at least, in relation to one principle, that of the social factor. For example, in considering thought or language, it is frequently and variously asserted that these are social phenomena historically generated and incorporated within collective existence. But these assertions having been made, either as introductions or declarations of intent, are then forgotten or at least they never emerge in actual research or in theoretical explanations. This major contradiction marks much of contemporary science. Nevertheless, we do from time to time find researchers who seem to take the social factor seriously and try to reduce the contradiction. One such worker was Labov, who attempted to create a sociolinguistic system which would re-establish language within its position in society. And this is also the case with Doise and Mugny and their coworkers in Geneva, who have sought to identify, within the development of intelligence as described by Piaget, the dynamics of relations which might account for it. Although they are not the first to have contemplated such an identification, they have, so to speak, taken the bull by the horns and achieved much, and with some success. This clear and well-thought-out book contains the results of very remarkable research carried out over several years which we are sure deserves to be made known to a wider public, not only to child psychologists but also to educationalists, sociologists, doctors and indeed all those interested in the development of ideas in this field.

S. Moscovici

Contents

1

The social significance of the study of intelligence

The success of intelligence tests and their use in the identification of the gifted and the retarded has turned these tests into a real social institution. Debates among specialists, whether on the different roles of heredity and environment in intellectual development, or on possible differences between the intellectual capacities of various social, cultural and ethnic groups, have become public and even political debates. Thus scientific techniques and research have taken on a social significance without any similar appreciation of the weaknesses in research methods or the weakness of the statistical data put forward as evidence in such debates.

At a more theoretical level there exist two very different approaches to the scientific study of intelligence, one more psychological, the other more sociological. For a French-speaking audience these two approaches are represented by two names, Piaget and Bourdieu. The first studied intelligence, and particularly its development, as a characteristic of the individual. The second studied the social determinants of the expression of intelligence in society, that is academic success. These two approaches have developed separately; each has attracted attention through its coherence (and systematisation) but neither has tried to incorporate the contribution of the other. Their analytic frameworks have been devised to deal with very different problems; one is about the study of individual dynamics, the other about those of society; the one clarifies what the other leaves in the background.

Piaget makes only very general assertions about the origins of differences in cognitive development as between individuals or groups. Thus, the differences between individuals are believed to be due to heredity: 'There is certainly a hereditary factor in the functioning of the intellect in the sense that no one has ever succeeded in raising the level of intelligence either of an average individual or of a defective one'. (1980: p. 80). Elsewhere, various sociocultural differences are explained in terms of the nature of interindividual interactions rather than in terms of the educational inequality of different groups: 'We may note that Boisclair has, together with Laurendeau and Pinard, begun in Martinique, the examination of a population of pupils who were far from being illiterate, since they are pursuing a primary school education based on the French programme, but who showed a backwardness of about four years on the main operational tests of intelligence; in this case the backwardness seems clearly to be due to general characteristics of social interaction . . . rather than to a deficiency in education'. (1966: p. 10). We can be certain that these social inequalities in Martinique would be given a different kind of explanation by Bourdieu. Nevertheless, remarks of this kind by Piaget contrast with his detailed analyses of cognitive development; such assertions do not explain, as they must, the mechanisms by which differences between individuals or between groups arise.

Bourdieu's analyses also leave questions unanswered. Certainly, society reproduces itself and the school plays an important part in perpetuating social inequalities; but one can arrive at conclusions of this kind without making a detailed study of the cognitive functioning of children from different social backgrounds. Bourdieu and his collaborators assert that the ways in which people present themselves, in which they talk and in which they master certain 'cultivated manners' differentiate pupils within the educational system, with the result that some are more successful than others. Do such differences in cultural capital have repercussions reaching as far as the cognitive operations studied by Piaget? The theory of reproduction does not even need to pose the question.

If we still have no link between the psychology and the sociology of cognitive development, if a kind of theoretical vacuum still exists between these two systems of explanation, society – and that includes the intellectuals – is not going to wait for the elaboration of a unified theory to fill this void before constructing its own social representations of intelligence. The application of intelligence testing, scientific controversies that are also ideological debates, influential scientific works, all without apparent links, provide the rough outlines for such social representations. It has been shown in the field of psychoanalysis (Moscovici, 1961) how different social groups construct different social representations out of the same theoretical standpoint. This standpoint fragments under the pressure of social dynamics arising from the specific positions occupied by different groups within a sociocultural domain. In the representation of intelligence such fragmentation is already present in the various scientific approaches. In effect a powerful social determinism ensures that all representations of intelligence, even those that emerge from scientific research, are shot through with tensions and oppositions.

Thus, in Ancient Egypt a division of labour between 'manuals' and 'intellectuals' had already led the scribes to contrast the advantages of their profession with the inconveniences of manual work and to indoctrinate their pupils with arguments of the following kind:

– thou shouldst set thy heart in pursuit of writing. And I have observed how one may be rescued from his duties (sic!) – behold there is nothing which surpasses writing . . .
– I have seen the metal worker at his work at the mouth of his furnace. His fingers were somewhat like crocodiles; he stank more than fish-roe . . .
The small building contractor carried mud . . . He is dirtier than vines or pigs from treading under his mud. His clothes are stiff with clay . . .
The arrow-maker, he is very miserable as he goes out into the desert (to get flint points). Greater is that which he gives to his donkey than its work thereafter (in worth) . . .
The laundry man launders on the (river) bank, a neighbour of the crocodile . . .
Behold there is no profession free of a boss – except for the scribe: he is the boss . . .
Behold there is no scribe who lacks food from the property of the House of the King-life, prosperity, health! . . .
His father and his mother praise God, he being set upon the way of the living.
Behold these things – I (have set them) before thee and thy children's children.

Quoted in Donaldson (1978: p. 84)

With others, Moscovici has no hesitation in seeing in the division between intellectuals and manual labourers a source of inequality that persists even in socialist societies:

> The equity which these societies have wished to introduce will remain beyond reach however (. . .) so long as the means of production maintain, among other things, a division of labour as between manual occupations and intellectual tasks. The separation of workers 'with the hands' and 'with the brain', of doers and rulers, preserves a divide which tends to perpetuate itself, the children of each category following the careers of their parents and harvesting the advantages or disadvantages of their position (. . .) Eliminating the consequences of this situation by other means of redistributing wealth would be ineffective. It would be necessary to transform work itself, acting on the sum and structure of knowledge created up to the present. A definitive solution resides in the invention of new skills, of another apparatus of production, of different exchanges with matter. From this the conviction that 'technical progress is the principal means of reconciliation between manual and intellectual work' (. . .). Progress is presented as the symbol of a new end state, overcoming millenary divisions, in societies that seek to institute collective relations founded on the harmonious association of human groups.

(1968: p. 9, translation)

It is also suggested that in socialist countries an intellectual caste has appropriated political power and that this historical fact explains the perpetuation of their privileges (Konrad and Szelenyi, 1979).

In all societies where a contrast between intellectuals and manual workers provides the basis for social division, the evaluation and appraisal of intelligence are invested with considerable social importance. It is not therefore surprising that judgements about the intellectual capacities of individuals are strongly influenced by those individuals' social backgrounds. Thus, for example, (Bourdieu and De Saint-Martin, 1975), in Paris in a prestigious higher school, negative appraisals are frequently made of provincial pupils while more positive ones are made of pupils with a background of Parisian intelligentsia; the work of the former will be described as 'simple, inane, servile, vulgar, insipid, flat, heavy, turgid . . .'; the latter are more likely to write essays that are 'clever, ingenious, subtle, intelligent, cultivated, personal, lively, and showing mastery, philosophical quest and spirit.' Such contrasts persist even in the obituary notices for former pupils of the Ecole

Normale Supérieure; sons of peasants, labourers and lower grade clerical workers are frequently described as resigned, discreet, ascetic, simple, modest, whilst the sons of professors or of people actually from the Ecole Normale Supérieure are more often said to be clever, delicate, brilliant, bright, intelligent, rigorous, spiritual, lucid, original, creative, and are identified as writers, poets, essayists, men of learning, great philosophers, theoreticians, masters.

If such contrasts persist in the assessment of individuals despite their success in a stringent selection process, it is because they reflect the stereotyped views of a culture which postulates the existence of a link between social origins and cognitive competence. In this area, as in others, the exceptions are used only to prove the rule. Is it possible to escape from simplifications which only serve to reproduce an established order and ensure the transmission of privileges to those who are already the designated *heirs*, (Bourdieu and Passeron, 1964)?

One might have hoped that the scientific and objective study of intelligence would help to settle debates in which the social consequences are so significant. In fact, the issue of possible differences in cognitive capacity between individuals belonging to different social groups will be resolved only if one has available a clear definition and a flawless measure of intelligence. The two dominant traditions in the study of intelligence – one inspired by Piaget and the other based on the use of tests – aim to provide such a definition and to elaborate such instruments of measurement or diagnosis. Now, as we see it, they are far from providing a convincing answer to the question of possible differences between social groups. On the contrary, their concern to 'desocialise' the problem of intelligence has led them either to neglect the study of social factors in the growth of intelligence or to use biological factors to explain differences that are clearly a function of social dynamics.

The Piagetian tradition

If any study of intelligence has been acknowledged as scientific, it is that of Piaget and his school. Now his work does not treat intelligence as a social issue. Some critics even suggest that this work reinforces social discrimination in the area of intelligence:

> everything occurs as if to the subject's ontogenetic development (temporal variable) came to be combined a variable locating the subject on a scale in which socioeconomic categories and 'civilisations' appear metaphorically, like more or less 'evolved' *social species*, in the sense that the theory of phylogenetic evolution gives to this term.
> Haroche and Pêcheux (1972: p. 104, translation)

According to some, a perspective on class is expressed in various of Piaget's writings. On the one hand he asserts that a favourable environment and the liberal educational style of an advantaged background lead to cognitive autonomy, decentration and reciprocity; and on the other hand, an unfavourable environment and the authoritarian educational style of a disadvantaged background lead to cognitive heteronomy and egocentrism. This particular reading of Piaget refers to the criticisms commonly aimed at Bernstein's work and in particular his distinction between elaborated and restricted codes, the former associated with more privileged social groups, the latter more characteristic of disadvantaged backgrounds.

Such critiques well indicate the social significance of all study of intelligence; they derive from a legitimate mistrust of all hierarchical classifications of cultures or subcultures, the social implications of which are quite enormous.

We accept, with Piaget, a developmental view of individual intelligence and we will return to this in the following chapter. But we do not adhere to a hierarchical division of cultures or subcultures as expressed in assertions such as: 'in many societies, adult thought does not progress beyond the level of concrete operations and thus does not reach that of propositional operations which are elaborated between the ages of 12 and 15 in our society.' (Piaget, 1970: p. 79). In our view different cultural systems all indicate that systems of social interaction influence individual cognitive development while at the same time social interactions in different cultures have common elements influencing the initiation of cognitive development.

This thesis does not directly contradict the Piagetian view of cognitive development which, as we will see, accords an important function to social coordinations and regulations: 'human intelligence develops in the individual as a function of social interactions which in general we far too often neglect.' (Piaget, 1967: p. 260). However, it should be recognised that the Piagetian epistemological system has elaborated a sort of defence mechanism justifying omission of the study of any causal links between the cognitive and the social. For Piaget the two domains will be regulated by identical operations and the development of these operations will simultaneously have repercussions in both the cognitive and the social domains. In the extreme, it would be sufficient to study the development of cognitive structure in order to grasp the development of regulations of social interaction. But much more important, such a view explicitly rejects the possibility of a causal intervention by the social in the cognitive:

> If logical progress thus proceeds in tandem with that of socialisation is it necessary to say that the child becomes capable of logical operations because his social development qualifies him for cooperation or should one assert on the contrary that it is these individual logical acquisitions that allow him to understand others and thus lead him to cooperate? Since the two sorts of progress are on even terms the question seems without solution except to say that they constitute the two indissociable aspects of a single and identical reality, at the same time social and individual.
>
> Piaget (1965: p. 158, translation from French).

In commenting on our own work, Piaget writes:

> It seems established therefore that the factor of exchange (or here of communication) generates the cognitive work. Whether it is, on the contrary, a matter of causality or of training (point 1), it remains clear that coordinations of actions and of operations are identical whether these liaisons are intra or interindividual and this more especially as the individual is himself socialised and that, reciprocally, joint performance would never function if each member of the group did not possess a nervous system and the psychobiological regulations which it comprises. In other words, the operational 'structure' which plays a part is of a general nature or 'common' and thus biopsychosociological and because of this is at its foundations logical.
>
> Piaget (1976: p. 226, translation from French)

At a certain level of generality it is obvious that all cognitive functioning is at the same time biological, psychological, social and logically structured. But this should not prevent us engaging in more localised theoretical and experimental analyses, for example of the capacity of physiological factors to impede or facilitate cognitive development. Thus Piaget's position does not allow elucidation of the mechanisms by which malnutrition, to mention but one factor, might interfere with cognitive development. More generally, the assertion that 'all is biopsychosociological in cognitive development' does not exempt us from researching into how neurological functioning and cognitive functioning are linked, nor how possible feedbacks between the two forms of functioning are established. The report of discussions between Piaget and Chomsky is in this respect very deceptive (Piattelli-Palmarini, 1980); much is said about a possible link between the innate and the acquired with reference to neurobiology, but philosophical and epistemological debate alone hardly advances our understanding of the intervention of the physiological in learning. The same is true for intervention of the social in the cognitive.

Research inspired more or less directly by the Genevan master does, however, bear on the links between cognitive and social development; but it hardly goes beyond the empirical study of correspondences between these developments. Some work (Nielsen, 1951; Dami, 1975; Moessinger, 1974, 1975), also carried out in Geneva, inherited a strictly parallelist association of progress in cognitive operations and social interactions.

Elsewhere, other researchers (Damon, 1977; Waller, 1978) have studied the development of different social competencies in the child and claim that social interaction has a functioning specific to itself. They refuse to view such social interactions simply as epiphenomena of cognitive development. Thus, with regard to moral development, Gersen and Damon (1978) write:

> In general, of course, most who study and write about moral knowledge believe it to be very much concerned with human behaviour. To believe otherwise would be to consider moral reasoning as little more than a cognitive epiphenomenon . . . (pp. 41–42) With this conclusion, nevertheless: The relation we found between children's reasoning and their conduct suggests that the way children derive positive justice solutions is limited by their developmental abilities to understand the real-life situation. (p. 47)

There is in fact a very high correlation between on the one hand mastery of cognitive operations, based on classification and compensation, and levels of moral judgement on the other. Certain cognitive competencies are considered as necessary but not sufficient to attain certain levels of moral development:

> Because no general or partial structure will account completely for the development of any social concept, we have said that general structures are necessary but not sufficient for social knowledge. Specifically, if a certain level of classification has a parallel in a certain level of positive justice, this means that the classification level makes the parallel positive justice level possible, but not that it causes it. Classification cannot cause positive justice development because there is more to justice than the logic of classes. Certain levels of classification behaviour can make certain levels of positive justice knowledge possible because certain modes of justice reasoning about people and events could not take place without the fundamental ability to construct collections in a certain manner.
>
> Damon (1977: p. 321)

Should one conclude from this that certain aspects of cognitive development precede certain social capacities? The problem is more complex:

> In fact, the necessary-but-not sufficient model does not exactly justify a prediction of onto-genetic priority. The relation between a general structure like classification and a social concept like positive justice is a bit more subtle than this. *Within* positive justice thinking it is necessary for a child to use certain modes of classification if he is to reason at certain justice levels.
>
> Damon (1977: p. 322)

Thus it could quite possibly be that certain cognitive operations are actually activated in the first place to resolve relational and social problems. Nevertheless, at the level of empirical investigations, the issue of a possible feedback effect of the social on the cognitive is not considered; research goes no further than ascertaining the existence of correlations between the two domains:

> What specific empirical relations, then would we predict from the necessary-but-not-sufficient model? Although we should entertain no expectations concerning the directionality of development in any two concepts, we could expect to find strong correlations in children's performance levels across concepts that share reliance on the same general structure. In other words, we do not assume that a child's performance in any one area informs us absolutely of his attainment of the general structure across areas. Rather we assume that the general structure appears in a number of manifestations and that the child's attainment of it in one manifestation makes likely, but not certain, his attainment of it in another.
>
> Damon (1977: p. 323)

This is not very distant from the parallelist conception offered by Piaget.

The inadequacies of the Piagetian approach are also denounced by Waller (1978):

> These remarkable and relatively early attempts by Piaget to integrate aspects of social development within his theoretical and structuralist model of development have as an important characteristic that they only consider social development as an epiphenomenon of cognitive development. More particularly, Piaget (. . .) directly reduces the expression of processes of social development to explanations of psychogenetic regularities in the cognitive structuring of non-social realities.
>
> (p. 13, translation from French)

The following concludes that cognitive development is, on the same basis as development of communicative capacities, a prerequisite for participation in complex social interactions:

> Our conception nowhere implies that the ontogenetic development of interactional capacities unfolds independently of cognitive, linguistic or communicative capacities. In the course of describing our model of the construction of interactional expectations, we have shown in several places that cognitive development plays an important role as an antecedent condition in the elaboration of interactional expectations. The same goes for the development of linguistic-communicative capacities (. . .). the question is therefore not *if* but in fact *how* the ontogenetic development of interactional competence is fashioned by the bias of a psychological development of cognitive and linguistic-communicative capacities. Within our conception – and this concerns the central thesis of our system – the influences of these capacities are exerted on the schema of behavioural anticipation in the transformation of social interaction experiences and are reflected in the progressive changes in these behavioural expectations in the course of development.
>
> (Waller, 1978: p. 200, translation from French)

If the authors of the passages quoted here differentiate themselves from Piaget in laying claim to a certain specificity for the analysis of the social, they still accept that individual participation in social interaction is conditioned by cognitive development and do not study the feedback effect of the social on the cognitive as such. In conclusion, specialists in the development of social knowledge have elaborated neither paradigms nor procedures offering a satisfactory association between cognitive and social factors. They do not study the cognitive as a social construction and, in this respect, they do not differ from the Piagetian tradition.

The psychometric tradition

In the last few years the literature on psychological tests has grown considerably, and we could not hope to make a complete inventory of all the arguments issuing from the prosecution or the defence. We may note, however, that even with the most ardent defenders of tests, the criticisms are acknowledged to have a tendency to be stronger than the arguments for the defence:

> At the beginning of the 1950s (. . .) no one disputed that IQ tests provided a valid measure of intelligence and that differences in degree of intelligence were due to genetic causes (. . .). In about the last ten years the position has changed considerably. Many psychologists have cast doubt on the value of IQ tests as measures of intelligence, and others have cast doubts on the importance of the genetic contribution in the origins of intellectual differences.
>
> Eysenck (1978: p. 8)

Intelligence tests may have some value in diagnosing the characteristics of an individual's cognitive functioning, but their use has become a social practice, the purpose of which eludes the testers as well as the testees. The legitimacy of their social utilisation is thus at the heart of this controversy, even more so as recourse to tests has a tendency to 'psychologise' – indeed to locate within neurobiological inheritance – aspects that often derive from social dynamics. This is the well-known debate on the innate and the acquired, on the respective importance of neurobiological inheritance and the environ- ment in explaining individual differences in test results. Yet these are not two factors that are able to intervene independently and separately from one another. Certainly, biological inheritance gives individuals potentials, but these are only activated by the intervention of the educational, social, family and cultural environment. The innate and the acquired are both equally indispensable to the production of cognitive development. Differences in the biological inheritance of individuals can possibly facilitate or inhibit the appropriation of a cultural heritage and differences in the level of cultural heritage can guide the expression of innate potentials in one direction or another. There is a growing awareness of the existence of complex interac- tions between the two factors; environments do not influence the develop- ment of all innate potentialities in an identical manner, while innate differences are not all expressed in the same manner in diverse environ- ments (Jaspars and De Leeuw, 1980).

There is an important element missing in this research however; its objec- tives extend only as far as measuring the differential effects of the innate and the acquired, the one as a function of the other; it has provided no psycho- logical or psychosocial model to explain these effects. It lacks any theory of the forms of environmental influence and particularly of social factors, on cognitive development. The sophistication of its mathematical models is not matched in its study of the processes whereby the characteristics of the social environment and the dynamics of cognitive development are related.

Another point of issue which has much greater social significance has developed out of the desire to use tests in the study of differences between social groups. Certain contributions (Eysenck, 1971, 1975; Jensen, 1969, 1972) have rekindled a debate on possible inequalities of genetic potential between social groups that evokes some embarrassing historical precedents. But such comparisons between social groups also pose a technical problem of size (Jacquard, 1978); estimations of the part played by differences in genetic heredity between individual members of the same group are used to calculate the differences in genetic inheritance between groups. Now, the techniques for estimating this heritability within a single group are them- selves disputed. But independently of the value of such estimations within the same sociocultural group, nothing justifies extrapolation of the result to groups inhabiting different environments; heritability can intervene to a considerable degree in the variations between individuals within one environment and to a much more limited degree in variations between individuals in another environment. One cannot therefore use estimates of heritability based on a single group to make calculations about different groups; 'heritability which cannot be defined or measured except within a single group cannot in any case be used for the analysis of spread between groups.' (Jacquard, 1978, p. 182, translation). In this controversy, there-fore, we endorse the prudent conclusions to which more than a thousand geneticians subscribed in 1975:

> The limits of the significance of IQ are particularly important when one compares children from different groups with different cultures;
> – although a major component of the variation in IQ within a group may have a genetic basis, this hypothesis remains to be verified;
> – there exists no convincing proof of a genetic difference in intelligence between races;
> – we believe that geneticians can and should express themselves as opposed to uses of genetics that draw social and political conclusions from inadequate data.
>
> Cited in Jacquard (1978: p. 185, translation)

The difficulties in any comparison between cultural groups or between sub-groups within the same culture derive also from the impossibility of measur-ing exactly the same characteristics in different sociocultural groups. In attempting to do this, tests no longer measure individual characteristics alone but include cognitive functioning as social functioning. The content and con-ditions of each test any way give rise to reactions and attitudes which vary as a function of the cultural, ethnic and social origins of the individuals tested (Katz, 1973a, 1973b; Zigler and Butterfield, 1968).

Let us examine the case of cross-cultural comparisons proper in a little more detail. One category of tests does seem to have attracted a certain con-sensus amongst those psychologists who have been concerned with such comparisons. These tests (Witkin, 1967) are concerned with perceptual field-dependence versus independence and with global versus analytic cognitive styles. The underlying theory considers the development of the individual as resulting from a series of differentiations, starting from an initial state of syncretism. Hence, these tests measure the individual's capacity to isolate various elements within the perceptual field and organise them into some shape, or his ability to separate the elements of a cognitive problem in order to construct a line of argument. The social connotations of these global styles of perceptual and cognitive functioning are not ignored. These are reflected in the more general strategies of information search, some individuals relying rather more on their social environments to structure ambiguous situations, others basing themselves on the information that is directly available to them. Research carried out both in Western cultures and in other cultures (Witkin and Berry, 1975) indicates that dif-ferences in more general educational and social practices may be at the root of differences in these cognitive styles (Jahoda, 1980).

The most detailed model of the link between styles of differentiation and culture (Berry, 1975) attributes considerable importance to social factors such as socialisation practices and role differentiations. Sadly, one seldom finds this emphasis in the empirical research dealing with correspondences between ecological factors or major types of civilisation (classified in terms of food accumulation practices) and cognitive styles (Berry, 1971). If the data impress by their coherence, it is to be regretted that specifically social factors are not analysed as such. Their influence is postulated in the empirical research, but their function is not studied. The same observation can be made of other work positing a link between ecological variables and success on various Piagetian tasks (Dasen, 1974).

Just as the Skinnerians study behaviour as resulting directly from environmental variables (Skinner, 1957) so recent cross-cultural research studies the links between the ecological or cultural environment and cognitive functioning directly, omitting any study of the social processes which mediate these links. This 'oversight' is most unfortunate as cross-cultural research offers a unique opportunity to study the links between the social and the cognitive, and between the universal and the contingent in social interactions and cognitive operations.

Innovatory work by two American researchers (Cole and Scribner, 1974) emphasises the need for careful study of the communication systems and social structure of a culture before investigating conditions for the production of cognitive processes, and describes an example of such an investigation with the Kpelle of Liberia; thus they are able to show that the adaptation to another culture of a test devised to demonstrate cognitive functioning is impossible without a profound knowledge of the communication conditions within that culture.

What is true for the application of tests in cross-cultural comparisons is true also to some degree for their application to comparisons between different groups within the same society. What is the meaning of a comparison indicating the average intelligence quotient of different socioeconomic occupational groups (Eysenck, 1975)? Their average scores are: higher professional – 139.7; lower professional – 130.6; clerical – 115.9; skilled – 108.2; semiskilled – 97.8; unskilled – 84.9.

Various interpretations of these results are possible. It is evident that they correspond to the educational levels required for these different occupations. The tests have been devised to predict scholastic achievement and the sociooccupational success to which it is linked. These findings thus suggest that the tests are effectively reductions of the system of educational evaluation and can be interpreted within the perspective developed in the work of Bourdieu and Passeron (1964, 1970) on the reproduction of social inequalities. Primary teaching, the foundation of the school system, is actually strongly uniform in its treatment of the child just as is the practice of testing. This uniformity induces a quite precise accentuation of social inequalities:

In order for the most favoured to be favoured and the most disfavoured to be disfavoured, it is necessary and sufficient that the school ignores, in the content of transmitted teaching, in the methods and techniques of transmission and in the criteria of judgement, the cultural inequalities between children of different social classes: in other words, in treating all pupils as equal in rights and obligations, unequal though they may in fact be, the school system is in practice led to sanction initial inequalities with respect to culture.

Bourdieu (1966: p. 336, translation)

This is how we would explain the results reported above. Who could possibly pretend that the social environments from which managers and manual workers come are the same? Or that these environments prepare children in an equally effective manner to cope with tests and school? The least one can say is that up to the present 'universal education' and 'universal tests' have hardly taken account of the cultural differences that exist also within our societies. If various reforms have been attempted, they are still a long way from succeeding. In our opinion this is also because the dominant definition of intelligence is centred far too much on the individual and neglects any study of the social conditions of cognitive functioning.

The IQ results mentioned above appeared in *The Inequality of Man*. Let us not conclude from this that there is an inequality in genes conditioning the intellectual development of members of different social classes; the social fabrication of this inequality is too evident. The social significance of studies of intelligence is located at the level of the explanations given for the observed differences and consequently at the level of the conception of intelligence that serves as a basis for these explanations.

Towards a new approach

The psychological study of intelligence cannot be reduced either to the Piagetian approach or to the psychometric approach. Nevertheless, these two approaches have furnished the most frequently used techniques of investigation. They have in common the study of intelligence firstly and almost exclusively as a characteristic of the individual. Such an approach seems obvious; the principal object of study is clearly the manner in which the individual organises his experience of the physical and social environment. Just as the brain is always identified as belonging to a particular individual, so in the same way is intelligence always studied as that of a distinct individual. But in this area, as in other areas of science, progress can also consist in rendering the self-evident less evident. Can the individual really, by himself, organise his experience of the surrounding world?

Traditional ideas in the psychology of intelligence constitute an abstraction. They isolate the individual from the social context in which his intelligence develops. This goes for Piagetian practice as well as for that of psychometrics. 'A large amount of the current research on cognitive processes treats them as independent of any context, as a property of the organism (or of its head), and not as a property of the organism in relation to a specific environment.' (Glick, 1974: p. 378). Intelligence is not just an individual property but also a relational process between individuals constructing and organising their actions upon the physical and social environment together. It is the relative failure of what were envisaged as *culture-free* tests, tests which were supposed to escape the specific contingencies and characteristics of different cultures, that has made us conscious of the inherent limits of the traditional definition of intelligence:

> It seems that the attempt to remove all cultural bias from a test of cognitive functioning proceeds from a deep misunderstanding about the nature of cognition. The cognitive is not independent of culture; one cannot conceive of it as a set of principles of functioning independent of particular circumstances and of the intentions of the subject. In reality, we should attempt to make our measures of cognitive functioning more sensitive to cultural variations.
>
> Glick (1974: p. 379)

We are entirely of this opinion, although judging its intention somewhat too general. Intelligence and culture are linked in several ways, but it is primarily in interaction situations that we will study here how the appropriation of such a cultural heritage is managed.

In the following chapter a definition of intelligence will be offered which is formulated neither exclusively in individual terms nor in general cultural terms, but which will postulate that human intelligence is elaborated in inter-individual relations established within specific social situations. This book does not pretend to resolve all the problems enumerated in the present chapter; it will try to offer a theoretical framework and paradigms for investigation that are more adequate to a study of the links between the cognitive and the social, thus allowing an escape from the impasse which characterises present studies of intelligence.

2

A social definition of intelligence

The challenges that contemporary research in intelligence offers us can only be met by a definition of intelligence that takes into account both its individual and its social nature. In offering just such a definition in this chapter, we do not claim to be the first to have tried to deal with cognition in such terms. Disciplines as diverse as anthropology, ethology, sociology, psychology and social psychology have all developed social definitions of intelligence at different points in their history and within widely divergent schools of thought. Unfortunately these definitions have had almost no impact on the types of research done and have, on the contrary, tended to remain as mere postulates in dealing with intelligence. Later in this chapter a social definition of intelligence that allows, and has been the object of, systematic experimental examination is put forward. The major directions in which our investigations have developed are described, and these are illustrated with concrete research examples in the following four chapters.

The postulate of the social nature of intelligence

An understanding of intelligence as social in nature was present even in the works of Wilhelm Wundt. The founder of the experimental method in psychology restricted use of this method to the study of the elementary processes of sensation and association, the bricks and the mortar of psychic life. He intended social psychology to include the study of more complex cognitive phenomena which found stable form only as collective products. Wundt claimed that collective phenomena could be studied only by a non-experimental method or observation:

> In the present stage of the science these two branches of psychology are generally taken up in different treaties, although they are not so much different departments as different *methods*. So-called social psychology corresponds to the method of pure observation, the objects of observation in this case being the mental products. The necessary connection of these products with social communities, which has given to social psychology its name, is due to the fact that the mental products of the individual are of too variable a character to be subjects of objective observation. The phenomena gain the necessary degree of constancy only when they become collective.
>
> Wundt (1907: 26)

14

While agreeing that mental phenomena must be studied in their social context, it seems nevertheless possible to transcend the dichotomy that Wundt saw between psychology and social psychology (Doise, 1982). We later demonstrate that the experimental method and not just observation can be an invaluable tool in the study of more complex mental processes. The social psychology that Wundt both preached and practised was in reality a *Völkerpsychologie* – a comparative psychology based on ethnographic procedures of describing the practices, traditions and customs of different human societies as reported by travellers, missionaries and explorers. Unlike Wundt, we attempt to clarify the links between social and cognitive processes in our own culture.

Durkheim visited Wundt's laboratory and was impressed by the experimental work in psychology with its concentration on 'precise and restricted' problems and its avoidance of 'vague generalisations and metaphysical possibilities' Lukes (1975: 90).

Durkheim also believed that complex mental processes should be studied as social phenomena, strongly defending with Mauss (Durkheim and Mauss, 1969: 83) the idea that logical operations developed socially and opposing the theory that the development of certain cognitive functions was based on interaction with objects and the environment:

> Far from it being the case, as Frazer seems to think, that the social relations of men are based on logical relations between things, in reality it is the former which have provided the prototype for the latter. According to him, men were divided into clans by a pre-existing classification of things; but, quite on the contrary, they classified things because they were divided by clans.

The theory held by these French ethnosociologists is indeed that:

> The first logical categories were social categories; the first classes of things were classes of men, into which these things were integrated. It was because men were grouped, and thought of themselves in the form of groups, that in their ideas they grouped other things, and in the beginning the two modes of grouping were merged to the point of being indistinct. Moieties were the first genera; clans, the first species. Things were thought to be integral parts of society, and it was their place in society which determined their place in nature. We may even wonder whether the schematic manner in which genera are ordinarily conceived may not have depended in part on the same influences. It is a fact of current observation that the things which they comprise are generally imagined as situated in a sort of ideational milieu, with a more or less clearly delimited spatial circumspection. It is certainly not without cause that concepts and their interrelations have so often been represented by concentric and eccentric circles, interior and exterior to each other, etc. Might it not be that this tendency to imagine purely logical groupings in a form contrasting so much with their true nature originated in the fact that at first they were conceived in the form of social groups occupying, consequently, definite positions in space? And have we not in fact seen this spatial localisation of genus and species in a fairly large number of very different societies?

Adherence to different forms of the idea that cognitive operations have social origins is currently widespread. The idea that the social organisation necessary for hunting food was an impetus to cognitive development in some hominids for example has become very popular as a result of recent books such as those by Ardrey (1977), Mendel (1977) and Moscovici (1976). This primitive form of labour organisation, and especially the interchangeability of roles it entailed, is considered a blueprint for other forms of structured behaviour, and in particular, for language. Leontiev (1976: 71) focuses on the example of the activity of 'beating' while hunting for game. For the beater, this activity seems to be approaching the business of hunting in the wrong way. It is only when his action is put in the context of, and meshes with the actions of, others that it becomes meaningful and loses its apparently contradictory nature:

> The beating of game leads to the satisfaction of a need but not at all because of the natural relations in the given material situation, quite the contrary. Normally, these natural relations are such that scaring off the game eliminates any possibility of securing it. What is it in this case, then, that links the immediate result of this activity with its final result? It is evidently nothing but the relation of the individual to other members of the collective that is the basis on which he receives his share of the plunder, a part of the product of the activity of collective work. This profit, this relation, arises through the activity of other individuals. This means that it is precisely the activity of other men that constitutes the objective material foundation of the specific structure of individual human activity; historically, in terms of its appearance, the connection between the motive and the object of an action does not reflect natural connections or relationships but objective social connections and relationships.
>   Thus the complex activity of the superior animals, subject to the natural relations between things, is in man transformed into an activity subject from the beginning to social ties and relations. This is the immediate cause which gives birth to the specifically human form of reflection on reality, human consciousness.

Intelligence is often defined today as the capacity to adapt to the environment. Ethologists rightly point out that primates and humans must adapt not only to the physical but also to the social environment. It seems in fact that the social environment would have produced more stimulation for the evolution of cognitive capacity. In this regard Humphrey (1976: 307) notes that individuals of the anthropoid species and even human tribes rarely use all their recognised cognitive capabilities to solve problems of biological survival in their natural environment.

> We are faced thus with a conundrum. It has been repeatedly demonstrated in the artificial situations of the psychological laboratory that anthropoid apes possess impressive powers of creative reasoning, yet these feats of intelligence seem simply not to have any parallels in the behaviour of the same animals in their natural environment. I have yet to hear of any example from the field of a chimpanzee (or for that matter a Bushman) using his full capacity for inferential reasoning in the solution of a biologically relevant practical problem.

Why then have the upper primates developed cognitively at all and why, as appears to be the case, have they done so to a greater extent than other species? The answer lies in their acquiring, through their membership of social communities, fundamental knowledge which was vital to their physical adaptation. The principal function of creative intelligence was thus adaptation to social life. And Humphrey argues that in fact the most complex cognitive demands made on upper primates are of social origin. Via adaptation to the social environment, which is much more complex, cognitively speaking, upper primates and humans adapted to their physical environment.

Similarly, Chance and Larsen (1976) have gathered data on primates that show the way in which constant maintenance of different status hierarchies in the same group in constantly changing situations demands that each individual member of a group must simultaneously attend to others and attract the attention of others. Doing so obviously entails highly complex cognitive operations.

Like several other authors, Stenhouse (1976–7: 53) argues that an important aspect of cognitive development is the ability to suspend or postpone an activity (his factor P, postponement).

> The essential feature of the P-factor is, in a given situation, to inhibit the previously normal instinctual response, at least temporarily, to provide an opening for the substitution of a new and intelligent (i.e., adaptive) response.

Social factors apparently have no place in this definition. However when Stenhouse goes on to describe the emergence of this aspect of cognitive development he refers to the momentary 'bracketing' of attention to hierarchical structure that allows social interaction in which individuals occupy positions interchangeably to be established.

> Accepting, then, that the achievement of bipedaly was followed by the enlargement of the 'unit' social group and the concomitant adoption of predation, what pressures can be postulated as operating upon the factors of intelligence in the new situation?
>
> If social co-operation is to be superimposed upon the hierarchical organisation characteristic of the vegetarian primates, one of the first desiderata must be the loosening of the social dominance mechanisms. These mechanisms cannot be abolished, since in some circumstances they will continue to be adaptive; also their total abolition could hardly be accomplished without undesirable disruption of other sectors of the behavioural repertoire. What is required is, then, the capacity to dispense with dominance interactions at some times (e.g. when hunting) but not at others (e.g. when apportioning sleeping 'territory' and mates and probably also when repelling predators).
>
> Stenhouse (1973: 173)

Anthropologists, ethologists and psychologists do not lack imagination when conjecturing about the social evolution of intelligence in the far distant past. Neither are they slow to postulate in so doing not a unidirectional line of causality, but a constant causal interplay between the development of intellectual capacity (in the neocortex) and the development of complex social organisation. Some given social system favours the emergence of new cognitive abilities which in turn makes possible the development of even more complex forms of social organisation and so on. Fox (1972) stresses the interplay of mutual causation between the development of society and that of the neocortex, showing, in the tradition of Lévi-Strauss, how fundamentally simple rules regulating marriage can produce very complex systems of parenthood, necessitating more and more advanced cognitive abilities. Indeed, the complexities of genealogical reckoning do not appear to have been created by anthropologists but rather to have been the foundation of ancient social practices.

Mead, Piaget and Vygotsky

Theories of the sociogenesis of intelligence have not been developed exclusively by those studying man's evolutionary development. Psychologists and social psychologists have also proposed explanations of a social nature to account for the human child's development of intellectual ability in the first few years of life. During the 1920s and 1930s, and in such different countries as the United States, the Soviet Union, and Switzerland, theories that saw children's cognitive abilities as social in origin were being put forward.

The posthumous works of Mead (1934) for example explicitly linked social interaction and cognitive development. Mead began with the idea of the so-called 'conversation of gestures'. Even before self-awareness or anything that could strictly be called thought appeared, interaction between two individuals provided a base on which symbolic thought could be built. In each specific action directed towards another, the reaction of that other is already anticipated:

> Just as in fencing the parry is an interpretation of the thrust, so, in the social act, the adjustive response of one organism to the gesture of another is the interpretation of that gesture by that organism – it is the meaning of that gesture.
>
> Mead (1934: 78)

Thought is the conversation of gestures internalised:

> The internalisation in our experience of the external conversations of gestures which we carry on with other individuals in the social process is the essence of thinking; and the gestures thus internalised are significant symbols because they have the same meanings for all individual members of the given society or social group, i.e. they respectively arouse the same attitudes in the individuals making them that they arouse in the individuals responding to them: otherwise the individual could not internalise them.
>
> Mead (1934, p. 47)

This internalisation is most probable when the spoken word merges with the conversation of gestures:

> If the individual does himself make use of something answering to the same gesture he observes, saying it over again to himself, putting himself in the role of the person who is speaking to him, then he has the meaning of what he hears, he has the idea: the meaning has become his.
>
> (*ibid*, p. 109)

Piaget, in whose later research paradigms the role of social factors in cognitive development remains implicit, outlined during this same period an approach to cognitive development in which the intervention of such factors was made explicit. In an article entitled 'Logique génétique et sociologie' published for the first time in 1928, Piaget drew a distinction between autism, which was seen as an extreme form of egocentric thought, and cooperation defined as

> any interaction between 2 or more individuals who are, or believe themselves to be, equal: in other words, any interaction in which there is no element of authority or prestige. It is of course very difficult to list, other than by degree, the behaviours that occur in coercive and cooperative situations: the product of a cooperation can be imposed later by constraint for example. But in principle the distinction holds, and in practice one can arrive at some approximation adequate for the discussion. This having been said, we believe that only cooperation constitutes a process in which new cognitions may be produced, while autism and social constraint can lead only to the various forms of prelogic.
>
> Piaget (1976a: 67)

And this article ended with the words:

> In conclusion we believe that social interaction is a necessary condition for the development of logic. We thus regard social interaction as transforming the very nature of the individual as it promotes him from an autistic state to one of intersubjective personality. As regards cooperation then, we see it as a process in which new realities are created and not merely an exchange between already fully-developed individuals. Social constraint is merely a step on the way to full socialisation. Cooperation alone ensures cognitive equilibration, which allows a distinction to be drawn between the factual nature of cognitive operations and the principles of the rational ideal.
>
> Piaget (1976a: 80)

Piaget (1976b: 114) expressed similar ideas at a colloquium held in 1931:

> To conclude, cooperation is the source of three kinds of transformation that occur in individual thought, all of which give the individual a better grasp of the reasoning inherent in all intellectual activity. Firstly, cooperation produces reflexivity and self-awareness. It thus marks a new change as regards both the individuals sensori-motor intelligence and social authority, which leads to coerced belief and not to true consideration of alternatives. Secondly cooperation allows the subjective and the objective to be separated. It is thus the origin of objectivity and transforms immediate experience into scientific experience, so that constraint is limited to bolstering the first by simply promoting egocentrism to the level of sociomorphism. Thirdly cooperation is the source of regulation. By transcending the simple regularity seen by the individual and the heteronomous rule imposed by social constraint in the cognitive as well as the moral sphere, cooperation promotes the rule of autonomy, or pure reciprocity, which is an important element of logical thought and of the system of notions and signs.

The relationship between cooperation between individuals and the development of individual cognition is clearly stressed. While these ideas were being expressed, Vygotsky was developing a similar line of thought in the Soviet Union. In 1934 his book was published posthumously, later appearing (in 1962) in translation. In this book Vygotsky attacked certain Piagetian ideas on children's language, which, he claimed, overemphasised the egocentric aspects (such as monologues and failure to coordinate simultaneous speech) in early language. To Vygotsky (1962: p.19) egocentric speech was only an intermediate stage.

> Egocentric speech as a separate linguistic form is the highly important genetic link in the transition from vocal to inner speech, an intermediate stage between the differentiation of the functions of vocal speech and the final transformation of one part of vocal speech into inner speech. It is this transitional role of egocentric speech that lends it such great theoretical interest. The whole conception of speech development differs profoundly in

accordance with the interpretation given to the role of egocentric speech. Thus our schema of development – first social, then egocentric, then inner speech – contrasts both with the traditional behaviourist schema – vocal speech, whisper, inner speech – and with Piaget's sequence – from nonverbal autistic thought through egocentric thought and speech to social-ised speech and logical thinking. In our conception, the true direction of the development of thinking is not from the individual to the socialised, but from the social to the individual.

In other words

The greatest change in children's capacity to use language as a problem-solving tool takes place somewhat later in their development, when specialised speech (which has previously been used to address an adult) *is turned inward*. Instead of appealing to an adult, children appeal to themselves; language thus takes on an *intrapersonal function* in addition to its *interpersonal use*. When children develop a method of behaviour for guiding themselves that had previously been used in relation to another person, when they organise their own activities according to a social form of behaviour, they succeed in applying a social attitude to themselves. The history of the process of *the internalisation of social speech* is also the history of the socialisation of children's practical intellect.

Vygotsky (1978: 27)

Vygotsky saw in the child's unsuccessful attempts to reach for some object the origin of the act of pointing, which develops as the child's attempts cause others to intervene for him:

The child's unsuccessful attempt engenders a reaction not from the object he seeks but *from another person*. Consequently, the primary meaning of that unsuccessful grasping move-ment is established by others. Only later, when the child can link his unsuccessful grasping movement to the objective situation as a whole, does he begin to understand this movement as pointing. At this juncture there occurs a change in that movement's functions from an object-oriented movement it becomes a movement aimed at another person, a means of establishing relations. *The grasping movement changes to the act of pointing.* As a result of this change, the movement itself is then physically simplified, and what results is the form of pointing that we may call a true gesture. It becomes a true gesture only after it objectively manifests all the functions of pointing for others and is understood by others as such a gesture. Its meaning and functions are created at first by an objective situation and then by people who surround the child.

Vygotsky (1978: 56)

This leads to an important generalisation:

An interpersonal process is transformed into an intrapersonal one. Every function in the child's cultural development appears twice: first, on the social level, and later, on the individual level; first, *between* people (*interpsychological*), and then *inside* the child (*intra-psychological*). This applies equally to voluntary attention, to logical memory, and to the formation of concepts. All the higher functions originate as actual relations between human individuals.

Vygotsky (1978: 57)

Although these 3 approaches clearly differ they have in common the impor-tance they accord to social factors intervening in cognitive development. What impact have these ideas had half a century later? Unfortunately they have not been seriously developed and have little impact on contemporary mainstream research in cognition. While Mead's notion of the conversation of gestures is cited in philosophical and epistemological works, it has not been subject to any systematic research. It has in fact been the other aspect of Mead's work, dealing with the social origins of self awareness and the internalisation of values that has retained the interest of researchers and out of which symbolic interactionism has developed. As for Vygotsky's ideas, Luria (1976) carried out his well-known research in Ouzbekhistan which showed how important social change such as collectivisation and the spread of literacy in agrarian communities gave rise to capacities for more abstract thought, while Vygotsky was still alive. While similar changes as the result of education and urbanisation have been found in other countries (Cole *et al.*, 1971), such research has not provided any explanation of the intervening processes which link cognitive and historical change. As well as insisting that cognition should be studied in its historical context, Vygotsky also emphasised the need to analyse interindividual interactions to account for cognitive development in children, and this aspect of his work has received less attention. Recently Schaffer (1977) and his colleagues (Murphy and Messer, 1977) have studied the origin of social relationships and particularly the act of pointing within a theoretical framework reminiscent of Vygotsky's.

In Chapter 1 it was argued that neither Piaget nor his disciples have adequately incorporated social factors into their many experiments. This has not prevented Piaget from using social interaction and cultural heritage, as well as biological maturation and equilibration, as factors in explaining the cognitive development of the child. Cooperation between individuals in fact remains

> the first of a series of forms of behaviour which are important for the constitution and development of logic (1950: p. 163)

Piaget (1967: 224–5) seems moreover to admit that

> human intelligence develops in the individual as a function of social interactions too often disregarded.

In some ways Piaget's work exemplifies the gap which exists between the general ideas which are put forward and the theoretical and empirical research carried out to clarify them.

Thus while important schools of thought in the human sciences admit the origin of intelligence (both phylogenetically and ontogenetically) to be social in nature, studies of intelligence tend to treat the social nature of its development as implicit. Social definitions of intelligence have in this sense remained mere postulates, for while the social nature of intelligence is recognised, intelligence is never explicitly studied as social. Such a situation creates the problems discussed in the preceding chapter. How are we to move beyond this situation and develop the investigation of intelligence while adequately incorporating its social nature and origins? In our opinion the solution lies in the theoretical elaboration of a definition of intelligence which not only embodies its social nature explicitly, but which can also be empirically investigated. Mead, Piaget and Vygotsky have all given us the ideas, but neither the paradigms nor techniques, necessary to substantiate their belief that intelligence is essentially social in nature.

A new social psychological approach

Several lines of research in social and general psychology have nevertheless pointed up ways in which cognitive functioning is effected by certain social variables. There is for example the work on reinforcement, which shows how an organism changes and adapts its behaviour to produce positive and avoid negative consequences. The theory of effect has been developed largely by Skinner (1971) and has proved effective in 'conditioning' both animals and humans. It is clear however that for humans positive and negative reinforcers are often of social origin. The theory of effect is thus one approach that shows how the cognitive and the social must be linked, at least to explain some forms of learning.

Traditional social psychology also provides such a paradigm in the form of imitation of models studies, as initiated in the classic work of Bandura and Walters (1963). Discovering the effect of social group membership shared by both model and imitator led to studies linking the relationship between individuals and groups, in an attempt to explain how cultural heritage might be passed on. Tarde's aim in 1898 of constructing a social psychology that explained complex social phenomena in terms of imitation processes has thus had an impact on modern social psychology.

Useful as these two lines of research may be, they do not seem, in their present form at least, the most appropriate ways of studying the emergence of complex cognitive operations in the individual. Piaget's theory, explaining as it does the way in which more basic cognitive schemata are integrated into increasingly complex structures in the course of development, deals more adequately and more explicitly with the major characteristics of individual cognitive development.

For Piaget (1976c: 187)

> cognitive operations are actions which are internalised, reversible (in the sense of inversion or reciprocity at the concrete level and of both at once at the formal level) and cooordinated into general structures.

Basic to this definition is thus the idea of an action, the effect of which can be negated by an inverse action or compensated for by another action. These transformations do not take place only by direct action on the world but may also occur symbolically in thought. Moreover, Piaget (1952) sees in imitation an intermediary process between 'the thought in action' of every young child and symbolism or internalised action. Internalised actions are then gradually coordinated into general structures which can be described by logical models. For many years the principal contribution of Piaget to psychology has been description of these structures in terms of logico-mathematical models. For Piaget, explanation of cognitive development involves the elaboration of models which allow an understanding of more complex structures arising from the transformation and combination of schemata at lower levels.

We wish to propose a social definition of intelligence that incorporates but goes beyond a Piagetian notion of cognitive development. While Piaget describes intellectual activity as coordination, we believe that this coordination is not only individual but to an equal extent social in nature. It is in the very coordination of his actions with those of others that the individual acquires mastery of systems of coordinations which are later individualised and internalised. The remainder of this book is concerned with the development and illustration of the general thesis that coordinations between individuals are the source of individual coordinations, and that the former precede and produce the latter.

To argue that interindividual coordination of action plays a crucial role in cognitive development does not imply a belief that the individual is passively moulded by external forces. Our approach is both interactionist and constructivist: in acting on the environment the individual elaborates systems of organisation of that activity on reality. For the most part, it is not a matter of merely acting on reality – it is rather in the coordination of one's own action with others that systems of coordination which can later be reproduced autonomously, develop. The causality we attribute to social interaction is thus not unidirectional but progresses in both a circular and spiral fashion – interaction enables the individual to master certain abilities which allow him to participate in more complex social interactions which in turn promotes continued cognitive development. At particular levels of development certain types of social interaction act as factors inducing new cognitive reorganisation.

Such a concept of mutually reciprocal causality linking social interaction and cognitive development is not unlike those used in accounting for the evolutionary development of cognition, as seen above. More complex social interactions favoured the emergence of advanced cognitive abilities which in turn allowed individuals to participate in even more complex societies and so forth. The postulating of mutually interactive and spiral paths of causality is an essential aspect of our definition and makes it clear that not just any form of social interaction will be beneficial at any time in development. Certain prerequisites are necessary to profit from social interactions, but those prerequisites are themselves the products of earlier and simpler forms of social interaction.

If the study of the evolutionary emergence of man's cognitive ability must depend on plausible conjecture, we have more means with which to evaluate our theory. When we suggest for example that certain forms of interaction give rise to cognitive progress in a child at a given stage of development, we can have this child participate in just such interaction and observe the results. In other words, and despite Wundt's belief, we are able to study experimentally the effect of social interaction (introduced as an independent variable) on cognitive development (considered as a dependent variable). The experimental method can show which interactions at which stages are effective in promoting cognitive development. It also enables us to go beyond any mere demonstration of a correlation between the two. In this sense we move away from the Piagetian tradition of studying the role of social factors only implicitly, but acknowledge from his work indications as to which processes and structures to study in the developing child.

Before describing the principal themes of our experimental work, it must be made clear that we deal here only with the development of concrete operational thought, that is, with the new abilities that children acquire toward 6 or 7 years of age which are demonstrated by actions on concrete objects in the environment. This choice in no way implies that the origins of earlier abilities are in any way less social. On the contrary, the work by Schaffer (1978) already cited clearly shows the truly social nature of behaviour patterns which develop in the first months of life in interactions with caretakers. Long before speech is possible, the infant participates in a form of dialogue, during which periods of the child's activity coincide with nonactivity in the mother and vice versa. In the same way direction and control of eye movements and attention develops in a social context. Together with the mastering of pointing, such social regulators then allow the baby to participate in more and more complex interactions.

If we focus specifically on the sociogenesis of concrete operations it is because these constitute a new phase in cognitive development which is all the more important because it makes education in the strict pedagogical sense possible. Neither does focusing on this period suggest that later progress necessarily occurs in an any more individual manner. The study of scientific activity clearly shows that even the hypothetico-deductive reasoning of scientists can be analysed as a social process of adopting a position in relation to other scientists and other schools of thought.

Research themes

Our theoretical and experimental development of the belief that cognitive abilities result not from a simple interaction between the child and the physical environment, but that such interaction is mediated by others, is consistent with a move toward a new approach in contemporary social psychology. This new approach stresses the necessity of transcending any approach that is limited to studying the individual's interactions with objects and calls for the study of more complex situations where several individuals are linked in terms of their interactions with or through an object. In line with these ideas, our study aims at moving from

> a bi-polar (ego-object) psychology to a tri-polar (ego-alter-object) psychology, a change necessary because the latter is a better representation of reality.
>
> Moscovici and Ricateau (1972: 141 translation)

The individual however must of course often interact with physical reality by himself. Is he necessarily 'handicapped' in such 'individual' situations as compared with a 'collective' situation where he interacts with others? The first theme in our research is the attempt to answer this very question by focusing on the differences between the cognitive performances of individuals working alone or in a group at the same task.

The constructive nature of social interaction

Many experiments in social psychology have been concerned with comparing group and individual performance. Kelley and Thibaut (1969) and Moscovici and Paicheler (1973) have both provided summaries of this research. They conclude that, depending on the nature of the task, the individual resources of the group members and their mode of interaction, group performance can be superior, inferior or equal to individual performance on the same task. But in most studies, interest is focused more on the comparison of performance than on the development of new cognitive abilities during interaction. In the same way, while Zajonc's (1965) well-known experiments on social facilitation show that the mere presence of others can improve individual performances on some tasks, such improvement usually occurs in familiar or already mastered responses and does not extend to the production of new responses (which in fact appear to be inhibited by the presence of others). The principle aim of these studies has thus been to confirm in one form or another the results of one of the first experiments in this area (Triplett, 1898), which was supposedly concerned with the performance of sportsmen competing alone or in groups.

While work on social facilitation shows that the presence of others can hinder the production of new responses, we subscribe on the contrary to the idea that social interaction can produce new cognitive coordinations. However not just any interaction at any stage of development is beneficial. There are in fact some types of interaction in which the individual is hardly motivated at all to coordinate his behaviour with others; for example when the collective product can be obtained merely by adding the individual contributions. Thus, when several children have to complete a collective drawing composed of houses or people side by side, there is less need to coordinate actions than when they must together draw a map of their village so that their respective houses appear in the right places (Cecchini, Dubs and Tonucci, 1972). Only in the latter case could progress due to interaction be expected.

Various authority structures and disruptions of communication can also result in certain members of the group taking little active part in coordination. No superiority of group over individual performance is to be expected when this occurs, as the nature of the interaction is such that the group product depends merely upon the individual capabilities of its members.

Even when certain abilities have been mastered by an individual, there is no reason to assume that these same abilities will be merely reproduced during interaction. Differences in motivation in the social situation might produce different performance, as the research on social facilitation has suggested. Moreover, given that the individual has mastered certain skills, collective performances may not always be superior to individual performance. An individual who has the necessary cognitive skills and who uses all available information can sometimes organise this information more quickly than several individuals who must not only check information contributed by members but must also deliberate on the organisation both of the information and of their interactions.

Cognitive prerequisites

Participation in certain social interactions requires that certain initial abilities be present before that interaction can benefit the individual. We thus support the important Piagetian notion of the genetic or evolutionary nature of cognitive development. Development takes place in stages, although several developmental paths can lead from one phase to the next (Longeot, 1978) and 'decalages' or lags in accomplishments can occur, depending on the nature and function of certain abilities. But the 'increasing equilibration' of which Piaget (1977: 179) speaks is itself the product of earlier cognitive restructuring:

> The crucial problem therefore is to understand the method for the improvement of regulations, in other words, the 'why' of the increasing equilibrations as revealed by their construction and increased coherence. The 'how' of the improvement is clear – their construction consists in the elaboration of operations dealing with the preceding constructions; these are relations of relations, regulations of regulations, etc. In short, new forms develop with previous ones and include them as contents.

In order that a new structure can integrate less advanced structures, the latter must of course exist. We do not agree with Piaget when he later asserts that 'this elaboration remains essentially endogenous', for elaboration is as social as it is individual in nature. Piaget (1977: 35) calls this process of construction 'reflecting abstraction'.

> The 'reflecting abstraction' includes two inseparable aspects: a 'reflecting' in the sense of projecting on an upper level what is happening on a lower level, and a 'reflection' in the sense of a cognitive reconstruction or reorganisation (more or less conscious) of what has thus been transferred. It should be mentioned that this abstraction is not limited to using a series of hierarchical levels whose function would be foreign to it: It is the abstraction that produces them by alternate interactions of 'reflecting' and 'reflection'.

This is an adequate description at the psychological level of what occurs in the individual, but integration of earlier regulators within new structures must also be studied at the social level – the collective elaboration of new structures reorganises pre-existing individual abilities. To profit from these collective integrations resulting in more advanced structures, individuals must already possess the necessary constituent elements.

One ability that seems necessary before a child can benefit from participating in social interaction in which perspectives are reorganised is the ability to realise that his position differs from those of others. Coordination is not the ousting of an existing centration but its integration into a new structure; and there is reason to believe that a conscious grasp of the differences between one's own centration and those of others is at the basis of such integration. It is still necessary however also to determine which initial abilities must exist before this realisation is possible.

The effect of social interaction on individual cognitive development

Most of our experiments demonstrate that participation in certain forms of social interaction leads to cognitive development. They thus lend substance to Vygotsky's claim (1962: 104) that 'what children can do with others today, they can do alone tomorrow'. In interacting either with adults or among themselves, children not only demonstrate more advanced forms of cognitive organisation than those they are capable of alone prior to interaction, but also are able to produce by themselves these more advanced forms after the interaction. It is these very abilities that then allow them to take part in more complex interaction and in this way to progress up the spiralling developmental path which characterises the interacting effects of social activity and cognitive development. It is these abilities too that later enable children to solve cognitive problems independently. Interdependence and autonomy are thus closely linked. However the longitudinal studies which would show the gradual social construction of more and more advanced abilities in the same children have yet to be done.

Of course it is necessary to ensure that progress observed after interaction is true progress and indicative of cognitive restructuring, rather than the mere repetition of verbal responses hastily learnt. Various means have been used in our research to test the authenticity of such progress, the most important of which are tests of the generalisation of operations to domains or material not used in the experimental phase, detailed study of the child's justification of behaviour, and the administration of tests of similar nature to the experimental task but requiring different responses.

Sociocognitive conflict

An important theme in Piagetian theory is that of centration. This term denotes the use of a cognitive scheme which has yet to be integrated in a more general structure.

Consider the examples which have been used in our research. A child agrees that two identical glasses contain the same amount of fruit juice. If the experimenter then tips the contents of one glass into a tall thin container and the contents of the other into a wide flat container the child thinks that there is more to drink in the thin glass. Such a decision results from his correct comparison of the level of liquid in the glasses but his failure to take into consideration the width of the glasses. He focuses solely on height and fails to coordinate the differences in height with differences in width. If this difference in width is pointed out, the child will just as readily centre on width and ignore the differences in the height of the level of liquid.

In the same way, if 2 rulers of 10cm are placed parallel to one another so that their end-points coincide, the child correctly judges the two to be of equal length. But it is only necessary to displace one of the rulers so that one end of it extends beyond the end of the other ruler to get the child to focus on this disparity. His evaluation of length is based on the disparity and he ignores the fact that the other ruler extends beyond the first an equal distance in the opposite direction. In a way that astonishes adults, a child does not appear upset by making successive centrations which cause him to give blatantly contradictory responses.

In such cases cognitive progress can result from the integration of the two different centrations into a single organised structure dealing with compensation of opposing equal differences. This integration is based on reciprocity (when the overextension of one ruler in one direction is judged equivalent to the other extension of the other in the opposite direction) and reversibility (when the 2 rulers can be mentally returned to their initial state). How do such cognitive reintegrations come about? In the book already cited, Piaget (1977) proposes a theory of equilibration which describes the way in which the child reacts to challenges to disruptions of his present understanding which reveal conflict among his own responses. While at an initial stage the child denies any contradiction, he later integrates the challenging centration either partially or completely. The role of this disruption is important in this model of equilibration as it is this which enables development to move toward a new equilibrium at a more advanced level. We believe this disruption to be above all social in nature. In fact when another asserts an opposing centration to that of the child, the child is faced with a conflict not only of a cognitive but also of a social nature. This sociocognitive conflict which allows two opposing centrations to exist simultaneously cannot be as easily denied as a conflict resulting from successive and alternating individual centrations.

We can thus speak, as Smedslund (1966: 165) does, of the social origin of decentration. Like Smedslund, we believe that the dynamic of cognitive development results in the main from a conflict in social communication. In an interaction between several individuals, centrations are more explicitly opposed than when an individual alone acts on an object.

> There is reason to believe that the only form which can lead to any change in an egocentric system based on a succession of *hic et nunc* situations is conflict of an equally *hic et nunc* nature. The type of conflict necessary is a conflict between several incompatible responses brought about in a given situation. There are two very different types of such intrasituational conflict: the first arises when anticipated results do not occur and leads to new learning without changing the egocentric nature of the system. The second type is brought about by social interaction and, more especially, some communication from another person about the given situation. The communication introduces the other's point of view and if this is different from that of the subject, there will be *hic et nunc* conflict . . . These remarks may be extended by proposing the following hypothesis: the occurrence of social interaction is a necessary condition for cognitive development . . . Such an approach calls for a change in the research in the area so that it no longer stresses interaction with the physical environment but with social interaction instead. This change seems necessary if we wish to reach a deeper understanding of the mechanisms and the content of cognitive development.

Such a view of sociocognitive conflict is in fact an elaboration of what Piaget had written 50 years earlier regarding the role of cooperation in the development of consciousness. Our understanding however also aims at giving empirical substance to this notion of cooperation as well as to the notion of communication conflict as used by Smedslund.

Social developmental constructivism and modelling theory

A social psychology of cognitive development cannot exclude the study of the phenomena of learning by modelling. One of the recent trends in learning studies using Piagetian tests, for example, deals with operational learning in children observing a model. (For examples of similar research see Charbonneau *et al.* 1976, 1977, Robert and Charbonneau 1977, 1978, 1979.)

On the other hand the role of sociocognitive conflict in development means that interaction effects cannot be explained by relying exclusively on modelling theory. What seems necessary is an integration of the modelling effect within the framework of our social interactivist and constructivist theory of intelligence. We demonstrate below that improvements in performance often derive not from copying a correct model but from the confrontation of opposed centrations that are socially produced. In certain situations the presentation of a solution cognitively less advanced than what a child is capable of can also lead to progress – it is indeed possible to learn from the mistakes of others. Of course viewing correct models also contributes to learning, but this contribution depends on the extent to which the model gives rise to sociocognitive conflict. To be effective, the model must introduce opposing centrations and at the same time offer to the thus confronted child important elements for a reorganisation of his ideas.

Social marking

One area of research currently being developed deals with how children conceptualise social reality (see, for example, Damon 1977, Furth *et al.*, 1976, Jahoda, 1979). Most of these investigations are still limited to describing a correlation between the development of social awareness and cognitive development as described by Piaget, and lack conclusions regarding causal links between the two.

We have introduced the term social marking to examine the causal intervention of social regulations as norms in cognitive development. This notion refers to links which exist between social relations in an interaction between individuals in a given situation and the cognitive relations inherent in certain properties of objects which mediate the social relationships.

Social marking occurs when there is homology between social relationships established in a situation and the cognitive relationships between characteristics of objects important in the situation. The specificity of a social relationship in a given situation depends on a system of norms and representations which predate it. Of course these norms and representations can be modified in situations but these changes do not take place arbitrarily – the principles and schemes which govern the unfolding of social interaction are characterised by a certain necessity. There is moreover good reason to invoke a similar necessity, such as that used in descriptions of operational structures in Piagetian psychology, in the description of cognitive organisation. The notion of social marking allows us to study the links between the principles of social organisation and the principles of cognitive organisation.

In some situations social markers provide the solution to sociocognitive conflict in that new cognitive structures will develop if they function to establish or maintain social organisation. These ideas have also been experimentally evaluated and we have been able to show for example that adherence to a socially sanctified principle of equal distribution helps children resist perceptually misleading centrations of transformations of equal amounts, just as the conservation of inequality is aided when it is mediated by assymetrical relationships such as that existing between an adult and a child.

The sociological factor

Psychologists and sociologists have each developed their own theories of intelligence, and places where these two streams of thought flow together are rare. At first glance it may seem that the effect of social conditions intervening in cognitive development would be to produce arbitrarily diverse forms of intelligence as a function of these different social conditions. This however is not the case: the social intercoordination of individual abilities is characterised by respect for apparent invariants such as, for example, the relationships between in front/behind, left/right and above/below in the representation of space. Of course social markers can assign different significance to these different positions, for example by valuing differently what is above rather than below, on the right rather than left, in front rather than behind. But this does not prevent each of these positions from necessarily implying a complementary position, or mean that they can be coordinated arbitrarily.

The aim of our book is not to pass judgement on debates over the universality or specificity of cognitive processes. However, it seems unwise to conclude prematurely that important differences between cultures and social groups exist. As already noted Cole and Scribner (1974) demonstrated that apparent differences in the cognitive functioning of cultural groups disappeared when the researchers succeeded in creating situations which activated appropriate cognitive abilities.

A similar and exhaustive attempt to activate demonstration of ability should be made before concluding that differences between children originate in different social category membership. Our social interactionist approach has led us to develop paradigms to study cognition that are less individualistic than the traditional ones. The traditional method of intelligence testing deals in our view with only a single, individual, aspect of cognitive development, and isolates the child from the social conditions in which cognition develops. It is this social aspect that is the central focus in our experimental procedures and one of our primary interests was to see whether use of these more complete approaches necessitated some modification in currently dominant beliefs about differences in children from different social backgrounds.

Conclusions

The rest of the book illustrates the way in which the social definition of cognitive development put forward in this chapter has been translated into experiments concerned with the seven themes just discussed. Of course no one piece of research has integrated all seven of the themes, and frequently we have been able to tackle only a few of these issues in a single study. However, the research taken as a whole must be considered as bearing witness to the validity of the approach, with each single study illustrating only certain elements of the much larger theoretical framework.

One way of organising this book would have been to take up each of the themes discussed here again and to describe the results of research relevant to it. Such a procedure has the disadvantage of making continual repetition of the different experimental procedures necessary. We have chosen therefore to group the research according to the paradigm used and thus to keep to a minimum the description of experimental technique.

The following chapters deal with research using a cooperative game demanding coordination of interdependent motor responses (Chapter 3), distribution tasks dealing with the conservation of liquid and number (Chapter 4), tests of the conservation of equality and inequality of length (Chapter 5) and a spatial transformation task involving the reconstruction of a model village (Chapter 6). Table 2.1 lists references to all the experiments described in the book together with the main issues tackled in each.

TABLE 2.1. *List of Experiments and Their Principal Themes*

	Comparisons between individual and collective conditions	Interaction phase performance level	Forms of interaction	Prerequisites for benefiting from interaction	Individual progress	Generalisation of progress	Sociocognitive conflict	Modelling effects	Cognitive composition of the group	Social marking	Sociological factors
The Cooperative game (Chapter 3)											
1. Doise and Mugny (1975)	X	X									
2. Doise and Mugny (1975)		X	X								
3. Doise and Mugny (1975)		X	X								
4. Mugny and Doise (1979)	X	X		X	X						X
Social sharing (Chapter 4)											
1. Perret-Clermont (1980a)	X				X						
2. Perret-Clermont (1980a)				X	X	X			X		X
3. Zoetebier and Ginther (1978)	X			X	X	X			X		
4. Perret-Clermont (1980a)					X				X		X
5. Pinxten and Bressers (1979)	X				X	X				X	
6. Perret-Clermont (1980b)					X			X	X	X	X
Sociocognitive conflict (Chapter 5)											
1. Mugny, Doise and Perret-Clermont (1975–76)	X				X	X	X	X			
2. Mugny, Giroud and Doise (1978–79)	X		X		X	X	X				
3. Mugny, Giroud and Doise (1978–79)	X				X	X	X				
4. Doise, Dionnet and Mugny (1978)			X		X	X				X	
Spatial transformation (Chapter 6)											
1. Doise, Mugny and Perret-Clermont (1975)	X	X			X						
2. Mugny and Doise (1978a)		X			X		X		X		
3. Mugny and Doise (1978b)	X				X		X				X
4. Carugati and Mugny (1978)			X		X	X					
5. Mugny, Lévy and Doise (1978)	X	X			X		X	X			
6. Lévy (1981)		X	X		X		X				
7. Mugny and Rilliet (1980)	X				X					X	

3

The cooperative game and the coordination of interdependent actions

> Neither the individual in itself nor society in itself exists. What do exist are interindividual relationships, some of which have no effect on individuals but others of which transform both the individual and the social mind
>
> Piaget (1976a: 80)

When Piaget wrote these lines in 1928, he was referring to two diametrically opposed types of interaction: constraint, which is characterised by some authoritative intervention, and cooperation, which is characterised by equality between interactors and involves no element of authority or prestige. Piaget believed that only this second form of social relationship was a process in which new social realities could be constructed, and which avoided reducing these new realities to the more imposition of social rules. Central to his approach was the idea that development progressed from a state characterised by social constraint towards an equilibrium characterised by social cooperation between equals.

How does such cooperation develop? In tackling this question Nielsen (1951) carried out a series of experiments on the social development of the child. Her results show children to be capable of cooperation only in the later phases of development, and suggest that true cooperation is actually the final stage of development. To illustrate these findings we can look more closely at one of the tasks (similar in many ways to the task discussed in this chapter) Nielsen used in her experiments, a task called 'drawing with attached pencils'. Two children sitting facing one another across a table are each required to make the same drawing, for example of a house. To do so they must each use a pencil attached to the other child's pencil by a string, which is deliberately made too short for both children to work on parts of their picture close to the respective table edges at the same time. To let one child draw the basement of his house, the other must work for example on the roof of his.

Nielsen found in fact that children up to the age of 10 had great difficulty in performing the task successfully. Nearly 50% of the 7 year olds failed to 'interact reciprocally' and even in the 10 year old age group nearly 30% of the children still engaged in egocentric behaviour. Only amongst the oldest group studied, 13 year olds, did the coefficient of egocentrism drop to zero.

Such research appears to show that 'true' cooperation is the final stage in cognitive development. It is clear that cooperation *per se* presents problems that are not always solved immediately by children (nor, what is more, by adults either). Our approach to the issue differs from those such as Nielsen's however to the extent that we consider cooperation not as a dependent variable (where it is *a priori* defined as a balanced sociocognitive relationship the achievement of which is to be studied) but as an independent variable, by using a task in which the actions of several individuals are meaningless unless they are coordinated. Considering cooperation as a constructive social process in this way means that the actions of much younger children, even if not organised in very advanced ways, may also be considered cooperative.

On closer examination, 'drawing with attached pencils' does not really allow cooperative behaviour in itself to be studied – in fact the task does not intrinsically demand real cooperation, since each child's drawing can, indeed must, be completed individually. Cooperation is demanded of the children only via verbal instruction, and whether the difficulty in obtaining cooperation arises more from characteristics of methodology than from characteristics of children's thought is debatable. While trying to study co-operation, Nielsen paradoxically appears to have activated a norm of competition.

Whatever the case may be, we felt it essential to ensure that cooperation was an intrinsic part of any cooperative task given to children, and found the work of Madsen (1967) for example, where the cooperative and competitive behaviour of children in various subcultures has been studied in its own right, to be more helpful. This research has adequately demonstrated that younger children are capable of cooperation when task completion entails such behaviour.

To study cooperation as part of the dynamic process of cognitive development our task also had to be of this nature, with cooperation being activated not by verbal instruction but by the very demands of the task. This was important moreover because we wished to study not only the origin of cooperation but also its development in experimentally manipulated situations. Above all however we were interested in evaluating cognitive progress following interindividual cooperation, for by doing so we could attribute to cooperation a dynamic status which had previously been denied to it.

The cooperative game

The cooperative game can be played by a single child or by several children. Its basic principle is the coordination of children's actions on a varying number of pulleys aimed at moving a central part attached by strings to those pulleys along a predetermined path. It is only by coordinating the various actions possible on the pulleys that the central part can be made to move forward along the path. When several children play the game together, only social coordination of these actions allows such movement. The game thus intrinsically entails social coordination, without relying on verbal instructions explicitly demanding such behaviour – thus we felt justified in christening it 'the Cooperative Game'. The technical details of the equipment can be seen in Plate I.

The equipment consists of a round flat table-like surface 60cm in diameter placed at the centre of a metal base surrounded by three (or up to as many as six) vertical posts to which the pulleys are attached.

The pulleys comprise a cylinder with a disc at either end forming a 'wheel' shape. One end of the string connecting the pulleys and the central part is attached to the cylinder while the other is attached to the central moving part by a small screw on a swivel. Use of fairly thick fishing line as the 'string' avoids breakages.

The technical arrangement of the pulleys means that the operation of the equipment can be regulated in three ways. One of the discs at the end of each cylinder is drilled with small holes in which a screw can be inserted to regulate the pulley's resistance to being moved. When the screw is screwed right in, the pulley is jammed, and cannot be moved, regardless of the force used on it. When the screw is loosened slightly it allows a 'notch by notch' movement, each movement allowing about half a centimetre of string either in or out. The equipment is generally operated under these conditions, as it allows the child to move the string easily when he intends to do so while allowing him to 'jam' the pulley when he thinks it necessary and to avoid mistakes like unintended movements. The 'notch by notch' method also prevents one pulley being activated automatically by mere pressure from another pulley and prevents the string from unrolling all the way as the result of pressure, accident or mistake. This is necessary when children attempt to resolve the difficulty of cooperating by using brute force! When the screw is right out the pulley runs freely and can thus easily be moved by pressure from another pulley. This mode of operation was in fact used only in the experimental phase of the last experiment to be described, where it allowed subjects (especially those working alone) to use indirect pressure on another pulley to complete the task.

The task consists of moving the central part to which is connected a felt pen (the marker) along a course drawn on large sheets of paper attached to the round surface. The marker thus traces the precise course the central part follows giving the subjects immediate performance feedback. The height of the pulleys is fixed in such a way as to prevent the central part and marker from leaving the surface regardless of pressure from the pulleys.

By manipulating the discs (which are large enough for the child to grip comfortably) at the end of the cylinders, subjects can move the pulley and thus the string attached to the marker in three ways. By just holding the pulley steady the child can 'block', that is, prevent its string from moving at all. By rolling the 'wheel' towards himself the child can pull in on the string thus moving the marker towards him. When the wheel is turned away from the child, the string is played out. These actions on different pulleys must be coordinated to move the marker down the course. In fact some of the youngest children studied were unable to play the game even when there was some resistance on the pulleys (notch by notch for example) as they were incapable of coordinating the direct (pulling in the string) and the reciprocal (playing out or blocking the string) movements.

Task instructions

When a child takes part for the first time (and in some experiments the child plays the game several times) he is collected from class and willingness to participate is checked (refusals are rare and usually not final). He is then taken to the experimental room and shown the equipment.

The experimenter explains that the game is to make the moving part and thus the marker follow the course drawn on the table. The experimenter places the marker at the start of the track and guides it along the path with his hand, stressing all the time that it must follow the path and stay right in the middle of it as much as possible. The child then repeats the instructions.

The experimenter then goes on to explain that the game would be too easy if the marker was kept on the track with one's hand and that it is more fun to do it using these 'wheels' (indicating the pulleys). Using a single pulley (to avoid demonstrating that coordination with other pulleys is possible) the experimenter shows the child the three possible movements: 'you see, if you roll the wheel towards you, you pull in the string; if you roll it away from you, you play out the string; and if you just hold the wheel the string does not move'. The demonstration aims at ensuring difficulties with manipulating the equipment will not arise, and the experimenter checks the child's knowledge of the actions by asking 'What do you do to pull the string in? And to let it out? And what happens if you just hold the wheel steady?' and so on. If the child can not recall the right movements, the experimenter repeats them and again checks that the child can perform them. Only a few subjects, the very youngest, proved incapable of performing and remembering the actions. It is important to emphasise that while the experimenter ensures the children can carry out the three operations, he carefully avoids indicating that coordinations of simultaneous action on more than 1 pulley are required to complete the task.

The circuits

The difficulty of the circuits used naturally differed according to the number of subjects who had to coordinate their actions, and the ones used here were designed for use with either 2 or 3 pulleys. In the early studies a 2-pulley course was used and the task could as easily be done by one child operating one pulley with each hand as by two children. Later a circuit demanding three children each to manipulate a pulley was used. Although difficult, it proved easier than expected for one child to complete the 3-pulley task.

The 2-pulley course is of course simpler than the 3-pulley circuit. It consists in fact of 2 tracks, as can be seen in Fig. 3.1, which the children complete one after the other.

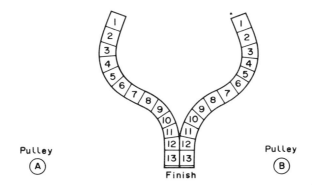

FIG. 3.1   Plan of the circuit for the cooperative game using two pulleys.

A schematic version of what actions must be coordinated to complete successfully the left hand track in Figure 3.1 would be as follows, with A and B being the 2 pulleys manipulated by either one or two children.
– from 1 to 2 the string attached to pulley A must be pulled in while no action is necessary from pulley B (at the start of the game the marker is placed at 1 with all strings taut),
– from 2–6 both strings must be pulled on, whether simultaneously or by using alternate and successive tugs on each string (which is the strategy most children adopt).
– from 6–9 pulley B must be used to pull in its string while pulley A plays out string,
– from 9–13 both pulleys must again be used to pull on the 2 strings together.

As can be seen, this circuit mainly demands the use of direct (pulling) actions, while the more difficult reciprocal actions are hardly necessary, especially if the marker is kept in the middle of the track. Reciprocal actions are not entirely unnecessary however, as the children often make mistakes and must try to get the marker back into the middle of the track. This is not always possible, as the marker is not attached to a third pulley which would allow it to be moved backwards, and this is a problem with this type of track. It also makes the 2-pulley game less discriminative as it is practically impossible to return to the centre of the track if the marker has left the course. The best subjects are thus not able to demonstrate their full potential.

This difficulty is overcome in the circuits for 3 pulleys (A, B, and C), as seen in Figure 3.2.

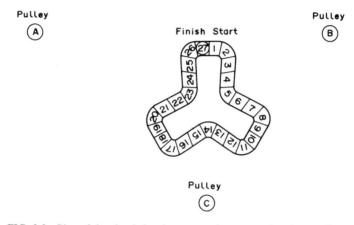

FIG. 3.2   Plan of the circuit for the cooperative game using three pulleys.

A schematic sequence of the coordinations necessary for this circuit would be
– from 1–2 pulley B must pull in, pulley A must play out and pulley C must pull in (without which the marker would not move round the bend),
– from 2–5 pulleys A and B must play out and pulley C pull in its string so the marker can advance,
– from 5–8 pulleys B and C must pull in while the other pulley plays its string out, and so forth.

In reality the task is more complex, as the actions of either pulling in or playing out simultaneously are not strictly that simple – one pulley must pull in more quickly than the other or one let out less string than the other for example.

The reason for the greater difficulty of the 3-pulley circuit is clear – at any given time at least one reciprocal action is necessary to allow the one or more direct actions to be effective. Our subjects had two problems here. Not only is it difficult to coordinate reciprocal action with its complementary direct action, but it is difficult to coordinate the various simultaneous direct actions too.

The general procedure for evaluating performance is as follows (exact details are given for each experiment). The circuit is divided lengthwise into a certain number of units, each of which is scored −1, 0 (zero), or +1. To assign the score, each unit (and thus the whole circuit) is divided breadthwise into thirds (although the circuit used in the last experiment had a central 'third' 12mm wide and 2 outside 'thirds' 10mm wide). When the trace made by the marker falls within the central third, the unit is considered to have been the result of a successful coordination and is thus scored +1. Once a successful evaluation has been assigned to a unit, this evaluation is not modified even if the trace reenters the unit backwards or in an outside third, as long as it has first crossed into the next correct unit. When the mark encroaches on or is wholly within either of the outside thirds, or leaves the unit in the wrong direction without having first crossed into the next correct unit, the unit is scored zero. This score indicates certain difficulties in coordinating. When the trace leaves the path altogether, the unit is counted as having presented serious coordination difficulties and is scored −1. Difficulties in scoring certainly exist, but are relatively infrequent and scores appear adequately to reflect the amount of difficulty the children have. An example of scoring is given in Figure 3.3.

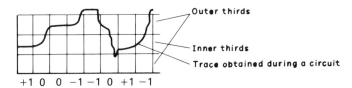

FIG. 3.3   An example of scoring of segments of the course.

For each circuit the performance score is obtained by summing across the scores of all the units.

Experimental overview

This experimental paradigm was developed primarily with a view to studying inter-individual coordination of actions in a task which demanded social cooperation when several children worked together. The first issue to be tackled was that of a comparison between the performances of groups of children and those of children attempting the same task alone. In the first experiment groups could structure themselves and function as they wished as long as the circuit was attempted with each child operating a single pulley. The comparison of individual and collective activity was made at different age levels. The superiority of group performance postulated in the preceding chapter was expected to appear only in the youngest children who had yet to elaborate the cognitive skills necessary for effective coordination of action. Once these skills had been socially elaborated and individually internalised at a more advanced age, this difference in performance was expected to disappear.

Using the same age groups as Experiment 1, a second experiment compared collective performances where the nature of the interaction allowed to develop during the game was manipulated. While some groups were free to work as they wished, some groups had a hierarchical structure imposed by requiring that the group obeyed a 'leader' who directed actions for each course. This was intended to make the collective performance more dependent on the ability of a single individual. Such 'individualisation of interaction' was expected to result in poorer collective performances amongst the youngest subjects, as these will depend more on individual ability. The difference between spontaneous and hierarchical collective performance was expected to disappear with the older children, as they should have internalised by this time the cognitive abilities necessary to complete the task.

In a third experiment, the interaction of certain groups was also disrupted, this time by forbidding verbal communication. Once again such a procedure was intended to make collective performance dependent more on the contribution of each member than on the thus limited cooperation. Our hypotheses were similar for both experiments – the disruption of interaction was expected to be more serious when the subjects were younger and had yet to develop the cognitive skills necessary for coordination.

An experiment of particular importance for two reasons concludes the chapter. Firstly, in this experiment the coordination scores of individuals before and after interaction were compared allowing us to test the hypothesis that interindividual coordination both precedes and promotes intraindividual coordinations. Moreover, by studying in more detail the performance of different age groups the theoretical sequence of development proposed could be better evaluated. While at a first stage neither individual nor collective activity was expected to lead to cognitive progress (as the cognitive prerequisites were lacking), at a second level collective activity was expected to be superior to individual activity in promoting improvement in individual performance following the experimental phase. Finally, at a still later stage, the two types of activity should produce approximately the same amount of progress.

This experiment also gave us the opportunity to tackle the issue of the impact of social environment on performance, as it involved children from two environments distinctly different in social, economic, and cultural terms. Such an experiment thus allowed the generality of our theoretical approach to be evaluated.

**Experiment 1. Intraindividual and interindividual
coordinations**

Do children coordinate their actions better when these actions are performed by several individuals or when they are performed 'intraindividually'
i.e. by the 2 hands of the same child? Our general hypothesis suggests that
collective performances will be superior to individual performances at that
time when such coordination is starting to develop. With older children such
a difference should no longer occur.

This hypothesis was first tested with the 2-pulley game, which a pilot study
had shown to be easier than the 3-pulley game for the reasons discussed
above. The experimental design involved four conditions resulting from the
crossing of two dichotomous variables. Coordinations were carried out
either by a single child or by two children (each operating one pulley). The
subjects were children of either 7–8 years of age (which pilot studies had
shown to be the age at which gradual elaboration of abilities necessary for
this task begins) or 9–10 years of age, an age at which the main difficulties of
coordination seem to have been resolved. Our hypothesis was thus that at
7–8 years a difference would appear between individual and collective performance while with the 9–10 year olds this difference would no longer be
apparent.

The subjects completed first the right-hand and then the left-hand courses
shown in Fig. 3.1. In the individual condition subjects had to complete the
task by simultaneously manipulating 2 pulleys (the notch-by-notch mode of
operation was used for the advantages outlined above). In the group condition subjects were randomly placed in front of, and had to operate exclusively, one of the 2 pulleys, while trying to complete the circuit together. The
nature and function of interaction was not restricted in any way by instructions, the experimenter merely making it clear that the children were free to
talk. During the task the experimenter always retreated a little so that
activity could occur as spontaneously as possible. When the task was finished
the children were questioned at length regarding their impressions of the
game, their collective or individual activity, what difficulties they had
encountered, and so forth. As these data are not however directly relevant
they are not reported here.

Twenty-four 7–8 year old children took part, eight in the individual
condition and sixteen divided into eight groups of two in the collective condition. Number and distribution of subjects was identical for the 9–10 year
olds.

The index of performance in this experiment was calculated from the
scores of the better of the two courses in Fig. 3.1, thus from the best performance of which the subjects showed themselves capable. Each of the
courses were divided lengthwise into 88 units and so scores range from a
possible best of $+88$ to a possible worst performance of -88.

Table 3.1 shows the mean performance scores for the four conditions.

TABLE 3.1. *Mean performance scores (n=8)*

	7–8 years	9–10 years
Individuals	+46.63[a]	+54.00
Groups	+59.25[b]	+59.00

Mann-Whitney U-test, conditions a and b, U=14, p<0.032.

The results thus partially confirmed our hypothesis. A significant difference did occur between individual and collective performances at the 7–8
year old level and only at this age does group activity produce performances
superior to those produced by the individual alone. Social interaction does
indeed seem to provide the ideal context for the elaboration of action coordination. As we had predicted, this difference was no longer apparent in
the results of the older children. It is interesting to note moreover that the
collective performances of the 7–8 year olds did not differ from the individual or collective performances of the 9–10 year olds. It seems as if collective
activity gives rise to coordinations which foreshadow in some way the coordinations which are manifested at a later stage by a child working
individually.

One difficulty did arise in the results however. The difference between the
individual performance of the 7–8 year olds and those of the 9–10 year olds
did not reach the level of significance that we had expected from a theoretical point of view. It seems likely that the experimental task used here
offers some explanation for this. As can be seen the scores obtained were
particularly high overall, indicating as foreseen that the 2-pulley game is
relatively easy, demanding as it does only minor use of the difficult
reciprocal actions. Thus it is possible that the results are influenced by a
'ceiling effect' which masked, however slightly, improvement of performance with age. Two later experiments thus used the much more difficult
3-pulley game, which discriminates more finely between performances of
different quality. One further experiment was however carried out using the
2-pulley game.

Experiment 2. Spontaneous groups versus hierarchical groups

The second experiment was concerned more specifically with the quality
of collective performance as related to the nature of the interaction between
partners in the game. In fact simply comparing individual and group performances does not provide information as to what factors in an interindividual
encounter are responsible for the superiority of group performances at
certain levels of development.

Of particular importance here is the fact that any manipulation which makes group performance more dependent upon the abilities of individual group members should reduce the level of group performance to that of which the individual members are capable. In other words, the best performance of a group under these conditions should not be too different from the performances of the individuals alone. To test out this prediction two new conditions were added in Experiment 2 to the four conditions used in Experiment 1. Thirty-two new subjects were divided into sixteen groups of two, eight at the 7–8 year-old level and eight at the 9–10 year old level. These subjects had to perform the same experimental task as used in the collective condition of Experiment 1, a condition now more precisely referred to as the 'spontaneous collective' condition, to stress that interaction was in no way constrained. The subjects in the sixteen new groups however had a hierarchical structure imposed upon them by making one child a 'leader' who had to direct action and who had to be obeyed.

One of the children was thus randomly chosen to be leader for the first course while the other child was leader for the second course. As the index of performance was based on the better of the two courses, changing the leader was necessary to ensure that the performance finally analysed would result from the better of the two leaders, as the variation in the children's ability to lead would otherwise have affected the comparison. Comparison was thus made possible between this and the spontaneous condition in which it was possible that one child (and usually the better) could direct both performances. Experiment 2 was carried out in the same school with the same classes as Experiment 1.

Table 3.2 gives the mean index of performance of the groups in the two new conditions as well as that of the subjects in the four conditions from Experiment 1. Again the possible range of scores is from +88 to −88.

TABLE 3.2. *Mean performances (n=8)*

	7–8 years	9–10 years
Individuals	+46.63[a]	+54.00[d]
Spontaneous groups	+59.25[b]	+59.00[e]
Hierarchical groups	+43.50[c]	+71.63[f]

Mann-Whitney U-test, conditions b and c, U=16, p<0.052
conditions d and f, U=12.5, p<0.05 two tailed test.

Our hypotheses were clearly confirmed: the hierarchical collective performances of the 7–8 year olds did not differ from those of individuals of the same age tested alone and were significantly worse than the spontaneous collective performances of age mates. With the 9–10 year olds the reverse effect can be seen – not only was there a slight tendency for hierarchical groups to be better than spontaneous groups, but the individualised groups also performed significantly better than individuals of the same age working alone.

The effect of imposing a hierarchy on interpersonal relations is thus particularly complex. At one phase in the elaboration of a notion it can prove an obstacle to performance to the extent that it makes collective performance depend on individual ability, while later, when coordinations have been mastered, making a child responsible for the management of interaction can ensure that capability is fully expressed. This 'individualisation of interaction' effect was also demonstrated in another experiment.

Experiment 3. Blocking collective functioning

Another way of reducing collective activity to the abilities of the individual members is to hinder the free interaction of the group. The manipulation used in this experiment consisted of forbidding verbal communication between subjects.

Our hypothesis here was based on the idea that communication conflict is one of the essential factors aiding progress when a notion is initially being developed. We had already observed strong disagreements in our subjects' verbal exchanges. Such exchanges are particularly necessary when the equipment is arranged in such a way (i.e. operating under 'notch by notch' conditions) as to prevent one subject exercising direct action to force another into reciprocal action (for example by pulling so hard on one string that another is forced to play out). In the face of not being able to get one's own way by force, verbal negotiation of proposals and disagreements was necessary!

Two experimental conditions were thus used and were again employed with both 7–8 year olds and 9–10 year olds. In the 'communication' condition instructions given were identical to those in the spontaneous condition used in the first two experiments. In the 'no communication' condition the subjects were explicitly asked not to talk and the experimenter, although retreating as usual, reminded subjects about the rule if it was broken. Even when the nonverbal communication (such as nodding and shaking the head, eye blinking and gesturing to indicate a desired action) used is taken into account, it was clear that in this condition the subjects were largely deprived of explicit indications or directions of how and when to coordinate action.

The 3-pulley game was used this time (see Fig. 3.2), necessitating only a single completion of the one circuit, with somewhat larger units than those used in other experiments. The circuit was divided into 27 units and thus performance scores could range from a possible high of +27 to a possible low of −27.

Seventy-two children took part and were divided into twenty-four groups of three, twelve groups in the communication condition and twelve in the no communication condition. Eight of the groups in each condition were comprised of 7–8 year olds while, for practical reasons, only four groups of 9–10 year olds could be studied in each condition.

Table 3.3 gives the mean performance scores obtained in the four experimental conditions.

TABLE 3.3. *Mean performances*

	7–8 years (n=8)	9–10 years (n=4)
communication condition	+3.50[a]	+8.75
no communication condition	−4.50[b]	+7.00

Mann-Whitney U-test, conditions a and b, U=13.5, p<0.03.

Results confirmed our expectations and were consistent with those of the previous experiments. Whereas the no communication groups had serious difficulties at the younger level which caused them to perform much less well than groups at the same age level who were allowed to communicate, such a difference was no longer apparent in the older children's results.

This again demonstrates that when the notions being examined are first developing free communication is important. Any disruption of it leads, as in the previous experiment, to the collective performance being dependent more on the coordination abilities of individuals than on cooperation, which cannot develop. These results clearly show that interaction cannot simply be regarded as the sum of the initial abilities of its participating members and that it does not lead to a mere reproduction of these initial abilities but on the contrary enables the construction of new and more advanced cognitive skills. The use of other paradigms later enabled us to show that the essential element in the social dynamic of development is indeed interindividual communication conflict.

Of equal importance here is the fact that the younger subjects had great difficulty in completing the 3-pulley task. While the scores obtained by all subjects in the 2-pulley game had been high, the youngest subjects all scored close to zero, which confirmed our previous argument that the coordinations (and especially the reciprocal actions) necessary in the 3-pulley game were more complex.

One criticism can be raised in regard to all three experiments discussed so far. It could be argued that the age groups considered are not representative of a range wide enough or fine enough to deal adequately with the complexity of the development of social coordination as proposed in our theory. Therefore in a further experiment the age groups studied were more finely distinguished and ranged over the crucial stages of elaboration of coordination.

Experiment 4. Cognitive development following collective activity in two social milieux

This last experiment differed from the preceding ones in several important ways. The equipment was now in its final form and the number of subjects was much greater. Moreover the experimental procedure this time involved an individual pretest, a collective or individual experimental phase and an individual posttest designed to reveal any cognitive progress that individuals might make. Finally the same experiment was simultaneously carried out in an environment which was both socioculturally and economically disadvantaged and in a more favoured social milieu.

A 3-pulley cooperative game (see Fig. 3.4) was used, but the methods of evaluating performance differed in the various phases of the experiment, which are discussed in more detail below.

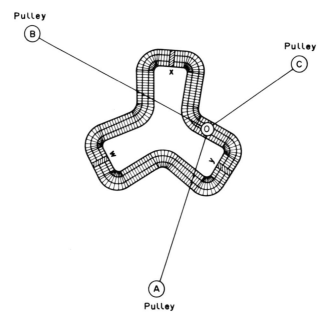

FIG. 3.4   Plan of the course in experiment 4.

During the individual pre and posttesting, subjects had to complete the first two-thirds of the circuit using pulleys A and B (while the string attached to pulley C ran completely free), and the last third using all 3 pulleys. The scores of this last third alone were used to compute the performance index.

On arriving in the experimental room (located at their school) for the pretest, subjects were shown how the equipment worked in the usual way. They then started the first part of the circuit from x to w, using pulleys A and

B between which they stood. They then proceeded from y to w. Thereafter at point x, all 3 strings were pulled taut and the subjects used all 3 pulleys to complete the circuit from x to y. To do so they had to move around the equipment although they were initially directed to start at pulley C. (A pilot study had shown that being positioned between B and C inhibited some subjects – those who had difficulty coordinating direct actions were often incapable of coordinating direct and reciprocal action and could not have even started the course from this position.)

Again the instructions stressed that the marker was to be kept to the middle of the course as much as possible. This time the pulley(s) not being used by the child were 'jammed' by the experimenter so that subjects could not use force to obtain a complementary action from another pulley. Subjects who were not able to work out how to complete the 2-pulley part of the course were not retained for the experimental phase. The time taken to complete the course varied from about 10 to 20 minutes, with the last 3-pulley part of the course causing most difficulty. When a subject stayed 'stuck' at one place for 10 minutes or when a subject could not get started, the game was terminated. In the latter case subjects were first reminded about the 3 possible actions and the need to use all 3 pulleys. If subjects tried to use brute strength to succeed these same instructions were repeated and the subject was reminded that the pulleys had to be manipulated before they would move.

About 1 week after the pretest the experimental phase (described below) took place and a week after this subjects were again individually posttested. In this test subjects were positioned between pulleys A and B which they used to complete the course from y to w and then all 3 pulleys were used to complete the x to y stage. Instructions were repeated for subjects who became stuck and if no progress had been made for 10 minutes (something that occurred only on the last part of the course) the posttest was terminated.

Performances were evaluated by scoring the 3-pulley part of the course which had been shown to be more discriminating than the 2-pulley stage. Completing the 2-pulley stage first however gave the subjects some practice and functioned to eliminate those completely incapable of operating the pulleys. The final part of the course was divided lengthwise into 60 units and thus possible scores ranged from a high of $+60$ to a low of -60.

The experimental phase required the children to complete the whole circuit using all 3 pulleys starting and finishing at x by passing through points y and w.

In one condition subjects worked alone. After the instructions had been given and all 3 strings made taut with the marker at x, the subjects were placed in front of pulley C. They thus had to move around the equipment in the same way as before although this time, unlike in the individual tests, the pulleys were not jammed. Subjects could thus bring about reciprocal action from one pulley by pulling on another. This made the individual situation more like the collective situation. The experimental phase was terminated after 10 minutes which was sufficient for almost all subjects in both conditions to finish the task.

In 2 other collective conditions either 2 or 3 children worked together. Each subject was reminded how the equipment worked and the group was told it could communicate freely, which had been shown to be important in the social elaboration of abilities by the preceding experiments. The groups then had 10 minutes in which to complete the circuit.

In the 3-person condition, each child operated a single pulley which he was instructed to hold firmly so that unintended action due to pressure from another pulley would be avoided.

In the 2-person condition, one subject manipulated pulley A while the other worked both B and C. This child had to work both pulleys at once in order to make the situation different from one in which the child could occupy various positions successively. While some differences between subjects operating either one or 2 pulleys was expected, no such systematic difference was found.

As the experimental phase necessitated completing all of the course and not just the final third, scores in this phase ranged between +180 and −180. These scores were divided by 3 so that scores in all 3 phases ranged from +60 to −60.

In assigning children to the groups in the collective conditions several criteria of homogeneity were adhered to wherever possible. The groups always consisted of 2 or 3 children of the same sex, age, and social origin from the same class where possible. Because this last was not always possible for children in the disadvantaged social milieu, an equal number of groups with partners from different classes was assigned to all conditions to avoid bias in the data.

The most important criterion of group make up was the degree of homogeneity in pretest scores, both within groups and in terms of groups with similar scores being distributed equally across conditions. Care was similarly taken in distributing children with particular scores equally amongst the 3 pulleys.

The experiment thus had 3 main variables – group versus individual activity, 5 to 6, 6–7 and 7–8 year old age groups, and advantaged versus disadvantaged social group membership. Ninety-five children, mainly the children of immigrant workers from the south of Spain whose sociological and cultural characteristics were known, were tested at a school in a working class suburb in Barcelona, Spain. These subjects were considered to be the disadvantaged group. The members of the other milieu were 95 children from a small industrial town outside Barcelona who attended a similarly run but private school. Their parents could all afford such private education and came from various professions and cultural backgrounds. The respective school buildings themselves reflected the differences between the 2 groups – on the one hand consisting of prefabricated temporary buildings and on the other of a luxurious villa surrounded by garden.

In each social group sample thirty-two 5–6 year olds, thirty-two 6 to 7 year olds, and thirty-one 7 to 8 year olds took part. Eight children were assigned to the individual conditions for both 5–6 and 6–7 year old groups with seven being so assigned from the 7–8 year old group. The other twenty-four were assigned to the collective condition, with four groups of three and six of two at each age level. One child from the disadvantaged group in the collective condition could not be posttested and is not considered in the analysis.

Three important points need to be made before the results are considered. First, the performance scores in the pre and posttests are considered as the scores of independent individuals, which is true in the pretest but not quite so true of the posttest since subjects in the collective condition had worked with at least one other child. The results relevant to progress made between pre and posttest can, however, to respect the basic principles of statistical method, only be dealt with by considering the progress scores of interacting partners as dependent, which they objectively are. To do this, the mean progress scores of the two or three partners are considered, which considerably reduces the numbers in the experimental condition but which makes the analysis more valid.

Secondly, as the results of the two collective conditions did not differ, they have been combined and considered together, which in fact makes more equal the number of entries per cell.

Finally, the results from the two different socioeconomic groups are considered separately first, as a temporal decalage appeared in the results which confounds the main effect of the experimental manipulation. A comparison of the two groups is made below in focusing on the sociological issue. We look first at the results for the disadvantaged group.

It is clear first of all (see Table 3.4) that the task proved very difficult for most of the subjects. The large negative scores produced by the youngest children indicates that the marker strayed from the course on many units. Even at the 7–8 year old level, pretest means are close to zero. Conditions were thus good for examining in more detail the development of coordination in the individual and collective experimental phases.

Consideration of these results shows once again that in general interindividual coordination of actions was superior to their intraindividual coordination. The results show this in two ways. Not only is collective performance superior to individual performance but groups also produced mean scores much better than those of which the individual group members had shown themselves capable in the pretest.

In line with our theory, the superiority of collective performance was not

TABLE 3.4. *Mean performances of disadvantaged group*

	Pretest	Experimental	Posttest
Individuals, 5–6 years	−20.13 (8)	−13.21 (8)	−25.00 (8)
Individuals, 6–7 years	−11.25 (8)	− 8.13 (8)[a]	−13.25 (8)
Individuals, 7–8 years	+ 1.00 (7)	+ 0.52 (7)[b]	+24.14 (7)
Groups, 5–6 years	−24.70 (23)	−16.87 (10)	−26.52 (23)
Groups, 6–7 years	−12.75 (24)	+17.03 (10)[c]	+17.79 (24)
Groups, 7–8 years	+ 1.08 (24)	+18.70 (10)[d]	+16.92 (24)

n in parentheses.
Mann-Whitney U-test, experimental phase, conditions a and c, $U=17$, $p<0.025$; conditions b and d, $U=21$, $p<0.10$.

stable across age groups. At the youngest age group, subjects in the collective condition did not improve on their initial individual performances, which suggests that the prerequisites, some initial competencies essential to the development of coordination, were not yet present.

If at the early age level groups merely reproduced in some way the performances of which their individual members are capable, at 6–7 years an improvement in collective performance was apparent, with groups being significantly better than individuals. At 7–8 years groups were still superior but not significantly so. These two conditions largely confirmed the results of Experiment 1.

Our essential aim however was to see if the effects of working in a group gave rise to some cognitive progress which members of groups can later demonstrate individually in the posttest. Table 3.5 presents the differences between mean performances in the pre and posttests (these figures are calculated from the mean performance obtained by the two or three members of the same interaction.)

TABLE 3.5. *Mean differences between pre and posttest performance,*
disadvantaged social group

	Individuals	Groups
5–6 years	− 4.88 (8)	− 1.83 (10)
6–7 years	− 2.00 (8)	+30.54 (10)*
7–8 years	+23.14 (7)*	+15.83 (10)*

n in parentheses.
*Wilcoxen T-test, $p<0.05$.

With one exception, individual progress was consistent with the results of the experimental phase. At 5–6 years neither individual nor group activity produced any progress. At 6–7 years collective activity, which produced better performances than individual activity, also led to better individual performances in the posttest (which were equal to the performances in the interaction) than the pretest. On the other hand, individual activity produced no progress in ability to coordinate. At 7–8 years collective activity had the same effect, encouraging individual progress. A surprising result appeared at this age for subjects working in the individual condition. Although they had shown no improvement on pretest performance during the experimental phase, they demonstrated considerable improvement in the posttest. Rather than regarding this as a simple practice effect, it could be argued that it is the result of a gradually developing autonomy in the child's ability to deal with cognitive problems. Before substantiating this argument however, an examination of the extent to which the results of the advantaged group are consistent with these is necessary.

Table 3.6 gives the mean performance scores across experimental conditions for members of the advantaged group.

TABLE 3.6. *Mean performances, advantaged social group*

	pretest	experimental	posttest
Individuals, 5–6 years	−10.88 (8)	+ 1.38 (8)	− 9.88 (8)
Individuals, 6–7 years	− 1.13 (8)	+ 1.42 (8)[a]	+ 0.75 (8)
Individuals, 7–8 years	+ 4.43 (7)	+15.57 (7)	+24.86 (7)
Groups, 5–6 years	−23.50 (24)	− 6.67 (10)	− 9.25 (24)
Groups, 6–7 years	+ 4.88 (24)	+26.90 (10)[b]	+18.17 (24)
Groups, 7–8 years	+12.71 (24)	+18.83 (10)	+25.67 (24)

n in parentheses.
Mann-Whitney U-test, experimental phase, conditions a and b, $U=8$, $p<0.01$.

While the pretest scores of these subjects are clearly higher than those of subjects in the disadvantaged group, it is nevertheless clear that the task was difficult for these children too. We were thus again able to examine the evolution of coordination during the experiment. Considering first the results of the experimental phase, it is clear that at 5–6 years individuals and groups both improved their performances. This improvement is maintained in the posttest however only by those subjects in the collective condition. This apparent progress by the individuals can thus be accounted for in terms of factors in the experimental procedure. As noted above, in the individual tests the pulleys were jammed when not being used while in the experimental phase this was not so. Children of this age group and social background often used brute pulling force to produce reciprocal playing out actions in the experimental phase which allowed them to avoid the difficult task of coordinating the actions. Their performances dropped again in the posttest therefore, where this technique was no longer possible.

The predicted difference between individual and collective activity conditions appeared again at the 6–7 year old level. While individuals did not improve their initial performances, groups clearly did so. At 7 to 8 years the results are a little less clear cut – individuals alone progressed a little while such progress was not clearly present for the groups. However these subjects had already produced good scores in the pretest and thus had relatively less room for improvement.

The data in Table 3.7 help clarify these results via a consideration of progress following the experimental phase.

TABLE 3.7. *Mean differences between pre and posttests, advantaged social group*

	Individuals	Groups
5–6 years	+ 1.00 (8)	+14.25 (10)*
6–7 years	+ 1.88 (8)	+13.29 (10)*
7–8 years	+20.43 (7)**	+12.96 (10)*

n in parentheses.
*Wilcoxen test, p<0.05.
**Wilcoxen test, p<0.10.

With one important exception which will be discussed below, the extent of progress shown was similar to that shown by disadvantaged group members. At 6–7 years significant progress was made by subjects in the collective but not the individual condition. The same effect appeared in the 7–8 year olds' results for both socioeconomic groups – both individual and group activity led to substantial improvement. These results strongly suggest that cognitive development gradually acquires a progressive autonomy after the initial elaboration of a notion.

Another effect is evident in the results of the advantaged group. Even in the 5–6 year olds, collective activity produced significant progress, which was not the case for the disadvantaged 5–6 year olds.

Results pertinent to the effect of individual and collective activity can be summarised as in Table 8, where each condition has been assigned 0 or + depending on whether no progress, or significant progress respectively, was demonstrated following the experimental phase.

TABLE 3.8. *Progress (+) and no progress (0) in posttest*

	Disadvantaged		Advantaged	
	Individual	Group	Individual	Group
5–6 years	0	0	0	+
6–7 years	0	+	0	+
7–8 years	+	+	+	+

The same pattern of development thus appears in both groups. The children in the disadvantaged group follow the basic model – at an initial period of development, certainly because cognitive prerequisites are not present, neither individual nor group activity allows the child to progress. At a second stage, only group activity allows collective coordination to be elaborated which are then individually appropriated. At a third later stage, progress is produced both by individual and group activity. As predicted interindividual encounters appear to provide a uniquely favourable context for the initial extension and elaboration of coordination skills. After this initial elaboration, however, autonomy is gradually acquired so that having once elaborated a particular notion in a collective situation, the individual appears capable of continuing to develop this notion via his own activity. Autonomy develops out of, and is the result of, interdependence.

The same pattern of development characterises the advantaged children except that interdependent activity is effective and beneficial as early as 5 to 6 years of age, a year earlier than in their disadvantaged counterparts. It may be conjectured that advantaged 4 to 5 year olds would probably find neither individual nor group activity beneficial, indicating that the necessary cognitive prerequisites were yet to develop.

A final important point arises. Pretest results show that advantaged children were superior to the disadvantaged children (who had greater coordination difficulties) although this difference was only significant for the 6 to 7 year olds. What is important however is that the progress following collective activity has marked consequences for this group difference. By comparing the results of Tables 3.4 and 3.6 it can be seen that while the pretest difference between the groups at the 6 to 7 year old level remains, in the posttests of the subjects in the individual condition, this difference is not apparent in the posttests of those in the collective condition. Moreover differences are no longer significant in either pre or posttest at the 7 to 8 year old level, indicating that the potential for coordination in the two groups does not differ. The posttest results of the disadvantaged subjects at both levels either equals or surpasses the pretest performance of advantaged children of the same age. A relatively short period of interaction thus enabled disadvantaged children to attain the initial level of the more advantaged children. Similar results will be reported again in later chapters.

This is not to say however that social interaction simply wipes out the effects of social discrimination. While it seems to allow children from disadvantaged social backgrounds to express a potential that individual activity does not, it also permits children from advantaged backgrounds to progress and what is more, at an even earlier age. The progress made by these 5 to 6 year olds following interaction was such that posttest results again showed a significant group difference.

As this issue is discussed below, it is sufficient to stress here that essentially the same pattern of development occurs in both groups. In both cases children progress towards autonomy after an initial period of interdependence. The age at which this interdependence can be taken advantage of to elaborate notions appears to be a function of social background.

Conclusions

The results of the four experiments using the cooperative game can now be summarised. Because the game demands the coordination of actions it was possible to evaluate our theoretical approach in relation to three of the basic themes discussed at the end of the last chapter.

First, the way in which collective activity generates coordinations that individuals alone are capable of only much later has been demonstrated. The superiority of group performance does not however occur at all stages of development but is to be found reliably at that time when the relevant notion is first being elaborated. Moreover social interaction is not necessary for further development at all stages – after this period of particular effectiveness (when group is better than individual performance) individual activity is also beneficial.

The second theme dealt with the individual appropriation or internalisation of abilities collectively elaborated. It is clear that this does occur, since in posttests individuals produce coordinations of a similar level as those produced by the group but superior to those of which they were capable in the pretest. But in the same way that group performance is superior to individual performance only when notions are being initially elaborated, progress following interaction is only significantly different from progress following other types of activity during this same period. A pattern of development is apparent which largely confirms our social concept of cognitive development. In the absence of certain prerequisites neither individual nor group activity produces progress. Later, progress results only from social interdependence – collective activity seems fundamental in elaborating the coordinations demanded by the cooperative game (and other tasks discussed below) while individual activity does not provide the same possibility for elaboration. Finally the child moves beyond this initial social interdependence towards increasing autonomy.

In conclusion, this research has stressed particularly the importance of the characteristics of interaction. To enable a group to develop its coordination capacities to the full, interaction must be such that it ensures total cooperation. The emergence of such cooperation may be blocked by disrupting the functioning or structure of the group so that collective performance is reduced to a dependence on the individual abilities of one or more of its members. When individual abilities are inferior to group abilities at the stage that a notion is being elaborated initially, the performance of restricted groups is inferior to that of freely functioning groups. Thus not just any kind of social interaction promotes cognitive development.

While these experiments suggest that interindividual confrontation and thus the conditions which foster it seem necessary for interaction to be beneficial, they have not dealt directly with the factors that make interaction so fundamental to cognitive development. Other evidence however also suggests, as we do, that sociocognitive conflict is central.

Leontiev (1970–1971) has described a series of experiments using a tracking task necessitating the coordination of interdependent actions similar to those demanded by the cooperative game. Although working with adults and interested in parameters such as speed, Leontiev reports several experiments that are directly relevant. In one concerning the effect of feedback, the experimenter asks interacting subjects to try to increase error. Paradoxically this seems to result in a significant improvement. It could be argued that what has been introduced is a procedure that intensifies sociocognitive conflict and the search for effective coordination. Whatever the case may be, it becomes clear from research described in the following chapters that sociocognitive conflict is in fact a central mechanism in the production of cognitive development through interaction as illustrated in this research using the cooperative game.

4

The benefits of sharing

How many little family dramas have originated in childish disputes over sharing? The significance of such disputes by far outweighs the material gains and losses that may result from them; once 'fair' shares are achieved children can very quickly give up the share that has been accorded to them, on the condition that other participants do not lay too blatant a claim to it. Experimental research has confirmed that 5 year old children know how to share on the basis of egalitarian principles (Lane and Coon, 1972; Lerner, 1974; Leventhal and Anderson, 1970), though the principle of fairness sometimes also leads them to produce unequal shares (Coon, Lane and Lichtman, 1974; Leventhal, Popp and Sawyer, 1973). Equality and fairness can be in competition, and can act differentially as a function of the experimental situation, particularly in the allocation of rewards by 5 year olds (Damon, 1977; Swerts, 1978). A form of social intelligence is revealed in such complex behaviours.

Now consider a child of this age participating in a classic Piagetian task, conservation of quantities of liquid. The experimenter has at his disposal two identical glasses (A and A1), and also a taller and narrower glass (B) and a wider and shallower glass (C) as shown in Fig. 4.1. He pours the same quantity of water or fruit juice into glasses A and A1 and asks the child if there is the same quantity to drink in the two glasses. The child agrees, though occasionally asks that a little bit more be added to one of the two glasses in order to bring the levels to exactly the same height. The experimenter then decants the contents of A1 into B and asks the child again if there is the same quantity of liquid in these two glasses. The child replies that there is more in the tall narrow glass (B), pointing out that the level is higher in this glass. The experimenter disagrees, possibly telling the child that once another child told him that there was the same amount to drink in glass A. Our subject replies that he would prefer glass B to drink anyway because there is more in it. In other words, he resists counter-suggestion. Then the experimenter replaces the contents of B in A1 and the child again agrees with him, affirming that there is the same to drink in the two glasses. Then the content of A1 is poured into C. In comparing A and C it is now A which contains the most in the child's view since its level is higher.

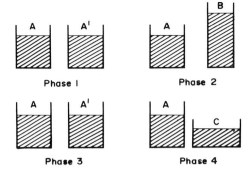

FIG. 4.1   Sequence of different phases of a conservation of liquids task.

Scenes of this nature have been observed thousands of times in Geneva and elsewhere in the world. We have described only one part of the test of conservation of quantities of liquid (see Piaget and Szeminska, 1952, and in more detail, Inhelder, Sinclair and Bovet, 1974). Of course, the child's replies are not always so clear; they can be more hesitant, waver in their opinion or agree with the counter-suggestions of the experimenter; they can also become openly conserving in asserting that the quantities of liquid remain the same, independent of their presentation in the different glasses.

Usually, according to the responses they give to the entire test, children are divided into three categories, or 'stages' to use the Piagetian terminology.

First stage: Absence of conservation (NC)

The child at this stage, presented with the same quantity of liquid in identical glasses, has no difficulty in recognising this equality. But if the liquid is put into containers of different shapes, he then believes that the quantity of liquid increases or diminishes depending on the shape of the container and in particular the height reached by the liquid in these containers.

Confronted with counter-arguments by the experimenter, the child either persists in his judgement or formulates other equally non-conserving responses. Reminding him of the initial equality in quantities does not modify his opinion in any way.

Second stage: Intermediate response (I)

These subjects waver between conservation and nonconservation of quantity. The reasons given are therefore generally incomplete and not very explicit. They do not follow any physical or logical necessity. They fluctuate between a coordination of the relations involved (height and breadth) and centration on one dimension.

Third stage: Necessary conservation (C)

The child immediately asserts the conservation of quantities of liquid, independently of the number or nature of decantings performed. He resists the counter-suggestions of the experimenter. As arguments for such conservation he gives one or more of the following explanations: identity, compensation, reversibility.

The identity argument is based on the claim that there is the same in the two glasses because we have not added anything or taken anything away during decanting; those of compensation relate the differences in height and breadth of the two glasses; those of reversibility are based on the fact that returning the contents of B or C to A1 would produce an equality between A and A1.

Such a test can then identify the successive development of cognitive functioning as do other tests including conservation of number, matter, length, weight or area. We will describe some of these tasks later. Although the cognitive status of responses in these tests has been relatively well studied, their social status has been neglected. These responses are in effect given within a social context; not only are they related to the successive configurations of given material, they are also related to the interventions, questions and suggestions of the experimenter. These interventions cannot be treated as if they were a measuring or diagnostic instrument having no effect on the situation observed. Examining various of Piaget's experimental methods in greater detail, one discovers that the act of questioning is often the cause of progress in the child (Van de Voort, 1977). Considerations of this kind do not enter into the analyses that Piagetians normally make of their experimental methods; these analyses are based exclusively on cognitive factors and ignore the simultaneous effect of social influences on the child's responses.

A contrasting approach has been adopted by our colleague Anne-Nelly Perret-Clermont (1980), who reexamines the paradigm of decanting liquids, putting it back into a social context in order to show how a social interaction based on this paradigm can foster cognitive development. This chapter describes an initial study which provides evidence for the cognitive benefit that children can derive from social interaction, a benefit which is confirmed in subsequent research. It is shown that the progress observed is not limited to the concept directly involved in the social interaction, and that it can also be found following social interaction involving sharing that is based on the conservation of number. Finally, we describe the results of research (by

Perret-Clermont and Leoni) which introduces more sociological factors into the experimental design. Within this account of our colleague's research, we will include descriptions of two pieces of research carried out at the University of Tilburg in Holland which replicates the principal results obtained in Geneva, and of which the second is based more directly on the role of social marking.

Experiment 1. Individual progress following sharing

The children who participated in this experiment (Perret-Clermont, 1980; see also Doise, Mugny and Perret-Clermont, 1975) were aged between 5 years 6 months and 7 years 5 months, their average age being about 6 and a half years. All had first taken part in individual pretests by which they were assessed as either NC, I or C, using a variant of the conservation of liquids task. Two weeks later the majority of them completed a task involving social interaction (experimental condition) before taking part a week later in a further individual test (first posttest). A second posttest followed one month later. The other children took part only in the pretest and posttests (control condition). This control condition allowed us to estimate the rates of spontaneous development which could have occurred in children of these ages irrespective of any experimental intervention. During the 3 weeks which separated the pretest from the first posttest the children obviously continued to attend school and were involved in numerous social interactions which could affect progress. Also, the pretest by itself may have stimulated their curiosity, as was the case of a little girl in the control condition who, during the posttest, described how she had asked her mother to repeat the test with her.

In the social interaction phase, three subjects took part together on each occasion. Two of them (C1 and C2) had been classified as conservers on the pretest, the third (S, the experimental subject as such) and also the only one to take part in the two posttests was in most cases a nonconserver (28 NCs), and otherwise an intermediate (9 Is).

The interaction was conducted as follows. S was placed at the head of the table and had at his disposal a glass capable of containing 25 cl. The two other children (C1 and C2) were seated near him facing each other, C1 having at his disposal a glass A1 identical to that of S and C2 had at his disposal a taller narrower glass, B (see Fig. 4.1) S was then given an opaque bottle containing syrup or fruit juice and another glass A2 identical to his own and to that of C1. He was asked to pour a drink for the other two children so that they would both have the same amount to drink and so that they would both be satisfied. The experimenter also told S that, after carrying out the sharing for C1 and C2, he should then ask them if they were satisfied, that he could make use of glass A2 if this seemed helpful to him, but that he could not serve himself until all three agreed on the quantities (Plate II).

The sharing session lasted about 10 minutes. Typically, the subject, being either NC or I, immediately poured the syrup or juice into glasses A1 and B until it reached the same height in each; by doing this he provoked protests from C2 who had received less syrup in his very narrow glass. When the discussion between the children was slow in getting under way, the experimenter invited them to give their opinions and helped bring out the possible differences between these opinions. He also took care to ensure that S was able to express himself and be heard, repeating his contributions if necessary as they were sometimes ignored by C1 and C2 who were more sure of themselves. The latter often persuaded S to use glass A2 which he would then fill before pouring it into B. The number of explanations and arguments given by the two children C varied considerably across groups. Nevertheless, all the NC or I children in this condition took part in a situation in which equality had been established as the norm, and they often established an agreement on equality that persisted after a transformation in the configuration of the quantities concerned. This specific characteristic of the sharing situation will be the subject of some later research. When C1 or C2 persuade S to use glass A2, in effect he learns the use of an instrument of measurement. This situation could also create numerous conflicts of centration between the height of the liquid in the glass and its width in the other, or vice versa. Several characteristics of this sharing situation lead the subject S to reconsider his nonconserving (or intermediate) response. Given so many grounds for expecting progress, does it actually occur?

Progress clearly did take place; in the first posttest 24 subjects out of 37 in the experimental condition showed progress on the Scale NC-I-C, as against only 2 out of 12 in the control condition. This advantage was shown to persist: progress was still apparent in the second posttest in 20 out of 24, some indication that it was genuine. However, the tasks used for the posttest were quite similar to those used during the social interaction. It was therefore necessary to find out if a change between the pre and posttests actually corresponded to a cognitive restructuring and was not just a reproduction of responses and justifications learned during the interaction.

A detailed study of the children's responses to the posttest tasks has provided some proof of the authenticity of this cognitive progress. During the interaction, at least one of the arguments of identity, compensation or reversibility was used in most groups. Yet the children who progressed on the posttests and attained the level of conservation (23 children) did not simply repeat the arguments used during the interaction. More than half of them (13 children) gave arguments which had not been used in the collective situation. Amongst these new arguments there were three identity arguments, seven compensation arguments and seven reversibility arguments.

The relative rarity of new identity arguments should cause no surprise: in 18 out of 23 cases it had been used in the interaction, and therefore only five children could have used it as a new explanation. This example indicates the degree of rigour used to prove that progress was genuine; this is not to say that repetition of an argument used during interaction does not reflect genuine comprehension. On the contrary, studies of memory do show that this is based on comprehension. On the other hand, when more than half the children, having reached the stage of understanding conservation, introduce new justifications, this shows that their arguments in the posttest cannot be explained by a simple process of imitation. These are undoubtedly indications of a new elaboration.

Another way of studying the nature of progress consists in using conservation tasks not based on pouring out liquids; this is employed in the following experiment.

Experiment 2. Generalisation of progress following sharing

This experiment had several aims. First, it was concerned with replicating the results obtained in the preceding experiment, whilst at the same time studying in greater depth the nature of the observed progress. With this aim the subjects were pretested and posttested with different tasks, in order to find out whether progress on conservation of liquids tasks is accompanied by progress in other areas. Secondly, it was concerned with examining the role of group composition; is it necessary to have two Cs in order to make an NC progress, or would a single C carry enough weight in the interaction? In other words, is it possible to exclude any explanation in terms of the effect of a majority? The experiment consisted of several conditions, but we will only be analysing here the results of conditions involving an NC subject (n=5) interacting with two C children or two NC children (n=12) interacting with a C child. It was these particular experimental conditions which led to greater progress compared to a control condition (an NC alone) and compared to a condition in which three NC subjects interacted.

As in the preceding experiment, the interaction involved a task of sharing a drink among three children. The pretest and the posttest were much more extensive than in the first experiment; in the pretest and posttest all subjects responded to problems involving the conservation of liquid and the conservation of matter; in addition, they took part during the pretest in a number conservation task and during the posttest in a length conservation task. We will describe here only the basic characteristics of these task (Perret-Clermont, 1980).

The liquids task was based not only on conservation of equal quantities, as in the preceding experiment, but also included questioning on the conservation of unequal quantities. Two identical glasses were filled unequally and then the contents of one were poured into a tall, narrow glass so that the two levels were both at the same height; then a further decanting took place into a wide, shallow glass. This task tested whether the child conserved the inequality in spite of the transformation that occurred.

In the number task, the child had to line up a row of eight counters of the same colour and then align above them the same number of counters in another colour. Once this task was completed, with or without the experimenter's help, the experimenter made several changes in the arrangement of the two series of counters, placing one lot closer together and spacing the others out, to determine whether the child would conserve the equality in numbers despite the changes in configuration.

In the task for conservation of matter, two equal quantities of modelling clay rolled into two balls were used. One of these balls was transformed into a 'pancake', then into a 'sausage' and finally into several small pieces. The task made it possible to determine whether the child had mastered conservation of quantity in this context.

The conservation tasks for equality of length will be described in greater detail in the next chapter. For the present experiment, two tasks were used. One employed two 'sticks' 16 cms in length, first of all placed parallel so that their ends were seen to match. Once their equality had been acknowledged, successive displacements of one of the sticks were made, to see whether the child compensated for the overlap of one stick at one end with the complementary overlap of the other at the opposite end. The second test employed a single stick 16 cm long and four smaller sticks of 4 cm, which were rearranged in order to test whether the child conserved the equality acknowledged at the beginning when the four short sticks were aligned end to end and parallel to the long stick.

The children's responses to all these tests were classed as NC, I or C. The principal aim of the experiment was therefore to see whether progress made during social interaction involving the sharing of liquids would give rise to a cognitive reorganisation, with repercussions for the other tasks. Admittedly, the need to meet particular criteria on several tests as well as questioning the children limited the size of the final sample.

Results

Among the 17 NC children who interacted with one or two Cs, 9 cases of progress were observed on the liquids task in the first posttest which, except in two cases, carried over to the second posttest. Let us see if performances on the liquids task in the first posttest are linked to performances on other tasks. Even though the numbers are not very high, the links are statistically significant; the children who progressed on the matter conservation task were to be found only amongst those who had become I or C on the liquids task, following the interaction (Table 4.1). Also, only children who had pro-

TABLE 4.1. *Level on the Posttest 1 Liquids Task and Progress on the Matter Task*

	Liquids Task (Posttest 1)		
	NC	I	C
Matter Task			
No Progress	8	2	1
Progress	0	1	5

Jonckheere's test, Z:2.836, P<0.005

gressed in this way after the interaction were able to give an I or C response to the lengths task on the first posttest (Table 4.2). Hence, this experimentally created progress clearly consists of more general cognitive reorganisations.

TABLE 4.2. *Level on Length and Liquids Tasks in Posttest 1*

	Liquids Task		
Length	NC	I	C
NC	8	3	2
I or C	0	0	4

Jonckheere's test, Z:2.396, P<0.02.

However, in this experiment not all the children who participated in an interaction with one or two C children made progress. The presence of one C versus two Cs does not account for the difference in progress because the levels of progress are similar in the two conditions. Moreover, an analogous result was obtained in the next experiment, which also included conditions designed to be a control for any possible effects of group composition. One must therefore look elsewhere for the factor which, under the same conditions, led to progress in some children but not in others.

We cannot stress too much the complex nature of collective situations. They carry different meanings for individuals with different social backgrounds. However, such differential effects, although they need to be studied further, were not among the immediate aims of our research. Another important difference that may exist between children, relates to their initial abilities. Not all the children classified as NC on a pretest have the same cognitive equipment. Everything points to the idea that children who have already acquired broadly based abilities are better able to profit from social interaction than those of their peers in whom such abilities remain to be established. This hypothesis is derived from our socioconstructivist view of cognitive development: it received some initial verification in the final study reported in the preceding chapter, which showed that social interaction was only profitable given a certain level of development. The present experiment provides a further indication of the importance of such preconditions. It is known that conservation of number is generally acquired before that of quantities of liquid. Thus the children who took part in social tasks were not all at the same level on the number task given in the pretest. Table 4.3 indicates that children more advanced in conservation of number were more likely to make progress following social interaction.

TABLE 4.3. *Pretest level on Number Task and Progress on the Liquids Task between the Pretest and the first Posttest*

	Numbers Task (Pretest)		
Liquids Task	NC	I	C
No progress	7	0	1
Progress	3	2	4

Jonckheere's test, Z:1.766, P<0.04.

The results clearly confirm those of the preceding experiment. Amongst other things, they show that a generalisation of abilities acquired in the interaction did occur and that progress is not independent of initial abilities.

Experiment 3. A replication in Holland

Let us now consider some of the questions examined in research carried out at the University of Tilburg (Rijsman, Zoetebier, Ginther and Doise, 1980). The methodology employed to determine the operational level of the children was different from that used in Geneva. It relies on a less clinical and more standardised format, using items from a test for conservation concepts (Goldschmid and Bentler, 1968). When subjects respond incorrectly to an item, they receive zero; they receive one point for a correct response and two points when the response is accompanied by an appropriate explanation.

For the pretest, three items based on the conservation of liquid were used; depending on the scores obtained, the children were classified as NC (zero to two points), I (three or four points) or C (five or six points). These classifications do not necessarily have the same meaning as those used in the clinical method practised in Geneva. Progress occurs if subjects, who were initially all NC, become either I or C.

The results presented here are based on the first posttest with 105 children who were NC on the pretest (scores from zero to two) and at the same level in school (the first year of primary schooling). Eighty-eight of these children took part during the experimental phase in sharing situations (as in Perret-Clermont), which involved an interaction of either two NC subjects (n=31), or three NC subjects (n=9) or one NC and one C (n=38) or one NC and two Cs (n=10). Finally, seventeen subjects took part in the pre and posttests only, and thus constituted a control condition without social interaction.

Let us look at Table 4.4a which gives the amount of progress for the control condition, for the interaction conditions involving NC subjects only and for all the situations in which there was interaction between NC and C subjects. These results are compatible with those from Geneva, and when the results of the 48 NC children who interacted with one or two Cs are compared with those of the 40 NC children who interacted with one or two other NCs, one finds a very significant difference in favour of the former. The presence of one versus two Cs with an NC has, however, no effect in itself (see Table 4.4b).

TABLE 4.4a. *Frequency of Progress in the Different Conditions of the first Tilburg Experiment*

	Control Condition	Interaction between NCs	Interaction between NC and C
No Progress	13	34	26
Progress	4	6	22

X^2 columns 1 and 3: 2.602, P<0.06.
X^2 columns 2 and 3: 9.561, P<0.005.

TABLE 4.4b. *Comparisons of NC–C and NC–2C interactions*

	NC and C	NC and 2C
No Progress	20	6
Progress	18	4

TABLE 4.5. *Frequency of progress among NC givers and receivers*

	Givers	Receivers
No Progress	24	22
Progress	11	12

The very marked difference in results between NC subjects working with other NCs and NC subjects working with one or two Cs also indicates that an interpretation based only on the activity of manipulating glasses and liquids is inadequate. This is even more directly apparent when one compares all the situations in which two children participated; in each case one of the children must carry out the pouring, one being the giver and the other the receiver. No difference was found which favoured those children who, as givers, were able to manipulate the materials. (Table 4.5).

TABLE 4.6. *Frequency of Progress and Outcome of Sharing*

	Correct Sharing	Incorrect Sharing
No Progress	16	44
Progress	15	12

X^2: 6.776, P<0.01.

TABLE 4.7. *Frequency of Progress and Argumentation during interaction*

	Interaction	
	With arguments	Without arguments
No Progress	23	36
Progress	24	4

X^2: 16.695, P<0.001.

Other characteristics of the interaction, however, have a very clear effect on the progress of the children taking part. Thus when we compare the children who participated in an interaction leading to correct shares with those participating in an interaction in which correct sharing did not occur, we find far more progress in the former case than in the latter (Table 4.6). A similar contrast exists between groups that had provided conservation arguments and those groups that failed to provide any (Table 4.7).

In order to confirm the authenticity of progress, two items based on length conservation and one based on area conservation were used in the posttest. The hypothesis tested was that children who became I or C on the liquids items would also give a more advanced response to these other items. Table 4.8 shows that this was the case for NC subjects who interacted with one or two C children, when the results for the liquids items are compared with those for the other items given in the first posttest.

TABLE 4.8. *Posttest 1 results for the liquids tasks and the generalisation tasks*

Generalisation tasks	Liquid Tasks		
	NC	I	C
Scores below the median (0 or 1)	21	3	2
Scores above the median (2 to 6)	5	8	9

Jonckheere's test, Z: 3.756, P<0.002.

The role of initial competence can also be illustrated with this experiment. It will be recalled that only children with pretest scores from zero to two on the liquids tasks (NCs) had been included as formal experimental subjects. It is therefore possible to order these subjects according to whether they obtained zero, one or two points. We did this for subjects who took part with one or two level C subjects and found that there was indeed a very strong link between their results on the pretest and their progress subsequent to the interaction (Table 4.9).

TABLE 4.9. *Results on pretest items and progress following interaction* (*Liquids Task*)

	Pretest scores		
	0	1	2
No Progress	18	7	2
Progress	4	5	13

Jonckheere's test, Z: 4.041, P<0.001.

Another result emerges from the first three experiments described in this chapter. On the second posttest some slight progress was evident, compared to the first posttest. This can be seen in the context of an analogous phenomenon observed in research on learning (Inhelder, Sinclair and Bovet, 1974). This 'phenomenon of development after the event is already apparent in some cases between the end of the learning procedures and the first posttest but particularly between the first and the second posttest, some subjects progressing from an unstable response to a completely operational solution or showing a distinct advance of one or two sublevels. During the interval between the two posttests (from 2 to 6 weeks depending on the case), the acquisitions triggered off by the learning procedures become extended and a set of integrations produced, the detail of which necessarily escapes us, but the results of which seem to prove that they involve genuine internal reorganisations of the same order as those which we have observed during the learning procedures'. (p. 296, translation).

Between the two posttests the child does of course participate in numerous other social interactions which might in part explain such progress. But it seems too regular to be reduced to chance effects; also, it seems less common in children who participate only in a control condition or in a social condition not producing significant progress. This would indicate that subjects in experimental conditions may at least acquire a competence allowing them to gain more from interactions that are not produced experimentally. One could also view this as an example of the spiral of causality between autonomy and social interdependence that is at the foundation of our view of cognitive development; work begun in a situation of interdependence continues later in an autonomous fashion.

Experiment 4. Sharing and conservation of number

Various forms of social interaction can give rise to progress in the conservation of quantities of liquid. Could such progress also be obtained for the concept of number following a sharing interaction based directly on this concept? Results of a further experiment (conducted by Anne-Nelly Perret-Clermont) should resolve this question. Forty NC children participated in social interaction, either with a C (n=14) or with an I (n=10) or another NC (n=16). They had to divide sweets using special 'plates' (rectangles) containing circles on which the sweets could be placed (see Fig. 4.2).

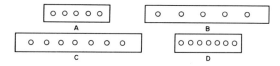

FIG. 4.2   Materials used in the experiment involving the sharing of sweets.

Plates A and B each have five circles, but one plate measures 9 cm in length and the other 17 cm; Plate C is also 17 cm long but contains seven circles while Plate D has seven circles but is 9 cm long. As the circles are placed at regular intervals along the entire length of the plate there is thus no relation between the length of this line of circles and their number; there are as many on Plate A which is short as there are on Plate B which is long.

At the beginning of the interaction the experimenter puts a pile of sweets on a little table at which the two children are seated face-to-face. Then he gives Plate A to one of the children and Plate B to the other. The two children thus see each other with different plates, both containing the same number of circles, but more tightly packed together on Plate A and set further apart on Plate B. The experimenter explains clearly that the circles on the plates correspond to 'places for the sweets' and then says, 'You can take the sweets and put them on the circles on your plates, but on the condition that you both have the same number. You should not have any less than your friend. You should both have as many as each other, and both be as happy as each other. Otherwise, it is not fair. How are you going to do it?' In some cases one of the two children carried out the sharing; in other cases each child served itself. When the act of 'taking the sweets' was completed, the experimenter addresses the two children, asking them if they have as many as each other, and why, or how the sharing should be done, encouraging them to find a means of coming to an agreement about an equal division. Once agreement is reached the experimenter swops over the plates between

I   The cooperative game

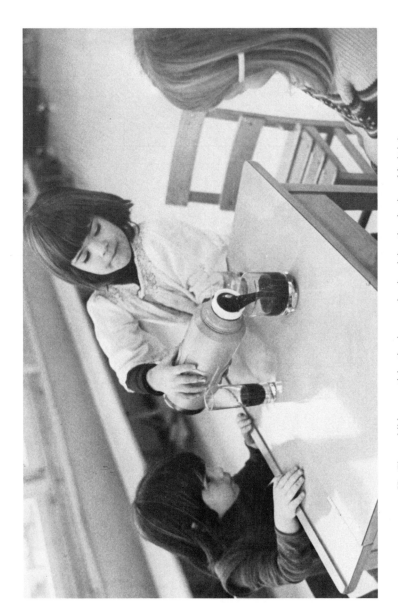

II   Three children participating in a session involving the sharing of fruit juice.

III   Interaction between two children involving conservation of equal lengths.

IVa　Two children copying the 'village' together.

IVb　Two children copying the 'class' together.

the two partners, in order to test the stability of the agreement. Then he continues the experiment in a similar fashion with other plates, saying 'There you are, you have understood the game very well; we are going to try again with other plates. Then we will eat the sweets.' The pairs of plates then used are, successively, B and C (both 17 cm long, but with different numbers of circles), and A and D (9 cm long, but with different numbers of circles). Following the final division, the experimenter allows the children to eat the sweets and asks them if they are both satisfied with their shares.

TABLE 4.10. *Interaction conditions and frequency of progress*

	Interactions		
	NC with C	NC with I	NC with NC
Progress	6	2	2
No Progress	8	8	14

Jonckheere's test, Z: 1.658, P<0.05.

Table 4.10 shows that progress is a function of the partner's level; the higher this level, the greater the chance that children will make progress following the interaction. In subsequent chapters we will see that it is not possible to generalise from this conclusion; in some cases children who are NC on a task benefit from interaction with another NC child, even though they may not derive any benefit from an interaction with a C. We should also make it clear that in the present experiment no C child regressed following an interaction with an NC, whilst of ten I children who interacted with NC children only one regressed, five reaching the C level. This result adds further support to the view that cognitive restructuring occurring during a social interaction cannot be reduced to the effects of imitation. Similar results will be presented in the chapter on coordination of perspectives.

As in the three preceding experiments, this one also shows that interaction can lead to real progress.[1] We will now examine how the dynamics of these sharing situations are linked to a more general social context and, in particular, how social norms can play a regulatory role in cognitive co-ordinations.

Experiment 5. Social marking in the conservation of liquids

A social situation is linked to the wider society by the norms that govern behaviour in this situation. As we have seen, the behaviour of very young

[1]These experiments confirm the results obtained by other researchers like Murray (1972), Silverman and Stone (1972), Silverman and Geiringer (1973) and Miller and Brownell (1975), though the present results offer some clarification of these earlier findings.

children is already governed by an egalitarian norm. It then becomes a matter of showing how this norm can influence the acquiring of an operational concept. In an experiment by Finn (1975),[2] two children were influenced less by transformations in two quantities of liquid when they had previously agreed to their equality in a situation in which each child had a right to the same amount of this liquid. Agreement on acquired rights and the fair sharing that derives from it seems to induce conservation of equality with respect to the object shared, independently of its configuration.

In order to evaluate the stability of this progress and its generalisation to situations lacking equality of acquired rights, a further experiment was carried out (Doise, Rijsman, Van Meel, et al., 1981). The experimental design included five conditions, together with a pretest and two posttests. The pretest was based solely on conservation of liquids; the posttests also included assessment of generalisation in terms of number and matter (Goldschmid and Bentler, 1968). We took great care to create a homogeneous experimental population. We included only NC children who agreed that there was the same quantity of liquid in two identical glasses equally filled, and who also asserted, in support of this response, that there was more liquid in a glass to which the experimenter had added some. Thus all these children had scored two points at the beginning. Their ages varied from 4 years 5 months to 6 years 1 month.

All the subjects, except the controls, participated in the experimental phase 1 week after the pretest. In one condition two subjects are seated at a table on which is a tall narrow glass (B), a broad shallow glass (C) and two identical glasses (A and A1). The experimenter reminds the children of their pretest participation, tells them that they had both worked equally well and therefore deserve the same reward; and that they will, as a consequence, both receive the same amount to drink. The experimenter then fills up glasses B and C with the same quantity of drink and asks the children if, in their opinion, there is the same quantity in each glass. He then says that he wishes to check whether there really is the same quantity in the two glasses and to do this pours the contents of each glass into the two identical glasses, A and A1. He then asks the children to explain the reason for this equality and reminds them, if necessary, of their equal claims. Once again he asks if the sharing is correct before pouring the two quantities back into B and C. If the children are then unable to agree on the equality of the liquids the procedure is repeated. At the end of the interaction the experimenter gives each child a glass to drink from.

Here we have a collective condition with social rights. A second collective condition without social rights is run identically with the first, except that no

---

[2]Unfortunately, Finn did not include a posttest which would have made it possible to establish the stability of this progress and its generalisation to situations not involving equality of acquired rights.

question of acquired rights is introduced. The experimenter reminds the children of the preceding session and announces, without referring to acquired rights, that he will pour the same quantity of liquid into the two glasses. Just as in the previous condition, he first uses glasses B (tall and narrow) and C (broad and shallow), before proceeding to the check on quantities with glasses A and A1 and to returning the contents to B and C. During discussion reference is made to the initial intention of pouring the same quantity of liquid into the two glasses. The procedure is repeated if the children do not both agree that there is the same quantity of liquid in B and C after the experimenter has carried out the check using A and A1. At the end the children are allowed to drink, one from glass B and the other from glass C.

In two 'individual' conditions, the child is alone with the experimenter. In the individual condition with social rights, the experimenter announces that 'in a minute another child will come in who has worked just as well and deserves the same reward'; in the other condition he says, 'In a minute another child will come in and take part in the same game, that of pouring the same quantity of liquid into the two glasses.' The rest of the procedure is the same as for the collective conditions.

The results from the first posttest show that the social rights situation is a source of progress, whether the partner is present or absent. Only four of the twenty-one subjects who made progress on the two conditions involving social rights regressed between the first and second posttest; in contrast, six subjects progressed still further (Table 4.11).

TABLE 4.11. *Frequency of Progress in the Experiment on Social Rights*

	With Social Right Condition		Without Social Right Condition		Control Condition
	Collective	Individual	Collective	Individual	
Progress	11	10	5	2	1
No Progress	4	4	10	12	13

Difference between conditions with and without social right, X^2: 13.533, P<0.001.

In posttest 1 as well as in posttest 2, observed progress in the various experimental conditions is very significantly related to scores obtained on the generalisation tests based on conservation of number and matter (Table 4.12).

Social harmony develops from cognitive restructuring of the situation, and the sociocognitive conflict is reabsorbed into an agreement based on a norm. This agreement leads to conservation of an operational nature corresponding to the conservation of a social nature. Social marking therefore

TABLE 4.12. *Generalisation scores as a function of pretest progress*

	First Posttest		Second Posttest	
	Generalisation	Scores	Generalisation	Scores
	0	1–6	0	1–6
Progress	8	21	7	27
No Progress	29	14	27	11

X²: 11.013, P<0.001;   X²: 18.336, P<0.001.

helps to establish cognitive regulations; in the absence of such marking one finds hardly any progress, even in the collective condition where the children share the same centrations. It is possible to create conflict in the observations of a situation without marking, only its infusion with social meaning accentuates sociocognitive conflict leading to a new cognitive regulation.

Experiment 6. The limits of sociocultural handicap

The sociological characteristics of participants in a particular social interaction are related to more general social dynamics. On this point, we may draw attention to two experiments by Anne-Nelly Perret-Clermont on the sharing of liquids, which were carried out in different parts of the city of Geneva. The children from the different areas were not equally successful on the pretests. This variation was without doubt related to socioeconomic differences between the inhabitants of the two areas. After the results of these experiments had been analysed it became possible to get information about the occupations of the parents of subjects in the second experiment on liquids and those in the experiment on number. It was thus possible, *a posteriori*, to divide the children into three categories according to parents' occupation (categories defined by the Sociological Research Service of Geneva):

Category A   Unskilled, semiskilled and skilled manual workers, public employees, etc.

Category B   Qualified employees, small businessmen, farmers, middle management, etc.

Category C   The professions, senior administrators, managers.

Crude as this classification is, it nevertheless corresponds to the success of the children on the pretests in these two experiments (Table 4.13).

Almost half the children from relatively disadvantaged social backgrounds (A and B) were nonconservers against about a quarter of the

TABLE 4.13. *Percentage of nonconserving children in Experiment 2 and 4 pretests as a function of social background*

| | Social Background | | |
	A	B	C
Experiment 2	51% (41)	44% (34)	25% (16)
Experiment 4	48% (52)	50% (66)	27% (22)

(In parentheses: Total numbers for each category).

children with the more favourable backgrounds (C). Several of these non-conserving children had the opportunity to take part in an interaction that was intended to generate progress. Thus in Experiment 2, seven NC children in Category A took part in an interaction either as an NC with two Cs or as one of two NCs with a C; five of these children showed progress on the posttest. It is not possible to draw definitive conclusions from such a small amount of data. Let us, nevertheless, extrapolate a little to stimulate thought.

Recall that in the pretest, 51% of children from Category A were NC; if they had all been able to participate in an interaction with at least one C, only 29% (2 out of 7) of these 51% would have remained NC, or 15% in all. A similar extrapolation applied to NC children from Category B gives a proportion of 22% after an interaction with one or two Cs. Now, 25% of the children in the most favoured category were NC on the pretest: an interaction lasting a few minutes therefore would suffice to allow a late developer to 'catch up' or to make good a 'sociocultural handicap' relative to a specific concept. Similar extrapolations based on the data from Experiment 4 give identical results. The effects in the two experiments are certainly weak but the results of the extrapolations are sufficiently consistent to regard them as more than chance effects.

A recent experiment carried out in another social setting (by Anne-Nelly Perret-Clermont and M. L. Leoni) studied the effectiveness of different forms of interaction among children from a less privileged background. One hundred and fifty nine children took part in a pretest on the conservation of liquids, their social class background having been established before the experiment. Table 4.14 gives the distribution of operational levels as a function of more or less advantaged social class background.

Once again the results vary in relation to social class membership. What happens to these differences following participation in different social interactions? The following gives details of the levels attained in the posttest by the relatively disadvantaged NC children who took part in the experiment. They were divided among three interaction conditions: a nonconserving child interacting with a conserving child (NC with C); an NC interacting with

TABLE 4.14. *Social background and pretest operational level in Experiment 6*

	Operational Level		
	NC	I	C
Advantaged background	17	4	30
Disadvantaged background	77	4	27

Jonckheere's test, Z: 4.400, P<0.001.

an adult who uses the arguments of a C (NC with adult); two NCs interacting together (NC with NC). Table 4.15 shows that these respective conditions represent a decreasing order of effectiveness.

TABLE 4.15. *Posttest operational level and experimental conditions: Subjects from disadvantaged background*

	Experimental Conditions		
	NC with C	NC with Adult	NC with NC
Posttest level			
NC	4	9	17
I or C	8	10	10

Extrapolating on the same principle as for the preceding experiments, it is possible to compare with the initial proportion of children in the relatively advantaged group who are NC; i.e., 33% (Table 4.16).

TABLE 4.16. *Percentage of children from disadvantaged backgrounds who are nonconservers on the pretests and on the posttest and extrapolations for the entire set of these children*

	Background	
	Advantaged	Disadvantaged
Pretest	33%	71%

	Experimental conditions (Disadvantaged backgrounds)		
	NC with C	NC with Adult	NC with NC
Posttest	33%	47%	63%
Extrapolations	24%	34%	45%

We can again see that taking part in a few minutes' interaction with a C child makes a difference. If cognitive functioning is considered as an aspect of social functioning, it must be concluded that the notorious sociocultural handicap is, in this specific case, not such a difficult obstacle to overcome as one might have been inclined to believe.

This experiment also provides an important result relating to the social meaning of a sharing task, which was varied here in a systematic manner. For half the subjects, the pretest was presented as a sharing between the experimenter and the subject; for the other half, sharing was carried out between two identical dolls ('twins who wanted to have the same to drink when they are invited to the child's house'). For the first half, the actions had implications for them personally; for the latter half the context is more that of a game and the child is less directly involved. This relational difference had the expected effect (Table 4.17).

TABLE 4.17. *Pretest operational level and conditions of task presentation*

	Operational Level		
	NC	I	C
Sharing with experimenter	40	6	35
Sharing between puppets	54	2	22

Jonckheere's test, Z: 2.292, P<0.02.

Conclusions

The experiments described in this chapter were especially concerned with individual progress resulting from various social interactions. Situations involving sharing with a more advanced partner are significant sources of cognitive progress; the social meanings that are activated in these sharing situations also play an important role in the production of new cognitive organisation.

In the following chapters we will see that interaction with a more advanced child is neither a necessary nor a sufficient condition for progress in the less advanced child. In certain cases a more advanced child can prevent the other from fully participating in the social interaction and thus coordinating his social approach with that of his partner. If much progress is made in experimental conditions involving children of unequal levels, it is clearly because these children were all deeply involved in their sharing tasks.

If it is thus shown that individual progress can be engendered by social interactions and that this may generalise to other cognitive tasks, it remains for us to elucidate further the processes by which social interaction generates progress. In the sharing situations the social interactions were very complex and entailed the simultaneous effects of a model, of sociocognitive conflict and of social marking. To study the nature of progress it was first of all necessary to optimise the chances that it would occur by creating situations which were both rich in potential and easy to reproduce. The paradigms described in the following chapters have had a different goal; they aim principally to clarify the specific role in the genesis of cognitive processes of three diverse aspects of social interaction, namely sociocognitive conflict, modelling effects and social marking.

5

Sociocognitive conflict

The two preceding chapters have shown that social interaction can be uniquely effective in initiating the development of a specific concept. The resulting progress is permanent and can extend to similar concepts which in itself provides evidence of a genuine cognitive restructuring.

However, we have also established that not all social interaction *a priori* possesses characteristics so favourable to development. It was found that a hierarchical structure, when imposed on children taking part in a cooperative game, made interindividual coordination more dependent on individual capacities. The same was true for children who were on another occasion prohibited from communicating freely in the same game. In a number conservation task, interaction between three subjects at a lower cognitive level (nonconservers) was not found favourable to cognitive development. Interactions concerned with the sharing of liquid did not lead to cognitive progress when the partners had not previously become aware of their social rights.

These varied social interactions do not produce sociocognitive conflicts that are strong enough to lead the partners to elaborate cognitive structures which allow them to resolve the conflicts; the constraints of the situations were such that they prevented the partners from developing a confrontation. Such apparent failures are certainly consistent with our theoretical position; social interaction is only constructive if it creates a confrontation between partners' divergent solutions.

One means of inducing such conflicts is to create a group with children of different cognitive levels. The difference can, as the preceding chapter has shown, lead to substantial progress. This is, moreover, confirmed by various results reported in the following chapter, which also specify more precisely the conditions necessary for the divergences to be advantageous, both to the group and to the partners as individuals.

However, these results cannot exclude the possible effects of imitation, even if they appear to involve an authentic reconstruction going beyond mere imitative appropriation. In order to isolate the mechanism of sociocognitive conflict itself, its effects need to be studied in situations where, in cognitive terms, no partner is more advanced than another. If it were

possible to trigger off cognitive progress in a nonconserving child on a conservation problem by confronting the child with a response that was both
contradictory to, and similar to (because based on the same preoperational
reasoning) its own, one would then have some confidence that this progress
could only have resulted from a process of construction or elaboration of
new responses within a conflict of a genuinely social kind.

Suppose we ask two 5 or 6 year-old children to judge the length of two
equal sticks. When these are placed parallel with their ends coinciding, both
children will acknowledge that they are equal. Suppose we now move one of
the sticks (see Plate III), the two children will judge that one is now longer
than the other; they centre on one of the differences, taking no account of
the complementary one. Let us suppose that each child's response is based
on the stick furthest away from it, and let us place these two children face-to-
face. One, judging the further stick to be the longer, will then contradict the
other; as this same stick is closer to the second, he will judge it as being the
shorter. In this conflict of responses, based on the same schema, it is possible
that if these children are led to coordinate their opposing centrations, they
may discover that the lengths are equal, since one difference is compensated
by another.

However, such conflict will not appear automatically, and even when it
does appear it is not necessarily resolved in terms favourable to cognitive
development. The conditions which favour sociocognitive conflict cannot be
directly assumed to exist. Following strict experimental reasoning, we will
first of all try to create the conditions necessary for effective conflict. Having
argued at the theoretical level that this conflict constitutes the fundamental
mechanism by which social interaction acts as a source of cognitive development, we will now seek to demonstrate the case.

Conflict of centrations and conservation of length

The same paradigm and the same rationale form the basis for the set of
four experiments which will be used to illustrate the cognitive conflict
mechanism through which social interaction produces cognitive
development.

First the paradigm; this entails a pretest, an experimental phase, an initial
posttest – identical to the pretest and given just at the end of the experimental phase – and a repeated posttest taking place 10 days after the experimental phase, to allow determination of the degree of stability of any
progress identified in the first posttest.

Let us look first of all at the individual tests. They are three in number,
each involving the same questions and the same instructions; they concern
the conservation of equal and unequal length.

Conservation of equal length

The pretest always begins with questions about conservation of length. The child is collected from his class, brought to the experimental area and sat at right angles to the experimenter.

After asking his name, what he does in class and so forth, the experimenter tells the child that they are going to play a game together. He then takes out two wooden rulers of the same colour and each 10 cm long.

'Look, here are two rulers and we are going to pretend that they are paths. Do you think you would have just as far to walk here (the experimenter indicates one of the rulers with his finger) as here (walking his fingers along the other ruler)? Or do you think you would have further to walk on one of these paths? What do you think?' If the child does not understand very well, the experimenter repeats the instructions but using the example of an ant. 'Do you think the ant would have just as far to walk along here as along here? Or do you think it would have further to walk along one of these paths than the other? What do you think?' If the child now responds, the experimenter repeats the question this time in terms of length. 'Do you think that the rulers are both the same length? Or do you think that one is longer than the other? What do you think?'

The same questions are posed for each item, following approximately the same formula. This formula is designed to overcome two difficulties. The child does not always know what length is while nevertheless sometimes demonstrating length conservation; thus a child may assert that the paths are the same (the path being understood as between the two ends of the ruler) and say that the point of arrival is effectively 'further' for one rod if it is displaced; such subjects do clearly dissociate 'length' (as determined by the path included between the two ends) which remains constant across perceptual changes, from differences in spatial positions. The words do not have the same meaning for the child as for the adult. Presenting the task in this way helps to avoid such misunderstanding.

The same question is therefore posed at various points during the test. For each new configuration, the experimenter draws the child's attention to the transformation he makes. 'Look carefully at what I am doing. And now what do you think? Are the paths the same . . .' Often, after a few questions, the child responds spontaneously, even before the experimenter has had time to repeat the entire instructions. In cases of nonconservation the child is also asked to recall how the rulers were placed initially. The successive steps in this cross-examination are presented in Fig. 5.1.

The two rulers are first of all placed in such a way that their ends coincide. Then one of the rulers is moved a few centimetres so that their ends no longer coincide. It is then moved back to the initial position before moving the other ruler in the opposite direction. For each successive configuration the same questions are asked.

FIG. 5.1   Successive configurations in the task for conservation of equal length.

What are the possible responses of the children? Subjects are classified according to three levels:

– At a lower level, the *nonconservers* do not conserve length when perceptual configurations are such that the ends of the rulers do not coincide. Thus configuration 1 produces a response of equality; these children have no difficulty in recognising that the rulers when corresponding in this manner, are the same length. In configuration 2, on the other hand, one of the rulers is longer, one of the ants will have further to walk than the other (it is often but not exclusively the displaced ruler which is 'elongated'). The child remembers perfectly well that initially (in configuration 1) they were the same length but now one of the rulers is judged to be longer because it 'sticks out'. In the same way, in configuration 4, length is judged to be unequal although the child recognises and recalls that when they were placed in perceptual correspondence (configuration 3) they were the same length.

– At an *intermediate* level, doubt sets in; occasionally with configurations 2 and 4 equality is asserted but then the inequality arising from the perceptual configuration prevails. Also, it is often impossible for the child to explain his equality responses.

– At the level of *conservation*, in contrast, not only do subjects recognise conservation of length but they are also capable of providing at least one valid justification. Either the child stresses identity – 'You still have to walk the same; you have only moved the ruler.' – or he appeals to reversibility – 'If you put them back as they were before they were the same' (recalling the initial configuration), or finally the child argues for a reciprocal compensation – 'You see, here this is longer but here (on the other side) the other one is the longer.'

Conservation of unequal length

After the child has responded to the questions on equal length, he answers the same question as applied to unequal lengths (for the precise wording one may refer to the description for equal lengths). Two small chains are used, of the same substance and colour, one 10 cm long and the other 15 cm. The usual questions are asked for each of the configurations presented in Fig. 5.2.

The response to this set of questions can also be classified in terms of three levels:

– At a lower level, the *nonconserving* child, though recognising that in the initial configuration (1 and 3) chain x is longer, fails to recognise this when presented with other configurations. For configuration 2 he judges the two chains to be equal, so that the ant would have as far to walk on both the paths. In configuration 4 he now judges that it is chain y (in reality the shorter) which is longer, and this in spite of recalling the initial configuration; the child only judges length in terms of perceptual difference on one side.

– At an *intermediate* level, the child accepts that chain x is still the longer in configuration 2 where the extremities of the two chains coincide, there being a perceptual difference between the two lengths. However, he still finds it difficult to argue for this. Furthermore,

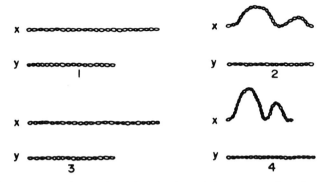

FIG. 5.2   Successive configurations in the task for conservation of unequal
length.

he ceases to conserve this inequality for configuration 4, perceptually the most salient, and
judges like the nonconservers that chain *y* is now longer; the illusion has become stronger
than the compensation. Occasionally, some subjects hesitate on this item, but without being
able to argue the case finally fall back on their original response.
¯ At a third, *conserving*, level the initial inequalities are conserved independently of perceptual configurations and subjects are capable of giving at least one conservation
argument, either of identity or reversibility or compensation (these various explanations
following the same principles as for conservation of equal length).

For the pretests, the sequence is, first of all conservation of equality and
then conservation of inequality. For the posttests the order varies according
to the nature of the conservation studied in the experimental phase. As a
posttest is given immediately following this phase, we begin with the type of
conservation that it has not included in order to avoid a simple transposition
of responses from one phase to the next. The second posttest is run by an
experimenter, who is 'blind' as to the experimental condition to which each
subject belongs.

The experimental phase

In this phase, the tasks presented to the children involve only one type of
conservation. The actual procedure for each experiment can vary fundamentally. However, a single principle is incorporated in the entire set of
these experiments which were conducted to illustrate that sociocognitive
conflict is indeed the critical element within social interaction that generates
cognitive development; the situations are organised in such a manner that a
conflict of centrations that are opposed but derived from the same preoperational reasoning is made possible.

The conservation of equal lengths task is the one most often used in this
phase. It will be recalled that subjects who are nonconservers with respect to
equal length (and only subjects at this level are used in these demonstrations) judge one of the rulers to be longer. Taking, for example, a child who,

given the following configuration (Fig. 5.3) judges ruler y to be longer 'because it sticks out here' (portion of y corresponding to x'), it is possible to create sociocognitive conflict by introducing a second child (or an experimenter in which case the conflict can be made more systematic), who, following the same reasoning (that one ruler exceeds the other), is inclined to the opposite centration, contradicting that of the first child. The second subject (or experimenter) therefore responds that ruler x is the longer 'because it sticks out here' (portion of x corresponding to y').

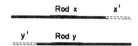

FIG. 5.3   Arrangement in a configuration involving partial overlaps.

Given such a situation, sociocognitive conflict is possible but still depends on other conditions being fulfilled; in particular, it must be ensured that one subject does not simply conform to the other's response thereby eliminating all conflict. It will be seen in the first three experiments how it was possible to create a conflict and then to vary it in terms of the interactions presented to the child.

Experimental overview

For the four experiments based on this paradigm we will specify the details only of the experimental phase, since the individual assessments are in each case identical to the foregoing description.

The first two experiments well illustrate the essentially experimental character of our approach; the experimenter himself intervenes to contradict the child. In this way it can be ensured that the sociocognitive conflict postulated theoretically will occur during the experimental phase. It is then possible to determine whether the anticipated progress actually appears.

In the first experiment we examined the hypothesis that a correct model is not necessary for cognitive development in the child; sociocognitive conflict based on opposing responses but derived from the same operational schema, and thus without exposing the child to a correct solution in the course of the conflict, should also lead to progress.

In this first experiment the conflict induced by the experimenter will be particularly strong. The child will be caught in a conflict from which he can apparently only escape by elaborating a coordination of these divergent centrations. In the second experiment the intensity of the conflict is varied, making it less constricting. Such a situation corresponds more closely to normal circumstances and allows various relational dynamics to emerge. For example, the child will be able to avoid interindividual conflict by agreeing with the adult view. The progress anticipated in this case is weaker and inversely proportional to the extent to which compliance appears.

Is it possible for sociocognitive conflicts to arise 'spontaneously' between two children placed face-to-face in this type of situation? The third experiment is addressed to this 'open' question, with the complementary hypothesis that it will be in those groups in which such conflict appears that cognitive progress will be most evident.

In the fourth and last experiment relating to this paradigm, the effects of conflict in relation to conservation of inequality of length will be studied. The social relevance of the conflict will be varied; it is predicted that cognitive progress will appear following the interaction to the extent that cognitive regulation corresponds directly to social regulations. This will provide a test of the social marking hypothesis within the framework of this new paradigm.

Experiment 1. Sociocognitive conflict and modelling

This experiment is intended to show decisively that cognitive progress resulting from social interaction does depend on conflict that is sociocognitive in form. This demonstration must therefore be based on situations that can exclude various alternative explanations.

It will therefore be necessary to show that progress cannot be attributed to the social expression of a correct response; if this happened an explanation in terms of interindividual imitation would be just as legitimate. The model presented should not therefore be correct, but what model should be chosen?

A second alternative explanation should also be excluded. The situation created should not involve the existence of different schemata.[1] Consequently, the response model that the experimenter presents to the child will have to be at the same level as its own; one can then talk about a model similar to that of the child.

Let us note that the task used, conservation of length, insofar as it involves judgements that cannot be tested within the situations presented to the child, excludes an explanation in terms of conflicts between the child's hypotheses and their disconfirmation by observation alone. The impact of such conflict on cognitive development has been demonstrated elsewhere (Lefebvre and Pinard, 1972).

By using a similar model in our demonstration, it is necessary to ensure, both the possibility of a conflict and its effective continuation. The possibility of conflict is assured in conservation of equal length tasks since, in the

---

[1] Work by Inhelder, Sinclair and Bovet (1974) has clearly shown that such conflicts are particularly beneficial for cognitive development.

case of nonconservation, two responses are possible; either one ruler is judged to be longer or the other. Conflict can then be induced by a similar model who judges the ruler to be longer when the child himself judges it to be the shorter. In order to increase the full opportunity for sociocognitive conflict (which is a legitimate aim since our hypothesis is specifically that this is the process through which social interaction becomes a source of cognitive development), the experimenter will himself introduce a response that is contradictory, though at a similar level, making sure furthermore that the child can only, with difficulty, avoid this conflict through a purely relational adjustment, such as compliance.

Let us look in detail at the various conditions which involve 53 children with an average age of 6 years 3 months.

In what is for our purposes the critical experimental condition, (which will be identified for simplicity as the similar model condition), items are presented in the experimental phase which are rather like those in the individual tests for equality of length. In addition, the child is placed facing a collaborator of the experimenter (see the illustration on page III; the collaborator is seated in the position of one of the children).

On the table are placed two wooden rails 4 cm wide and 22 cm long. There are also toy wagons to give some context to the material and with which the children can play before the experiment begins.

The rails are first of all placed in perceptual correspondence and it is established that they are indeed of identical length. Once the child has acknowledged this equality, the experimenter asks the collaborator to respond. He also gives a response of equality.

The experimenter then modifies the configuration by moving one of the rails and poses the usual questions to the child who, being a nonconserver, replies that one of the two rails is longer. The experimenter then asks him to justify his choice which he does in terms of the sticking out by the rail judged to be the longer. The same question is then put to the collaborator who judges the rail not chosen by the child to be the longer and this also by reason of its overlap. The experimenter then remarks that they do not agree: 'How can that be? Can you both try and agree?'

If the child persists in his initial response the collaborator insists, 'I think it is this one; you see, it goes further over there' using the same incorrect reasoning as the child but choosing the opposite response. The experimenter moves on to the next item (an opposite displacement of the other rail) when the discussion has been going on for about 5 minutes. If, however, the child gives a response of equality, the two adults avoid agreement and the collaborator reiterates his counter-suggestion. If the child persists in his response we pass on to the next item, or the session is ended if the second item has already been reached.

If, as is often the case, the child adopts the collaborator's incorrect response, the experimenter intervenes by saying, 'But I agreed with you that this one (indicating the rail initially chosen by the child) is the longer; it sticks out here.' This game can continue for 5 minutes for each item, the child being well and truly caught within a double conflict – between his own initial response and that of the collaborator, and between the contradicting responses of the two adults themselves.

This similar model condition will be compared with a correct model condition where the same procedure will be followed, the only difference being that the collaborator will give a correct response, 'I think the two rails are the same length because this one sticks out here, you see, but that one also sticks out there, so it is the same.' In this condition the experimenter never intervenes and contents himself with allowing the child and the collaborator to speak in turn. He stops an item after 5 minutes of discussion or when the child has recognised the equality of the two rails and justified it. As in the preceding condition, there are two experimental items.

Finally, in a control condition, the subjects work individually with similar items. As the absence of sociocognitive conflict greatly reduces interaction time with the material, the number of items is doubled, the subjects therefore responding to four items. For this, one of the rails is moved first in one direction and then in the other to allow some possible chance of contradiction. The latter two items are similar except that it is now the other rail that is moved first in one direction and then in the other. It is of course true that, even here, the probability of conflict is weak because nonconserving children tend not to experience contradictions between successive responses.

Results

What happened during the interaction? Amongst the 13 subjects in the individual control condition no child gave the correct response. In the correct model condition, where the correct response was given by the adult collaborator, all children finished the items by giving a response of equality (even though all did not justify it). But here the effect is obvious. Rather less so is that 15 out of 20 subjects in the similar model condition should give on one occasion or another a response of equality, although it may be renounced when the collaborator repeats his counter-suggestion. Here, then is an indication that sociocognitive conflict can lead subjects to try new responses which may include that of equality in order to resolve a conflict which, it should be stressed, is particularly strong. The dynamics of the interaction, however, are too powerful, particularly because the collaborator's incorrect counter-suggestion follows immediately after any possible proposition of equality by the child which he then abandons. It is not possible to assume an absence of progress during this experimental phase. But what do the children do in the first posttest given immediately after this conflictual interaction?

The results are given in Table 5.1. We should remember that all the subjects involved in this experiment were nonconservers on both the equality and the inequality tasks.

TABLE 5.1. *Frequency of Nonconserving (NC), Intermediate (I), and Conserving (C) subjects on the first posttest*

| | Conservation of equal length | | |
	NC	I	C
Control condition *a*	13	0	0
Similar model *b*	11	1	8
Correct model *c*	1	2	16

| | Conservation of unequal length | | |
	NC	I	C
Control condition *d*	12	1	0
Similar model *e*	7	5	8
Correct model *f*	10	5	4

Jonckheere's test, conditions *a* and *b*, Z: 2.577, P<0.01; conditions *a* and *c*, Z: 4.862, P<0.00003; conditions *d* and *e*, Z: 3.053, P<0.002; conditions *d* and *f*, Z: 2.173, P<0.02.

The results largely corroborate our hypothesis. First of all, and it is hardly surprising, the control condition, lacking any intraindividual conflict, gives rise to only one case of progress, one subject becoming intermediate on the inequality test; with regard to equality no progress is apparent. At the opposite extreme, when the correct model or correct responses are given and justified by the experimenter's collaborator, the majority of subjects prove capable of giving the correct response in the equality test and justifying it. Let us note in addition that a large proportion of the arguments advanced by subjects in this condition are different from the compensation argument given by the experimenter's collaborator; only four subjects adopted this argument whilst the others for the most part adopted an identity argument. This originality in argument is similar to that shown in the preceding chapter in the first experiment on conservation of liquids. As to the effects observed with the conservation of inequalities task, even though progress is less marked, it still differs significantly from that in the control condition.

In the similar model condition, the important one for us, in which the collaborator systematically advocated an incorrect response, even after a correct response by the child, one finds progress on the equality test in almost half the subjects. Even though this progress is less than in the correct model condition, it nonetheless differs significantly from the control condition. This progress is also in most cases generalised to conservation of inequality and is there slightly superior to that in the correct model condition.

Finally, it may be noted that progress is substantially sustained, in the second posttest, 10 days after the experimental phase; the results of this are given in Table 5.2.

TABLE 5.2. *Frequency of Nonconservers (NC), Intermediates (I) and Conservers (C) on the second posttest*

| | Conservation of equal length | | |
	NC	I	C
Control condition *a*	12	1	0
Similar model *b*	11	2	7
Correct model *c*	2	4	13
	Conservation of unequal length		
	NC	I	C
Control condition *d*	10	2	1
Similar model *e*	5	8	7
Correct model *f*	8	6	5

Jonckheere's test, conditions *a* and *b*, Z: 2.168, P<0.02; conditions *a* and *c*, Z: 4.291, P<0.00003; conditions *d* and *e*, Z: 2.580, P<0.01; conditions *d* and *f*, Z: 1.715, P<0.05.

In the second posttest, as in the first, considerable progress may be observed in the similar model condition. The main characteristic of this situation is the introduction of a strong sociocognitive conflict which is not based on a correct counter-suggestion, indeed quite the reverse.

The results obtained from this experiment are particularly important and open up a new perspective. As we have seen in the case of several earlier studies involving social interaction, in most of these experiments children are confronted with progressive and even correct models. Substantial progress regularly appears. In consequence, the role of the information contained in these conditions seemed to be of prime importance for cognitive progress, and mechanisms based on imitation were regarded as quite feasible. The same kind of results were found in our correct model condition in which the conflicting response was also correct and led to substantial progress, which for a number of subjects extended to the inequalities task which was not included in the experimental phase.

The novel contribution demonstrated by the present experiment is that a similar model (in which the child is confronted with centrations that are certainly opposed but also as incorrect as its own) leads to substantial progress, and to generalisation to conservation of inequality equivalent to that with a correct model. Thus cognitive restructuring can result from two centrations at a lower level. Such restructuring results directly from the subject's attempt to resolve the conflict between himself and the collaborator. The experimenter will remind the children of this conflict if they are tempted to resolve it by straightforward compliance. Caught in such a conflict, the child moves towards an attempt to offer an alternative solution by proposing that the rails are equal. The collaborator, however, responds to the challenge by repeating his incorrect counter-suggestion. As one might expect, few children are able to hold out against this. But it is sufficient to then remove the counter-suggestions, as in effect happens in the first posttest, for the majority of children to demonstrate a new structuration.

Experiment 2. Intensity of sociocognitive conflict

What happens if the similar model condition is not as constraining as in the preceding experiment, where the child was caught in a strong conflict by two adult accomplices?

Certainly one might anticipate that in several cases there would tend to be compliance between the child and the adult, the contradicting response of the latter not being challenged. The effect of such social dynamics will be studied in this experiment in terms of several hypotheses. First of all, it will be determined whether or not presentation of a similar model alone, without a more forceful challenge on the part of the experimenter's collaborator is sufficient to set progress in motion. It should be sufficient in a similar model condition in which the experimenter forces the child to confront the contradicting responses without locking him too firmly within a conflict. It is also expected that this condition of moderately strong conflict will induce equality solutions among children who try to resolve the conflict with the adult in a cognitive manner. Therefore, the hypothesis is advanced that the most compliant subjects, that is those most often adopting without question the adult's incorrect solution, will be those who progress the least; compliance as a social means for resolving interindividual conflict will inhibit a cognitive restructuring of this conflict.

Three conditions were devised to test these predictions.

In a *no-conflict* control condition no form of conflict is introduced. Nevertheless, in order to match the other conditions the experimenter's collaborator is present but replies in the same manner as the nonconserving child, judging the same rail as that nominated by the child to be the longer and arguing in terms of the sticking out at one end, thus adopting the same formula as the child. Four items are presented in order to compensate for the brevity of the interactions.

In a similar model condition with *weak conflict*, after the child has given and argued for his nonconserving response, the collaborator gives his own response, judging to be longer the opposite rail to that nominated by the child on the grounds of the protrusion of this latter rail. The experimenter then simply asks the child to give his own final response and to justify it. As in the no-conflict condition, there are four items in order to compensate for the short duration of the interactions compared to those in the similar model condition with strong conflict.

In the *strong conflict* similar model condition, a conflict is introduced which is still somewhat less intense than that in the preceding experiment. For the two items comprising this condition the procedure is similar. After the child has given and justified his response, the experimenter asks the collaborator to give his own. Again he judges the opposite rail to be longer and gives the usual justification. If the child is compliant, if, in other words, he adopts the collaborator's response, the experimenter reminds the child of his initial response and asks him to justify this unexpected change. If the child resists the collaborator's counter-suggestion, the experimenter draws attention to the disagreement and asks the partners if there is not some way that they could agree. The experimenter then attempts to make explicit the contrast in centrations and to obtain a noncontradictory solution. Conflict, although strong, is therefore unquestionably less so than in the preceding experiment.

Results

To what extent does compliance appear in the two conditions involving a similar model? Out of 15 subjects in the weak conflict condition, 10 at one point or another in the interaction adopted the adult's response. In the same proportion, 11 out of 17 in the strong conflict condition adopted the collaborator's response, which was as incorrect as their own, at some point during the interaction. These data clearly indicate that, in the preceding experiment, by the active intervention of two adults we suppressed an inter-individual dynamic that has a strong probability of occurring in exchanges between child and adult.

Who are the subjects who discover, albeit at only one point or another during the interaction, the correct equality response, a response that the adult, it should be remembered, never gives?

In the no-conflict condition, 2 subjects out of 14 give such a response. In the weak conflict condition, 5 subjects out of 15 try to resolve the conflict in this way. This number increases in the strong conflict condition in which the experimenter asks the subjects somehow to find middle ground; in this case, 11 out of 17 subjects offered a correct response at some point.

What are the repercussions of these behaviours for progress in the post-test? The results are presented in Table 5.3.

First of all it can be established that the strong conflict condition shows substantial progress, mainly relating to conservation of equality. In contrast to the preceding experiment, in which the conflict was more intense, progress on equality and on inequality are only weakly related, which indicates that conflict, when moderated in this way, leads only to partial elaboration of the concept concerned.

TABLE 5.3. *Frequency of Nonconserving (NC), Intermediate (I), and Conserving (C) subjects on the first posttest*

	Conservation of equal length		
	NC	I	C
No conflict	13	0	1
Weak conflict	12	2	1
Strong conflict	10	4	3
	Conservation of unequal length		
	NC	I	C
No conflict	13	1	0
Weak conflict	14	1	0
Strong conflict	12	5	0

Jonckheere's test, conservation of equal length, Z: 2.140, P<0.02.

However, the strong conflict similar model condition differs significantly from the no-conflict condition in which only one subject progresses on the test of equality. The condition involving simple presentation of a contrasting though similarly justified response occupies an intermediate position and does not differ significantly from the control condition. For the test of inequality the tendency is similar but nonsignificant.

Progress in the second posttest is sustained in 8 out of 11 cases for equality but, and this deserves emphasis, in 6 out of the 7 in the strong conflict condition, stability of progress on inequality is of the same order (5 out of 7). Thus, in spite of the fewer cases of progress obtained, such progress proves to be largely stable and indicates the beginnings of restructuring.

The apparently strong results from the first experiment are thus placed in their proper context; when sociocognitive conflict is pushed towards manageable limits for the child it produces sizeable, generalised and stable progress. In this respect, our theoretical hypothesis, concerning the role of sociocognitive conflict, is clearly verified. The present experiment concerns the possible extension of such a conflict to situations closer to those to which the child is accustomed. It has been shown that a difficulty arises when the child is able to use compliance as a means of escaping the tension induced by conflict with an adult. Progress diminishes when adjustments that are actually relational take the place of strictly cognitive adjustments. Is it possible to find a more precise confirmation of this?

For this one needs to consider only the results on the test of equality, since it alone corresponds to the test practised during the experimental phase, and for the strong conflict condition since this alone shows substantial progress. What levels are attained by the children who adopt the adult's incorrect counter-suggestion on both the interaction items (maximum compliance), on only one item, and on no items? The results are given in Table 5.4.

TABLE 5.4. *Frequency of Nonconserving (NC), Intermediate (I) and Conserving (C) subjects on the test for conservation of equal length as a function of number of items on which compliance occurs*

Compliance on	NC	I	C
0 Items	2	2	2
1 Item	3	2	0
2 Items	5	0	1

Jonckheere's test, Z: 1.649, P<0.05.

Although the analysis is based on a small number of children, the differences between them as a function of their willingness to comply are significant and indicate that progress is, indeed, inversely related to the compliance displayed in relation to the adult; when a purely social adjustment of the conflict occurs it is to the detriment of cognitive progress (such a regulation was counteracted in the preceding experiment which led to more progress). This is, moreover, a result that will be found again on several occasions in relation to other paradigms.

Experiment 3. Sociocognitive conflict between peers

Can children engage in sociocognitive conflict 'spontaneously' when they are placed in situations analogous to those of the two preceding experiments? This question is not so much a theoretical extension as a study of the possibility of such conflicts in interactions between 'equals'. The basic hypothesis of course rests on whether progress will appear principally in groups displaying such conflict.

Let us suppose that in situations exactly like those in the two preceding experiments, two nonconserving children are placed face-to-face and have to respond successively, and then have to come to an agreement if their responses are contradictory and incorrect. Are the possibilities of such conflict identical for the conservation of equal and of unequal lengths tasks? (It should be added that in all the conditions in the experimental phase, small chains are used.)

In fact, the probability of conflict between two nonconserving children in the unequal lengths task is very low. The two subjects will almost inevitably share the same centrations. Thus, when the configuration is such that the ends of the longer chain are 'within' those of the shorter one (see Fig. 5.2, configuration 4), two nonconservers will agree in judging the latter to be the longer. In the same way, they would in principle both judge the chains as equal when their ends coincide (configuration 2). The possibility of conflict is thus almost nil. Looking ahead to Experiment 4 we stress that, despite this low probability, means may be found to introduce sociocognitive conflict into this type of task by contrasting the centrations of nonconservers with differing and correct judgements derived from a social form of necessity.

The probability of conflict is stronger for the equal lengths task and for each of the two items four possibilities exist (though it is still impossible to predict the exact probability of each):

– either the two children agree that chain x is the longer (if for example their criterion is that the longest is the one that has been moved by the experimenter), or chain y given the opposite criterion.

– or each child centrates on one of the chains, one choosing x as the longer, the other choosing y or vice versa. This is possible if for example each subject centrates on the chain that is further away (or conversely the one that is closer.)

The least one can say is that the probability of conflict is in this case not zero. It could be hypothesised here that conservation of equality produces more conflicting interactions than conservation of inequality. In consequence more progress would be expected in the first case. Equally, it should be emphasised that on the basis of the second experiment we expect less progress than in the first experiment since it is less certain that subjects would be caught in a conflict as intense as that in the first experiment. Let us now see how the experiment was carried out.

Ninety-six children, with an average age of 6 years 3 months, participated in the experiment, 24 in the individual control conditions and 72 in 36 groups of 2. Forty-eight children worked on conservation of equal lengths, 48 on conservation of unequal lengths, thus giving 12 in each individual condition and 36 in 18 groups of 2 in each collective condition.

Let us summarise the experimental conditions for the conservation of equal lengths task, the more important since it alone seems liable to provoke conflict. In all cases two chains of the same length but a different colour were used. The experimenter places them successively in three configurations, always parallel in front of the subjects. To begin with their ends coincide. Then one chain is displaced a few centimetres, and then the other chain is displaced in turn so that it exceeds the first chain in the same direction. The two chains always remain parallel.

In the two collective conditions, the children are seated facing each other across a small table and the experimenter assigns one of the chains to each child, emphasising the respective colours. For each presentation he asks them to agree on the respective lengths of the chains, repeating if necessary 'Is one longer than the other, or are they both the same length? What do you think?' For one-third of the pairs, their responses have no particular consequences. In the other pairs, each child receives two sweets at the start of the interaction with the following instructions: 'The winner is the one who has the longer chain and he can take a sweet from the loser, the one with the shorter chain. You must always agree about who has won and who has lost; if not, I will take one sweet away from both of you.' The chains are always manipulated by the experimenter.

As our hypothesis specifies that conflicts of centrations are necessary for the appearance of individual progress, the analysis of results will distinguish the groups in which such a conflict occurs from those in which it does not. An interaction will be considered as conflicting if at one point or another it gives rise to disagreements between the two children's incorrect responses, their discussions having been recorded.

In one of the individual conditions, the child must allot sweets to the longer chain. The experimenter places two sweets near each chain and says 'These sweets belong to the chains. The rule of the game is that each time a chain is longer, you take one of these sweets from the shorter chain and give it to the longer chain which will have won.'

The experimental design and procedures are exactly the same for the conditions based on conservation of unequal length, except that one child is allotted a longer chain and the other a shorter chain.

Results

We assumed that the appearance of sociocognitive conflict would be more likely in groups working on conservation of equality than in those working on conservation of inequality. Table 5.5 gives the number of groups in which conflict occurred between the two children's incorrect responses at one point or another during the interaction.

TABLE 5.5. *Frequency of groups with and without presence of conflict*

| | Conservation of length | |
	Equal	Unequal
Conflict	9	4
No conflict	9	14

As we expected, conflicts between incorrect responses tends to occur more often in the condition based on equality, where half the groups display such conflict. In the other half the subjects agree throughout the interaction on the same incorrect response. The remainder of our analysis will only concern this condition, which alone allows for a meaningful comparison between conflicting and nonconflicting groups.

The first question is whether the introduction of winnings has an effect on the occurrence of conflict? The answer is no since 3 out of 6 groups without winnings involve conflict, as do 6 out of 12 groups with winnings. It is true that the dividing of two sweets may not constitute a very strong incentive. But it is also not impossible that the introduction of winnings could just as easily favour a change in centration as the preservation of the subject's initial response. Be that as it may, this is only a secondary variable and it will not be taken into account in the remainder of the analysis. (We did establish, moreover, that it had no significant effect on progress found in groups with and without conflict).

Before giving the results for the groups with and without progress let us note that the individual or rather intraindividual condition with no conflict shows insignificant progress; in the first posttest only one subject becomes a conserver on the test for equality (whilst none become intermediate); in the case of inequality, only one subject gave a response classified as the intermediate level, none managing to give a conserving response.

Table 5.6 gives the results for the first posttest for the experimental groups with and without conflict.

TABLE 5.6. *Frequency of Nonconserving (NC), Intermediate (I) and Conserving (C) subjects on the first posttest*

| | Conservation of equal length | | |
	NC	I	C
No Conflict *a*	14	3	1
Conflict *b*	7	10	1
	Conservation of unequal length		
	NC	I	C
No Conflict *c*	12	6	0
Conflict *d*	7	10	1

Jonckheere's test, conditions *a* and *b*, Z: 1.944, P<0.03, conditions *c* and *d*, Z: 1.500, P<0.07.

The results indicate that it is the subjects who participate in conflicting interactions who progress the most. The effect is very clear for the equality task (on which the interaction is based), whilst there is a statistical tendency for the unequal lengths task.

On the whole, therefore, interaction between children is also confirmed as being a significant context for cognitive development but such progress appears only if there is sociocognitive conflict between the partners. Certainly, some progress does also appear in groups categorised as non-conflicting. This is not inconsistent, since the criterion used to distinguish the two types of group is that of social expression of disagreement between equally incorrect responses. There is the possibility that some disagreement could exist without it being expressed verbally. Let us remember that in the preceding experiment the mere presentation of a model without a conflict procedure, did result in some slight progress.

Progress is quite systematically maintained in the second posttest; of the 15 subjects who progressed on the equality test, 12 maintained their progress (with 4 actually improving on it). With respect to conservation of inequality, 13 out of 17 cases of progress that were apparent immediately following the interaction remained stable. This stability suggests genuine progress. The validity of this progress is further supported by the large number of subjects who progressed on both tests simultaneously. Furthermore, this is only true for the conflicting groups within which 9 children progressed both on equality and inequality (for the most part to the intermediate level).

In contrast to the first experiment, where a number of subjects gave conservation responses, in the present experiment in which children are opposed in 'spontaneous' interactions, one mainly finds responses at the intermediate level. Only particularly constrained social situations (as in experiment 1) allow more rapid conserving response. These situations are essential to an experimental demonstration of a sociopsychological mechanism (which is why they were conceived), but they are not necessarily representative of the social situations encountered daily by children.

Is the progress found specific only to certain individuals in groups that have experienced sociocognitive conflict or does it derive directly from the social dynamics that arise between the partners? Part of the answer is to be found in the distribution of progress amongst the groups. If progress is linked to the course of the interaction itself, we might therefore expect progress to occur for both participants. To examine this possibility one could consider the number of groups in which both partners progressed on the first posttest, the number in which only one of the two progressed and the number in which no progress resulted from the interaction. This analysis can be carried out separately for the equality and inequality tests (see Table 5.7).

TABLE 5.7. *Number of groups in which 0, 1 or 2 partners progress on the first posttest*

Number of partners progressing per group	Conservation of equal length			Conservation of unequal length		
	0	1	2	0	1	2
No Conflict	5	4	0	5	2	2
Conflict	2	3	4	2	3	4

Jonckheere's test, conservation of equal length, Z: 1.736, P<0.05; conservation of unequal length, Z. 1.079, N.S.

It appears that among the groups with conflict progress occurs for the most part for both partners, and this is more so than among groups without conflict. This is particularly evident for the test of equality on which the interaction was based. In fact the four cases of progress among groups without conflict occur in four different groups, whilst among the conflicting groups eight out of eleven cases of progress are to be found in four groups, which underlines the social interdependence of cognitive progress.

For the inequality test the results are less clear-cut, although they tend in the same direction. Eight out of the eleven cases of progress following conflict come from four groups. However, the proportion of cases of progress found to come from the same groups in the case of nonconflicting groups is similar; here, four out of six cases derive from two groups. Although it cannot be concluded that there is a difference between the two types of group, the consistency of the effects on the two tasks for the groups in which interaction was conflicting is noteworthy.

The last experiment represents the conclusion (albeit a provisional one) of the research intended to provide an experimental foundation for our thesis, namely that the impact of interpersonal interaction upon cognitive development lies in mechanisms of sociocognitive conflict. The first experiment offered a particularly rigorous demonstration, illustrating how socio-cognitive conflict, taken to its limits, is a source of cognitive progress. No correct response was suggested to the child; on the contrary, the adult persisted in advocating an incorrect response based on the same non-conserving reasoning as that which the child had shown itself to be capable of. From this highly constraining conflict substantial progress resulted. In the second experiment the intensity of the conflict was reduced and less progress resulted. This made it possible to show that it is actually the form taken by interindividual conflict which allows an incorrect 'model' to produce progress; the model by itself was only minimally effective. Finally, the present experiment has shown that such conflicts can occur between children and lead to progress. It has also shown that the probability of socio-cognitive conflict on the inequality task is slight. Is all sociocognitive conflict therefore ruled out in any social situation involving this task? It is to this question that the following experiment is addressed. It will be seen that the difficulty can be removed through systematic challenging of the child by the adult, but that this challenging is only really effective if the relation between the child and the adult posing the questions is relevant to the situation.

Experiment 4. Social marking

If two nonconserving children participate together in a task for conser-vation of unequal length it is very likely, as we have seen, that they will respond in a similar manner. Indeed, little conflict appears as the preceding experiment has shown. To show that sociocognitive conflict may have a role, in the present experiment an adult collaborator of the experimenter will be the child's partner. He will initiate sociocognitive conflict through systematic challenges as described below. This will also provide an oppor-tunity to illustrate the concept of social marking in another way. This concept refers to the correspondences that may exist between the nature of the relationships that are or may become established between social partners, and the nature of the cognitive relationships entailed in the task which mediates the relation between them. Under certain circumstances these correspondences can favour cognitive progress, especially when an isomorphism exists between them. This experiment will include a social marking condition in which such a correspondence will be made salient.

To illustrate the concept of social marking, an experimental situation is necessary in which the correspondence between a social norm and an intellectual concept is particularly strong. Conservation of length meets this requirement. Indeed, the size relation between different objects can, in the context of an adult-child interaction, correlate with the physical and social characteristics of the participants. Correspondence between a cognitive concept and a social norm will be established in an interaction phase involving sharing: the allotting of two bracelets of different lengths to the adult and the child. In a control condition this sharing will also be carried out, but with two paper cylinders.

The paradigm for this experimental situation can thus be defined in the following fashion. First of all, the relation to be established by the child is mediated by the sharing of objects between itself and another (the adult experimenter). Next, the social representations involved are those available to the child in its relationships with others (here, the adult experimenter). Thus, as the particular properties linked to this representation concern measurements, the social norm implies here that the adult has more right to larger objects than the child. In this case the social norm governing the assignment of objects of unequal size coincides with the correct conservation response at the conceptual level. Choosing to accord the larger object to the adult, independent of its configuration, coincides with conservation in the unequal length task.

The subjects are all nonconservers on the two length conservation tasks. They will be led by the experimenter's challenges to relate their judgements of the bracelets' lengths, judgements which are dependent on their level of cognitive development, to their assignment of the bracelets, dependent for its part on the social norms expressed in the functional relations already correctly established. Allocation between the experimenter and the child, which requires giving the larger bracelet to the adult, should increase sociocognitive conflict for the child and an associated search for a cognitive regulation. It could thus favour discovery of the constancy of length across variations in spatial position since the norm coincides with conservation of the identity of objects and their properties. In fact, as the adult is always bigger, the larger bracelet accorded to him should likewise always remain larger. There is no such social marking in the control condition, where the bracelets are allocated to paper cylinders. As a consequence, progress in the level of judgements of length conservation should be much smaller than in the experimental condition.

Thirty-five children were retained from a larger sample on the basis of responses on a pretest which showed they were clearly nonconserving with respect to conservation of equal and unequal length. They were drawn from classes at the second infant level (average age 5 years 9 months) and first primary level (average age 6 years 5 months). One day after the pretest they took part in an interaction session lasting for about a quarter of an hour. They were given an initial posttest immediately following the interaction. A second posttest was conducted 2 weeks later.

In order to control for the characteristics of particular experimenters, all subjects were dealt with by three different experimenters. One administered the pretest for half the subjects and conducted the interaction and first post-test for the other half, the second doing the same for the alternative halves. A third experimenter, blind as to the subjects' experimental condition, carried out the second posttest.

The material used in the experimental phase consists of two small chains of the same colour, one 15 cm long, the other 20 cm long. These materials are, in the control condition, accompanied by two cylinders made of card-board, 5 cm high, the diameter of one being 4.5 cm and of the other being 6.5 cm, so that their circumferences correspond respectively to the lengths of the two chains.

Interaction phase

In both experimental and control conditions, the procedure, task and terms used were identical. The only difference was that in the experimental condition the bracelets were allotted 'so that they fit the wrists easily' (those of the experimenter and the child), and in the control condition, to go round the two cylinders.

Following a preliminary phase for presentation of material and for specifying the size of the bracelets and cylinders, four items were presented to the child:

1. The configuration of the two unequal chains as employed at the start of the inequality test (see Fig. 5.2, configuration 1). First, the experimenter asks the child to judge the relative lengths of the bracelets, the answers being obvious to all subjects. He then asks the child to choose the bracelet 'which is the better one for me and the one which is better for you' or for the two paper cylinders. (For convenience, from now on, only the instructions for wrists will be indicated, the procedure being identical for the cylinders). Each time the child is asked to justify his response.

2. This involves the second configuration of the standard test with the ends of the bracelets coinciding (see Fig. 5.2, configuration 2). After making a judgement about the lengths, the child selects bracelets for

himself and the adult. The bracelets are then tried on and this, depending on the child's response, is accompanied by one of two counter-suggestions.

(a)   If the child has made an error in his choice, 'You chose that one because they are both the same length, but it still doesn't work. Do you think that's right?'

(b)   If the child has in spite of his incorrect judgement selected the right bracelet for each of them, he is reminded of his judgement: 'Since they are both the same length you could also have chosen that one,' (proposing an exchange of bracelets).

The child, normally ready to accept the experimenter's proposals, then finds himself successively opposed by these two types of counter-suggestion. At the end of the item he is again asked to make a judgement about the lengths and to make a further selection, this time without cross-examination; for all the children this choice is correct. A further justification is then requested of the child.

3.   This involves the last item in the standard test (see Fig. 5.2, configuration 4). Centrating on the extremities, most subjects judge the longer bracelet to be shorter. For those who allocate the inappropriate bracelet to the experimenter's wrist or to the larger cylinder, the counter-suggestion consists of a reminder that at the beginning of the trials they had chosen the other bracelet: 'How can that be? You said at the beginning that the big one would be better for me because I was bigger and the little one would be better for you because you were smaller. Now you are telling me that I should have the little one. Do you think that's right?' For those who, in spite of their incorrect judgement allot the bracelets appropriately, it is easy to remind them that their choice contradicts their initial judgement. Finally, a new choice is made, on which all children are successful as in item 2.

4.   A final item further accentuates the squashing up of the longer bracelet. This last item involves only a judgement followed by a choice without any counter-suggestion.

Results

What are the effects of social marking in terms of individual progress? The results are indicated in Table 5.8 which gives the distribution of levels on the first posttest for the equality and inequality tasks.

The results confirm our predictions, since the condition involving social marking generally leads to greater progress than the condition without it. This effect is obtained both for conservation of equal length and conservation of unequal length tests, even though it is more marked for inequality because the experimental phase involved this kind of task.

TABLE 5.8. *Frequency of Nonconserving (NC), Intermediate (I), and Conserving (C) subjects on the first posttest*

	Conservation of equal length		
	NC	I	C
Cylinders *a*	15	1	1
Bracelets *b*	8	2	8
	Conservation of unequal length		
Cylinders *c*	15	1	1
Bracelets *d*	7	1	10

Jonckheere's test, conditions *a* and *b*, Z: 2.576, P<0.005; conditions *c* and *d*, Z: 2.930, P<0.002.

In the first posttest, eight out of eleven subjects in the experimental condition who progressed in terms of the inequality on which the manipulation of social marking was based also progressed on the equality test. It seems that here we have an instance of genuine progress in cognitive structure. What is more, the progress in the control condition with respect to equality and inequality is hardly comparable. The stability of the progress recorded in the first posttest is considerable, since for the inequality test, eight out of the eleven subjects progressing on this test conserve this progress on the second posttest, and this is true for nine out of the ten subjects showing progress on the first posttest in terms of the equality test.

The responses the children made during the course of the interaction were compared and particular attention paid to the justifications advanced at the end of item 3 after the experimenter's last counter-suggestion. At this point, sociocognitive conflict was at its strongest (since most of the initial judgements regarding this item were incorrect, given the perceptual configuration and the subjects' level). What is more, having drawn conclusions from their eventual failure in the selection of bracelets, all the subjects in the two conditions finally allotted the bracelets correctly. The effects of social marking could already be seen at this level. We then classified the responses to the final counter-suggestion according to whether the arguments were conserving (identity, reversibility, compensation) or nonconserving (absence of coordination of different configurations of bracelets, functional arguments of the type 'It's fine like that') . . . The results show that thirteen out of the eighteen subjects in the social marking condition provided an operational argument while only four out of the seventeen in the condition without social marking did so. Thus, at this point in the experiment, children in the experimental or social marking condition give more conserving justifications; this forecasts the cognitive restructuring to which this condition gives rise in the individual posttest level.

Finally, we should draw attention to one result which does rule out an alternative interpretation of our findings. In simple terms, is it possible to interpret the difference in the difficulty of the task in the two conditions in terms of simpler learning because the material is easier? This is not the case. When, in the interaction phase of the experiment subjects give the first of their four choices regarding allocation of the bracelets, there is no difference between the two conditions in choices of the 'right' bracelet for each wrist or cylinder. On this first item the choices are always correct since the requirements correspond to the initial configuration and this does not even pose a problem at the judgemental level; the choice likewise cannot be other than correct. For items 2 and 3, in which the task is made more difficult, about half the choices in both conditions are correct. Only on the last item (item 4) is there in the experimental condition an increase in correct allocations, an increase which could indeed coincide with the beginnings of a restructuring observed at the end of item 3. However, the difference between the two conditions on item 4 is not significant either.

Conclusions

This experiment, like the preceding ones, confirms that if social interaction is of particular importance in cognitive development, it is to the degree that sociocognitive conflict arises. It is not necessary to demonstrate the appropriate response to the child explicitly; he constructs it in the interaction as in the first experiments he discovers the equality of lengths despite modifications in their configurations. If conflict is to give rise to cognitive restructuring, it must be particularly strong. This can occur when the child is caught within a conflict, by the adult, when compliance is denied to the child or when the child's response is directly relevant to its relationship with the adult. In each case only regulation of a cognitive order is able to regulate the social relation itself.

6

The coordination of viewpoints

The child's representation of space has interested psychologists for a long time.[1] The issue of coordinating different points of view has usually been approached in terms of the elaboration of space. Piaget and Inhelder's (1952) 'Three Mountains Task' is very well known; in front of the child is a sheet of cardboard on which three very different looking mountains are placed. The child's task involves imagining the perspective which a doll would have at different viewpoints. Several techniques involving more or less activity on the part of the child are used to highlight the difficulties encountered, and their progressive mastery. Analysis of them shows how egocentrism, in which what the child perceives constitutes the only possibility (which is then attributed to the doll, no matter what viewpoint it occupies) gives way to a progressive realisation of other perspectives. These are manifested first in terms of partial adjustments (for example, in correctly transforming the front-back or the left-right order), leading finally to a complete system in which the multiple spatial relations are expressed correctly transformed into all the dimensions involved in the different viewpoints.

As with other areas of research already discussed, these spatial coordinations have been considered solely as intraindividual processes, related to the structural characteristics of this representational space. Social dynamics are absent from these studies, the only social relations being imaginary and implicit (and therefore never considered as elements of the task); these are the relations with the doll whose perceptions must be imagined.

Now this representation of space could also result from the coordination of real viewpoints, occupied by real, not imaginary, individuals. The intellectual coordinations characteristic of the elaboration of space might then result in a very important sense from the social need to coordinate diverse viewpoints within a balanced system in which these various viewpoints can be acknowledged despite their diversity in perceptual appearances.

---

[1] In 1948 Piaget and Inholder published a long work on this question (English Edition, 1952); it provided a set of experimental techniques which inspired the research of numerous subsequent investigations. In this work one finds an essentially psychological perspective on this complex area of development while in more recent works, such as that by Laurendeau and Pinard (1970), are to be found various theoretical and methodological refinements.

Take the classic example of recognition of right and left. To the child who has just realised that there exists a spatial order qualified by the terms 'on the left' and 'on the right', this concept is absolute. An object can only be 'on the left' *or* 'on the right'; it cannot be both simultaneously for two different individuals, and even less for a single individual. After some training this child will easily distinguish his right-hand from his left and will designate them correctly. Let us place an individual opposite him and then ask the child to indicate the newcomer's right-hand. The left/right concept being as yet an absolute, the chances are that he will indicate the hand which corresponds to his own right-hand, that is the other's left-hand.

The social psychologist's interest in this situation is concerned not so much with the child's inability to consider the left/right relation as located in a space in which configurations can appear different according to viewpoint, as with the fact that such a response has a strong chance of generating socio-cognitive conflict. If the partner is also a child, it is possible that, to the degree that he recognises his right- and left-hands by the same criteria as the other, he will not accept the first child's judgement. Let us suppose that the second child is indeed at the same level as the first. He will himself suppose that the first child's right-hand is the one corresponding with his own right-hand (i.e. he will pick the other child's left-hand). Our hypothesis is that such sociocognitive conflicts are the origins of the intraindividual coordinations of which children are later capable. These will in effect be a consequence of the social need to coordinate viewpoints.

The following set of experiments is intended to illustrate the social-psychological mechanisms that are involved in such an elaboration. It is inspired by the Three Mountains task although it does differ on several points. This variation is not of great importance since the tasks involved have been devised primarily to allow the inclusion of various experimental manipulations. Let us first examine the spatial transformation paradigm that will be used.

Social coordination of viewpoints in the reconstruction of a village

The spatial transformation task used follows the same principle in all the various experiments. In each there may be differences in detail though these do not affect performances. They are principally in the form of the material (rectangular in the first experiments and square in the later ones, to accommodate further experimental manipulations; we will describe here this latter square form, which offers more possibilities for manipulation), and the position of the houses in the village.

The principle is simple; after observing a village consisting of several buildings, the child must reproduce it using identical houses on an identical base-board, the orientation of which can, however, differ from the perspective occupied by the child. Let us examine this procedure element by element.

The materials

As is shown in the photograph (Plate IV(a)), the material usually consists of two bases made of cardboard 50 cm by 50 cm. These are the 'plots' on which the villages will be built. The orientation of the plot was usually given by a blue-coloured mark (an isosceles triangle formed by a half square with 15 cm sides) the base of which is placed in a corner of the plot with the tip pointing towards the middle.

On one of these bases the experimenter constructs a village which the child is then asked to reproduce on the other base. This requires two sets of three or four houses (one for the experimenter and one for the child). For the individual tests three houses are used in all the experiments described. In the first two experiments, three houses were used in the experimental phase, whilst in the remainder, four were used.

Each house is a different colour (they may be called 'the red house', 'the blue house', and 'the yellow house'; the fourth, when used, being 'the white house') – and made in such a manner that it can also be oriented; the side with a door is regarded as the front.

Depending on the experiment and the experimenters, the precise details of each house may differ, though not in any important ways. Where possible, however, the same material is used.

All phases, but particularly the individual tests, use record sheets on which each item is depicted and on which the child's performance can be recorded together with any possible changes made in the positions of the houses.

Finally, and especially for the interaction phase, it is desirable to have video recording facilities available, to record the interactions on which the major independent variables bear. (When possible, this was done in most of the experiments.) Protocols are also carefully taken at the time of the experiment and if possible verified immediately by a collaborator of the experimenter.

The standard procedure

Let us describe the tasks given to the children in the various individual and collective phases (in the latter case supplementary instructions are given which, where they are specific to a particular experimental manipulation, will be mentioned at an appropriate point).

As in the other experiments, the child is collected from his classroom. In the experimental room (located in the same school) he is placed before a table, having been asked his name, his age, what he does in class, and generally put at ease. On the table the experimenter has put a cardboard base, the plot on which he has placed in predetermined positions the three houses making up the village.

The experimenter begins by indicating the village he has just constructed: 'We are going to play a game with the houses; we are going to say that this house is the red house, this house is the blue house and that this is the yellow house. I have made a village with these houses on the table; do you agree that this is a village? Look carefully at this here (the experimenter indicates the orientation mark with his finger). We could say that this is a swimming pool. Well, the game is to make exactly the same village on this table (he says this indicating the second or copy table). You must place these three houses so that they make exactly the same village.' Indicating the village he has just constructed himself, 'in this village if a man (note that this so-called man is not represented by a doll) comes out of the swimming pool here (he indicates the location of the swimming pool with his finger), he knows the path for getting to his own red house, the path to the blue house, and also the path for going to the yellow house very well. In the village, which you are going to make the man coming out of the swimming pool must find the same houses along the same paths as in this one. He must find the red house along the same path as here, the blue along the same path as here, and also the yellow one along the same path as here. Do you understand? So what do you have to do? Explain to me.' By the time the second item is reached it is generally no longer necessary to repeat the instructions to the child in full, and this is also true for the later (experimental and posttest) phases.

A crucial feature of the procedure is that no indication, either verbal or by gesture, be given regarding the dimensions relevant to a spatial transformation, correct or otherwise.

As indicated in the diagram (Fig. 6.1), the child is always placed during the individual tests in position x and can only move within the limited area indicated by the dotted lines (the boundaries are marked by obstacles, usually chairs).

On an initial item, which may be described as 'simple', the child is told what is expected of him; that he should examine the village created by the experimenter on table 1 and then reconstruct it on table 2, situated to his left at an angle of 90°.

The other items, characterised as 'complex', then follow. First, the orientation of the base on which the experimenter erects his village is modified. While for the simple item the marker (the swimming pool or mountain) is, when viewed from position x, 'in the far left hand corner', for the complex items the mark is positioned 'in the near right hand corner' (when viewed from the same position). Hence, a faithful reconstruction requires not only a rotation of the whole 90° to the left, but also an inversion

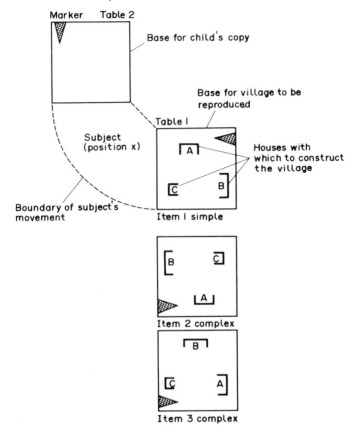

FIG. 6.1   Items used in the individual task situation.

of the left-right and front-back orders. Thus, in the second item, house A moves from right to left, while houses B and C find themselves on the right and are also reversed in terms of the front-back dimension. A correct solution in item 3 requires that B is placed on the right, with A and C on the left, but at the front and the back respectively.

Assessment of performance

Several evaluations of performance are possible. One can assess in centimetres the average deviation, from its correct position, of a house placed by the child. This deviation index, which has been used on several occasions, has three characteristics. First it is very laboured (after each item detailed measurements must be taken, which is time-consuming). Second, it is not without ambiguity: two different incorrect strategies can produce similar indices depending on how precise children have been in their reconstruction. Finally, it generally provides results very similar to those that can be obtained from a more qualitative analysis in terms of cognitive levels or stages in the task under consideration. It is this latter analysis which will be used for all the experiments here. Based on analysis of overall strategies (and not on deviation insofar as it is a measurable quantity) it offers among other things the advantage of accommodating itself very well to variations in detail between the experiments in terms of the positions of the houses.

Let us now look at this analysis in terms of levels, bearing in mind that the assessment of performances is based only on items 2 and 3, the complex items. Subjects retained for the experiments described were all capable of correctly reproducing the simple item, in other words of placing the houses correctly on the left (or on the right), and at the front (or at the back). Let us add that it is the structure of the whole that is taken into account and not the precise position of each house. It is the relation between the elements that is considered rather than the precision of the placements. Also, no account is taken of errors in the orientation of the houses; this would have made a classification almost impossible, particularly at the intermediate level where these errors appear.

The assessments are based on the two complex items. More specifically, assignment to one of three levels of classification is made on the basis of the best performance achieved by each subject. This is an important point because progress will not be evaluated as a function of the 'generality' of a strategy. A case will not be treated as one of progress if the subject responds correctly to two items but has already responded correctly to one item in the pretest. This would be evaluating not a cognitive capacity but its degree of extension. There is no progress in our sense unless the most advanced capacities evident in the pretest are improved upon in the posttest (or post-tests). Subjects may progress in terms of a scale defined by the following levels:

Level I: Subjects at the first level take no account of the different orientations of the village and simply submit the whole village to a rotation of 90°; they therefore only reproduce the perceptual tableau that they are able to observe in front of the model, without producing any of the inversions required by the 180° rotation that the experimenter has made to the base of the model village for the complex items. These subjects will be characterised as NC (subjects presenting 'no compensations'), insofar as they do not compensate for this rotation (Fig. 6.2, solution Ia).

Some subjects do give a solution which consists of a simple translation (Fig. 6.2, Ib represents this type of solution for three houses). This solution is rare and when it appears it is most often combined with an NC type solution. These few subjects are also considered as NC. In most of the experiments, only NCs presenting the Ia type of solution to the complex items in the pretest were allowed to participate in the experimental phase. In the few experiments where Ib type NCs were retained (primarily because of the small sample sizes), they were distributed in equal proportions among the various experimental conditions.

Level II: At this intermediate level, subjects are characterised as PC (partial compensation), being capable of achieving one of the inversions required; either they adequately transform the right-left order but reproduce the front-back order as it appears (Fig. 6.2, solution IIc), or they adequately transform the front-back order without transforming the left-right order (Fig. 6.2, solution IId). The transformations used are therefore still only partial.

It should be noted that in this case the structural index is more precise than the deviation index. There is a similarity in the reasoning which underlies such performances. But, when the left-right relation is transformed (solution IIc) one of the houses is placed correctly. The deviation index is therefore smaller in this case. In contrast, when the front-back order is adequately inverted (solution IId), the two houses involved nevertheless remain incorrectly placed, due to the fact that the left-right relation has not been transformed. Indices of deviation would in consequence be clearly higher than in the preceding case, even though the level of transformation achieved by subjects is identical. The structural index is therefore the more suitable for our demonstrations.

Various 'hybrid' solutions do occur that do not correspond in any simple way to the type definitions. In order to classify them, the kind of transformation attempted by the child is considered. In cases of doubt at the pretest stage, the child is excluded from the sample. If the doubt arises in a posttest the child is classified as NC and this usually (although not exclusively) avoids introducing a bias in favour of our hypothesis. However, such cases are rare.

Level III: At this final level the performance is correct, the 'compensations' are complete. We therefore characterise as TC (total compensation) subjects who correctly transform the two dimensions simultaneously for at least one of the two complex items.

In the individual tests, subjects are classified according to their best performance on the complex items as either NC, PC or TC. Progress between the pretest and any of the possible posttests is considered to have taken place if a subject initially NC is then classified as PC or TC (where possible, the nature of the progress is specified more precisely), and in the case of a PC subject if he shows himself capable of at least one correct or TC response. TC subjects are not able to demonstrate progress within the framework of the task as defined here and were not retained for the remaining experiments (though another experiment has demonstrated the stability of this kind of performance among almost all subjects initially classified as TC).

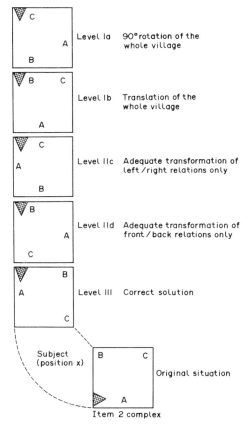

FIG. 6.2   Example of response types.

The experimental phase

The experimental variables whose effects on individual progress are to be studied are manipulated during this phase. The various experimental manipulations will be described in detail for each experiment, as will the details of the items which may also vary as a function of the situations devised.

In each experiment, however, the basic tasks remain the same. In this phase we begin by repeating the complete instructions to the child and also by asking him to recall what he did during the first session (the pretest). In cases where a collective performance is requested of the children, they are simply asked to complete the same village together and to tell the experimenter when they have agreed a solution. This requires the children to agree about the village in terms of 'the man finding the same houses along the same paths'. In the case of failure to agree, the children are asked again to try to reach an agreement and to tell the experimenter when this has been done.

As a general rule, each item is completed in a few minutes. In the first experiments, which were more exploratory some groups took up to 20 or 30 minutes. We decided that in the future we would stop the interaction after 10 minutes and would do this for every item. This kind of intervention was, however, rarely necessary.

During the interactions, as during the individual tests, the experimenter makes every effort to follow a standardised procedure, taking care to give no indication of the solution to the child (he never speaks of right or left, of front or back, of near or far, and so on). He confines himself to ensuring the proper conduct of the proceedings.

In the experimental phase, when children are interacting, the proximity of the experimenter can modify the interpersonal dynamics. Consequently, the experimenter may have a screen from behind which he can follow the interaction on a colour television monitor, if material and technical conditions permit. At all events, the experimenter and his collaborators separate themselves as far as is feasible from the children, to avoid overly blatant 'surveillance' of the work groups.

However, the role of the experimenter will be more important in some experiments. Occasionally (as has already been seen in the experiments on length conservation) the adult will be involved directly as the child's partner, in order to create conflicts. But given interactions between children, direct intervention is undesirable and is avoided despite frequent inclinations to intervene to help a group unable to begin an interaction. The experimenter cannot of course withdraw completely but it is necessary that he remain in the background and that he follow a standardised procedure in those matters he is able to control.

Experimental overview

One aspect of the experiments described here follows the same strategy as used in the other paradigms. An initial experiment compares individual performances with those of groups formed on a random basis; the latter appear qualitatively superior to the former. In a second experiment, various processes generated in the first will be isolated; we will seek to systematise the cognitive composition of the groups, hypothesising that more conflicts should occur between individuals at different cognitive levels than between individuals at the same level, and that in consequence, progress should be more frequent in the former. A more clinical analysis of the interactions is aimed at understanding the reasons why one of the experimental conditions seems not to fit this hypothesis. Note that, starting with this second experiment, individual tests are systematically carried out before and after the interactions. In a third experiment children who are at the same cognitive level will be involved on this task, but set in opposition by creating conditions more fitted to engender sociocognitive conflict. For this, the children will be required not to work side by side (as is the case in the first two experiments), but face to face, so that their different viewpoints may give rise to conflicts. In this experiment, the issue of sociological factors will also be raised again. In the fourth experiment we will go even further. We will totally remove any difficulty of a cognitive kind (the subjects themselves being confronted with simple items), but will create conflicts by placing the child face to face with another who is confronted with a complex item. The other child's erroneous response will, if the conflict is sufficiently strong, provoke the subject who faces no cognitive difficulty to elaborate new coordinations.

Two significant pieces of research carried out by May Lévy (1981) will then be presented which will once again raise the issue of 'modelling effects'. Most of the existing research in this area, as we have seen in the introductory chapters, has considered cognitive development as resulting from interaction with models providing correct responses. Might not such an effect be a particular instance of sociocognitive conflict? If this is so, it should then be possible, as our preceding experiments have already indicated, to induce progress without observation of correct models. Even models of a similar solution but based on different viewpoints or centrations should be able to lead to the elaboration of more developed concepts. Consequently we will study different types of model, keeping the mode of questioning constant. It will be seen that the effects of a correct model, a model that is incorrect, but more developed than that of the child (i.e. an intermediate level model), and particularly a model that is a little 'regressive', all lead to real progress. The same type of regressive model will be considered again but this time to study its effects in various situations involving presentation by an adult. This will provide an opportunity to show the value of systematic questioning as a specific means of creating sociocognitive conflict, as distinct from the influence of a model, even if only implicit. Hence, we will be experimenting, even if some centuries late, with what might be called the 'Socratic method'.

As in the preceding chapter, this will be achieved by an experiment demonstrating the role social marking plays in this spatial transformation paradigm.

Experiment 1. Individual and collective performance

The starting hypothesis, concerning the links between cognitive development and social interaction, is the supposition that, during the period of elaboration of a concept, the cognitive products of individuals working in small groups should be superior to those of individuals – drawn from equivalent populations – working alone. It is around this idea that the first experiment is formulated. If it is true that the coordinations of viewpoints of which individuals show themselves to be capable are socially generated, then one should be able to provide some evidence for a superiority of collective performances at a certain point in cognitive development.

The experimental design is very simple. The sample of subjects, composed equally of boys and girls, is randomly divided into two experimental groups, one working alone and the other in pairs. the average ages (5 years 9 months for half the children drawn from the second year of infant school, and 6 years 8 months for the other half, drawn from the first year of primary school) coincide with the stage for elaborating the cognitive structures involved in our spatial transformation task, as a previous study had indicated. This also indicated such development in 4 to 5 year old children, but their interactions are less spontaneous than those of the age range sampled making it too difficult to put the procedure into practice.

There is no pretest. Sixty children in all participated in the experiment, twenty in the individual condition, and forty divided into twenty groups of two. In each group children are drawn from the same class and are of the same sex.

Both individuals and groups respond to four items, first a simple item, then two complex items and finally another simple item (Fig. 6.3). The material used is rectangular (60 cms × 40 cms). During the interactions the two partners remain side by side and on the same side as those working individually.

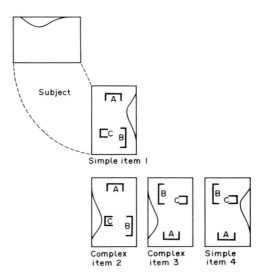

FIG. 6.3   The four test items.

Results

What proportion of the houses were the children tested capable of placing correctly and giving an appropriate orientation? This particular measure will only be used in this experiment. As this relates to the new paradigm it is perhaps not superfluous to provide this kind of data. Thus, Table 6.1 indicates, by item, the average number of houses correctly placed. It will be recalled that for each item the children have to place three houses.

TABLE 6.1. *Mean number of houses correctly placed*

	Simple Items	Complex Items
Individuals	2.38	0.65
Groups	2.53	1.65

Analysis of variance, carried out on this data, indicated a significant interaction between experimental condition and item type. Specifically, there is no difference between individual and group performances on the simple items which are frequently correct; as subjects have already acquired the cognitive structures necessary for their adequate realisation, groups are able to do no better. What happens with the complex items which introduce a major difficulty? Less than one-third of the houses are correctly placed by the individuals, which confirms that they are still at a stage of elaboration. Now, it is at the point of elaboration of a concept that our theory predicts a superiority of the group over the individual. The data show quite clearly that the interactions lead to structuring, since more than half the houses are appropriately placed.

What of the cognitive level that underlies these performances? Table 6.2 gives, for the two complex items, the levels attained by the groups and the

TABLE 6.2. *Cognitive levels attained on the two complex items*

	First Complex Item		
	Level I	Level II	Level III
Individuals	2	13	5
Groups	1	8	11
	Second Complex Item		
	Level I	Level II	Level III
Individuals	3	10	7
Groups	1	5	14

Jonckheere's test, First complex item, Z: 1.638, P<0.06; Second complex item, Z: 1.982, P<0.025.

individuals. Recall that at Level I, children offer no compensation for the 180° rotation imparted to the experimenter's village, at level II children manage an adequate transformation of one of the dimensions, the compensation therefore being partial, and those at the third level succeed in completing the village correctly (recall, also that for this more qualitative index, possible errors of orientation are not taken into account).

This more qualitative analysis clearly confirms the superiority of group over individual solutions. It is moreover particularly marked on the second item, group performances being somewhat improved here while individual efforts remain unchanged.

Why is the group particularly advantageous for cognitive elaboration? This experiment led to a more clinical examination of the development of interactions, aimed essentially at demonstrating the basic features of the paradigm and identifying the questions that need to be considered if the mechanisms involved are to be grasped more thoroughly. The following, albeit provisional conclusions, seem to be suggested.

First there arises the matter of individual progress within the group. From observation of the complementary actions of two partners it is difficult to evaluate clearly development in the strategies used by each one. The main point is that 'progress' does not only appear in subjects who start out with level I or II strategies and who are confronted by subjects responding correctly. The groups in which the two partners did not produce a correct solution straight away still appear to elaborate this in the course of the interaction. This then raises the issue of social constructivism, and the mechanism which underlies it, as well as that of the level of the cognitive models provided by partners. These two points will be considered in subsequent research.

That progress seems to occur, even when neither partner is initially capable of a correct response, is not the only significant fact. In such groups 'progress' can be linked to the existence of a conflict between individuals who possess different, though incorrect, strategies. This can be observed in disagreements between partners regarding the positions of one or more houses. It is most particularly true in those groups where this conflict cannot be transformed into the 'submission' of one of the subjects, but also in those groups where no decision structure is established that allows partners to juxtapose their placements without considering the view of the village as a whole. This point will be developed in Experiment 2.

What can be said about the subjects working alone? For them, there is no element of conflict. It should be remembered that the experimenter 'removes himself' from the situation, that he only intervenes to control the procedure, makes no judgements and provides no indications which could aid the child in evaluating his efforts or in considering aspects that he would otherwise have neglected. If the child 'forgets' the mark, or only transforms one dimension, no one will tell him so. The only possible conflict is between his own expectations and the observations he is able to make; this would be the case if he tried to put a house where he had already placed one. But, facing such difficulties on his own, the child will often be all at sea and will fall back on his original strategies, even if they are unsatisfactory.

This first experiment has therefore allowed us to shed some light on the situation and make a list of the problems. First of all, it was confirmed that the performances of individuals chosen at random to work in a group situation were superior to those of individuals working alone. It will of course be necessary to reexamine this hypothesis in further experiments. In these we will try to discover the initial levels of the partners, since the impact of this variable is apparently critical. This will in addition provide an opportunity to evaluate more directly the hypothesis that the source of the progress is the sociocognitive conflict implicated in the difference in individual strategies. In this initial experiment these could not be rigorously determined since there were no individual tests.

Let us begin with a fundamental question: will confrontation between individuals of different cognitive levels actually generate sociocognitive conflict leading to cognitive progress by the partners?

Experiment 2. Composition of groups as a function of cognitive level

It is important to note that in the preceding experiment, the subjects, working side by side, shared the same viewpoint. If in addition they were shown to be at the same cognitive level in a pretest (and if one could be sure that they would act in the same way at least at the start of the interaction phase), one could anticipate agreement between them, since their expectations regarding the placement of each house would coincide. There should thus be no sociocognitive conflict and consequently no progress.

This is valid to varying degrees depending on the cognitive level of the partners. Thus, if one considers NC children (those at the lower level), the probability of conflict is almost nil, the children sharing, so to speak, stereotyped behaviours, and impose on each house a 90° rotation to the left. In contrast, for the intermediates (PC subjects), there is some possibility of conflict. A PC subject can adequately transform either one or the other of the two dimensions, either left-right or front-back, without there being any certainty as to which one it will be. One cannot, therefore, *a priori* exclude the possibility that some conflict might occur between two intermediate level subjects since they may disagree over one or more houses because of their simultaneous consideration of a different dimension.

On the other hand, when the levels attained by the partners in the pretest are not identical (or generally similar), the probability of sociocognitive conflict is far greater. Disagreements must occur regarding the positions of the houses. Take the example of two children, one NC and one PC (who might correctly transform the left-right relation); Fig. 6.4 indicates the positions which each subject would choose for each house.

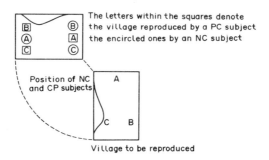

FIG. 6.4   Positions of houses as placed by NC and PC subjects when working on a complex item from the same position.

If each child made up his own village separately and if they were then compared, no house would coincide. However, group dynamics are not so simple. To the extent that children complete their village together on the same base, a division of labour may occur (with, for example, the NC child placing one house and the PC child placing the other two), thus tending to vary the intensity of any possible conflict. It is also possible that since the experimenter remains as aloof as possible from this group performance, the children could quite simply juxtapose their actions, each one doing his own task, without considering their view of the village together until after completing their reconstruction. For such interactions the hypothesis will simply be advanced that the probability of sociocognitive conflict will be higher, without this prejudging the mode of conflict resolution. It is expected, however, that substantial progress will occur.

This hypothesis must, however, be more specific with respect to individual progress. In effect, each child provides a mode of resolution for the problem presented, a kind of model (even though this may be implicit or at least not verbally explicit). The NC child could thus be confronted by a PC child whose cognitive level is more elaborated or higher than his own. If he progresses one could (at least partially) explain his progress by the fact that the other child may have shown him the more advanced solution, clarifying various doubts he might have had. Unless the initially NC subject becomes TC on the posttest (by replying correctly), the operation of a 'simple' modelling effect could not therefore be excluded. The situation is different for the PC child. He would have been confronted with a subject making placements at a cognitive level lower to his own. Progress by this PC child would be evidence of an authentic cognitive reconstruction and not of imitation. We could then hypothesise that the intermediate subjects, in spite of having been confronted with subjects at a lower level, could also benefit from social interaction and demonstrate progress in the posttest.

Consider now a condition in which an NC subject is confronted with a TC subject and therefore one who is capable of a totally correct reconstruction of the village. Precise hypotheses are difficult to formulate *a priori* for this condition. It is indeed likely that sociocognitive conflict would arise between these two children. But would it result in progress for the NC child? Will the TC subject's response in effect be at too great a 'cognitive distance' from the NC subject for him to understand (Kuhn, 1972)? Alternatively, as the TC subject is capable of the correct response, would he not quite simply impose it on the NC subject (Silverman and Stone, 1972; Silverman and Geiringer, 1973; Miller and Brownell, 1975), without allowing him to intervene or collaborate in a solution at a more advanced level than his own? The experiment will decide this question.

The experiment

More than 100 subjects took part in a pretest and were classified as NC, PC or TC on the basis of the level attained on the two complex items. Of these, 74 who displayed the same level of strategy on these two items were retained, the 'hybrid' case being eliminated for this experiment. As the experiment is based on the composition of groups according to the initial cognitive levels of the partners, such rigour was necessary. The 74 children were distributed in terms of their levels as follows: 40 NC (from 5 years 4 months to 7 years 1 month), 23 PC (from 5 years 5 months to 7 years 2 months), and 11 TC children, who were chosen from amongst those attaining this level to participate in interactions with NC subjects. All children came from the same school and in almost equal proportions from classes in the second year of infant school and the first year of primary school.

In the experimental phase, these 74 children participated in 37 interactions in groups of 2, and in four experimental conditions in which the composition of groups was based on the initial cognitive levels of the partners:

- 9 groups confronting two children both at level I (NC+NC);
- 11 groups confronting one level I child with one level II child (NC+PC);
- 11 groups confronting one level I child with one level III child (NC+TC);
- finally, 6 groups confronting two children both at level II (PC+PC).

A fifth condition confronting a level II child with a level III child was abandoned because of the low number of PC children and also because this condition is less interesting, the chance of progress being too high.

In terms of performances during the interaction, we therefore had four experimental conditions. However, in terms of individual progress following interaction, there are five conditions that can be considered (the subjects marked in italics are those whose progress is considered):

- a child at level I with a child at the same level ($NC+NC$);
- a child at level I with a child at level II ($NC+PC$);
- a child at level I with a child at level III ($NC+TC$);
- a child at level II with a child at level I ($PC+NC$);
- a child at level II with another at the same level ($PC+PC$).

The partners are always drawn from the same class in school and are of the same sex. The experimental phase begins about 10 days after the pretest and is separated from the posttest by the same interval.

Results

What are the levels attained during the group performances? Recall, that assessment is based on the best performance achieved by the group over the two complex items (that is, the best *final* performance since no account is taken of provisional solutions considered before a definitive solution is adopted for an item). Table 6.3 gives the results.

TABLE 6.3. *Classification of interaction phase performances*

	NC	PC	TC
NC+NC	7	1	1
NC+PC	3	2	6
NC+TC	1	1	9
PC+PC	0	1	5

In groups in which at least one NC child participated the average level of performance therefore depends on the level of the most advanced partner. Consider now in more detail what lies behind these results for each of the conditions.

NC+NC: when two NC children interact the majority of performances are at a lower level, the probability of a conflict appearing being very low. A more detailed analysis of these interactions indicates a very marked absence of conflict. From films taken of the interactions, it was found that in the 7 groups where the two NC children did not 'rise above' the strategy they were capable of in the pretest, they acted exactly according to their pretest strategy. In these groups the interactions are very short, the subjects always agreeing about the positions of the houses. Performances at a level superior to the initial level of the subjects occur in the two remaining groups. In both cases one of the subjects adequately transforms one of the two dimensions, thereby provoking an unexpected conflict. In these two groups the other NC subject disputes this move and relocates the house according to his own strategy. Nonetheless, in one of these groups, the subject who has progressed (to level II) makes the final decision. In the other group, the NC subject is seen to make a quite spectacular advance on his pretest level. He begins by placing the houses in a level II pattern, a copy which is then modified by the subject who has remained NC and who places the houses according to the same schema as in the pretest. The subject who has become PC changes things again despite the protests – 'but no' – of the NC subject. He then explains: 'Yes, definitely, it is by the mountain' (the orientation mark represents a mountain for this group.) the first item ends there. On the second item this subject, now a PC, manages to pursue the development of this concept. He first places a house according to level I; dissatisfied, he places it according to level II and finally places it correctly. Here we have two groups that do not really correspond to the definition we wished to give to this condition. Although these results do not support our hypothesis, we have nonetheless treated these groups as part of this experimental condition.

NC+PC: when an NC and a PC subject confront one another a particularly interesting finding emerges. Out of eleven groups, six manage to complete one complex item correctly in terms of the left-right and front-back inversions required. Now, neither of the partners in these groups was capable of achieving such a level of performance in the pretest. So is this effect due to the sociocognitive conflict that was anticipated in this condition? Analysis of the interactions showed that the subjects did disagree about the placement of the houses. The resolution of these conflicts varies considerably across these groups. Several groups quite simply juxtapose their actions in terms of their own respective strategies. In some cases each subject places only one or two houses without bothering with the whole village. Other groups 'share' the items. The NC subject finally decides on the entire configuration of the village in one item, while in the other item it is the PC subject who does this. Note that these groups do not make their points of disagreement explicit and none of the NC subjects progress. In the remaining groups negotiations do occur and it is usually the PC subject who is led to emphasise the importance of making the placements in relation to the orientation of the mark. This overt emphasis is useful not only to the NC subject who is thereby provided with some information about the main problem in the task, but also to the PC subject himself as he is then able to pin down the dimensions which are still posing a problem for him. Finally, the high level attained by these groups in this experimental condition is reflected in individual progress.

NC+TC: In terms of collective performances, interactions between an NC child and a TC child are easy to analyse. They are characterised (in eight out of eleven groups) by a one-sided approach in the decisions taken about the placements of the houses. As had been expected, moreover, it is the TC subject (in seven out of these eight groups) – the one capable of executing the task correctly – who dominates and, indeed, imposes his solution. It should be noted that this imposition occurs without any additional explanation, and explicit reference to the modified orientation of the marks occurs only very rarely. There is then a simple conflict of responses in an interaction dominated by one of the partners. In this situation the NC children do not progress.

In the other three groups there is more sharing of the decision making. In one group negotiations arise which end in a product at the intermediate level; both children seem satisfied with the solution and appear to be happier playing with the microphone. In the second group a systematic juxtaposition of actions is observed. In the first complex item, the NC subject, who is quick to pick up the houses, places them as he wishes. In the second item the TC subject is the quicker. This does not seem to bother them at all; in fact, they preoccupy themselves only with counting the centimetres separating the houses from the sides of the base (in these first two experiments a measure of deviation is possible because of a grid marked on the base). It is this precision which matters to them and not the preservation of the intrafigural relationships. It should be no surprise that neither of the NC subjects in these two groups progressed.

In fact of the eleven NC children studied in this condition, only one progressed. He also participated in the only group where genuine reciprocity occurred. Let us look at this situation in detail. Right at the beginning, on the first (simple) item the TC subject makes an error of orientation with the two houses, which he puts in place very quickly. A discussion then follows initiated by the NC subject about the correct orientation of the houses. In the second (complex) item, the NC subject reacts according to his initial level and is then given advice by the TC subject who, following an explanation, indicates the correct position for one house. The NC subject carries this out and then, on the basis of its 'complementarity', places another house correctly (one house being opposite the other). On the third (also complex) item the NC subject again begins by placing a house according to his initial strategy, or at least he makes a gesture in this direction. Then he places it correctly while the TC subject positions another house, also correctly. The NC subject then takes the remaining house, and considers placing it this time in terms of level II but the place is already occupied by another house. The TC subject then locates it correctly. The NC subject is therefore beginning to attempt transformations. These may be more or less correct, but they are not obvious to him, the proof of this being in the orientation errors which also derive from level I (even when the positions are generally correct). In the posttest this subject proves to be capable of completing at least one item correctly.

Another one-sided group in terms of decisions provides an example of a TC subject who sees himself as a teacher. He dictates the positions and supports them with a long argument. He explains how to 'do the thing' to the NC subject: 'When it is there (in the experimenter's village) it goes there (in their village)' and so on for each house. The NC subject never decides himself; he merely acquiesces. In the fourth item (which is again a simple one) it is the latter who rushes to the houses and constructs a village . . . which would be correct if the orientations of the bases were different, except that they are not! Thus, he has certainly learned how to do this 'thing' very well. But the thing does not correspond to a real cognitive restructuring, as is shown in the unwarranted generalisation of the 'thing' to a simple item. Nonetheless, it should be acknowledged in his defence that this NC subject then agrees with good grace to modify the village to give a correct response. He too does not progress on the posttest.

PC+PC: in the interactions of two PC subjects it is difficult to identify the part played by sociocognitive conflict, because if one child places a house correctly according to one dimension it is sufficient that the other transforms the second dimension adequately for a correct solution to emerge.

To conclude the analysis of effects during the interaction, the results can be summarised:

– with respect to interactions in which NC subjects participate, one may conclude that the group product depends in effect on the level of the partners. With another NC subject it is at a lower level and with a TC subject it is at a higher level. With a PC subject it is at an intermediate level. However, the level of this performance can also be above the level of the better subject on the pretest. Therefore social construction of new cognitive solutions does occur. It is this that emerges in the condition confronting an NC and a PC subject where more than half the groups manage at least one correct performance.
– It is difficult to draw conclusions about the interactions involving two PC children, for reasons linked to the intermediate cognitive system itself.

What then are the consequences for the cognitive levels attained by participants in these interactions on the individual posttests? Will they follow the same (very linear) 'logic' as the individual interactions? The results of the posttest are given in Table 6.4.

First of all, considering only the progress of the NC subjects, it can be established that they are not as linear as the interaction performances. In fact, only the *NC+PC* condition leads to significant progress, while con-

TABLE 6.4. *Posttest classification of subjects*

	NC	PC	TC
NC*+NC*a	13	1	1
NC*+PCb	4	4	3
NC*+TCc	10	0	1
PC*+NCd	0	1	8
PC*+PC*e	1	5	6

*Subjects classified.
Jonckheere's test, conditions a and b, Z: 2.285, P<0.01; conditions b and c, Z: 2.130, P<0.02; conditions d and e, Z: 1.560, P<0.10.

ditions confronting NCs with TCs or other NCs have only slight effects. For the *NC+NC* condition this poses no problem, since it is not conflicting. But what of the *NC+TC* condition where the latter in most cases imposes the correct response? Why, in spite of everything, does the NC subject fail to progress here? First, as we have seen in the more detailed analysis of the interactions, the TC subject is very sure of himself and imposes his solutions. However, he does this without making the reasons for his choices explicit and without allowing the NC subject any active role in the interaction. This is the basis of our explanation. However, it could be that the cognitive level of the TC subject was too far removed from that of the NC subject. Although the present experiment does not provide an answer to this question, the possibility should nonetheless be rejected since, as will be seen in Experiment 5, presentation of a correct model for resolution of the problem can actually lead to substantial progress in the NC subject.

The PC subjects show considerable progress in the two situations even though, as might be expected, this progress tends to be more frequent in the NC and PC condition where the probability of conflict was stronger.

We should add that these results have also been obtained in New Zealand in two different subcultures (Mackie, 1983). However, though these effects have been confirmed for the NC subjects, the progress made by PC subjects is considerable irrespective of the experimental condition. (In our experiment the differences between conditions were also not very strong for these subjects). There is without doubt an effect of progressive independence in development here.

The results of this experiment, and their replication referred to above, show that our hypotheses, although well-founded, should be explored further in additional experiments. First, the hypothesis that the individual's progress results from conflicting interactions (induced via the confrontation of children of divergent cognitive levels) is generally confirmed; sociocognitive conflict must occur for there to be progress. This is, however, a necessary condition, rather than a sufficient one. In reality, the effects of this sociocognitive conflict depend on its negotiation; if the negotiation is one-sided, if it is reduced to a kind of imposed force, it will not lead to new cognitive construction. In the same way a simple divergence of response is not sufficient; these can be juxtaposed in a division of labour in such a way that sociocognitive conflict does not automatically result. To be fruitful these divergences must be recognised and dealt with; they must lead to a search for a coordination of viewpoints.

A question of definition now arises: what is to count as true sociocognitive conflict? Is simple divergence of responses sufficient? Does one-sided domination, even if the differences are explained, really accord with a definition of sociocognitive conflict? We will not risk a more precise definition at this point: for example, one limiting the concept of socio-cognitive conflict to interactions that lead to a genuine coordination of viewpoints. This would be to define sociocognitive conflict by the progress it induces!

Might it not be more profitable to consider the ways in which differences may be resolved in such sociocognitive conflict? Thus it can be shown that alternative modes of resolution lead to differing degrees of progress. There are two contrasting attitudes in response to the disagreements involved in the situations selected by the experimenter.

One consists in managing the disagreement by focusing on the task. In this case cognitive regulations appear in response to an imbalance that is social in nature. The result could be cognitive progress deriving from social coordina-tion of the different viewpoints.

The other is to manage the conflict in relational terms. Faced with a dis-agreement, one could either give in to the other, or else accept the juxta-position of contradictory responses. In this case, sociocognitive conflict is dis-placed by a social adjustment. The conflict is resolved by focusing not on the task and the social coordination of viewpoints, but on the functioning of the group itself. In this case, cognitive progress has little chance of emerging.

This relates to some of the issues encountered in the experiments on length conservation. It was concluded there that a tendency to compliance was likely to appear in nonconserving subjects when the adult advanced a contradicting response. To obtain progress it had been necessary for the child to be caught in a conflict between two adults. In practice this ensured that cognitive regulations leading to progress would appear and that a purely social adjustment of the conflict would be prevented. When the experi-mental procedure was less constraining, and gave freer rein to such regula-tions, progress diminished considerably. The progress which remained, moreover, came from subjects who opposed the adult's incorrect response.

As in the length paradigm therefore, a variant of experiment 4 will present a procedure in which the NC+TC encounter occurs between a child (NC) and an adult (TC) who in this case avoids imposing himself and allows the child to be actively involved. Significant progress does result from this sociocognitive conflict. Thus it is true that an adult can sometimes prove to be a better teacher than a peer!

Experiment 3. Opposition of viewpoints

Within the child's daily experience it is difficult to distinguish the effects of individual cognitive work from those of sociocognitive work. The two aspects are so intimately linked that the question is without a clear answer. In contrast, when building a model of the dynamics of cognitive development, it is essential to illustrate the effectiveness of sociocognitive conflict as a central dynamic in cognitive development. The present experiment is intended to provide such an illustration (as is Experiment 4 which pushes this line of reasoning to its ultimate conclusion).

There is a second consideration underlying this research. If, as we have seen in the preceding experiment, encounters between two individuals who are both at the NC level neither produces conflict nor facilitates progress, might it not be possible to envisage situations in which such conflict could nonetheless appear (and which also have some chance of occurring normally)? In this connection, it should be recalled that subjects in the first two experiments are placed side by side and so share the same viewpoint. What would happen if instead two children, both at the NC level in the pretest, interact from different viewpoints? If both subjects respond according to the level initially attributed to them, it could result in different placements of the houses. It should thus be possible to induce sociocognitive conflict simply by modifying the situation.

Let us take an example. In order to achieve a similar degree of difficulty for the two subjects all that is required is to modify the positions of the mark in the two villages, orienting them in such a manner that the necessary inversions are of the same order for both subjects (the only difference being that for one the transformation is made from left to right and for the other, from right to left). The children are then placed face to face in a symmetrical arrangement as indicated in Fig. 6.5.

On the copy table the houses are placed as NC children would have done in terms of one or other of the viewpoints x or y. If the two subjects simply execute a 90° rotation – as subjects do at level I – one (x) will do it from right to left and the other (y) from left to right. The result would be that none of the placements would coincide! This is the situation employed in the third experiment on this paradigm.

Before considering the experimental design, we will indicate the four items (all complex) which were used in the interactions; these are given in Fig. 6.6

The positions of the marks as represented in Fig. 6.6 are used only for the interactions. In the pretest and the posttest the usual items are employed.

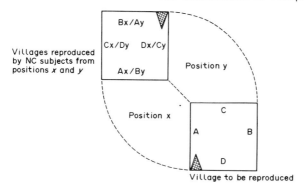

FIG. 6.5   Positions of houses as placed by two NC subjects when working on a complex item from opposite positions.

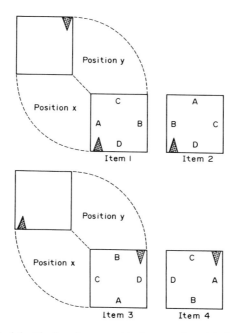

FIG. 6.6   The four items used in the experimental phase.

In all, 72 subjects of both sexes, aged from 5 to 8 years or thereabouts, participated in all the phases of the experiment. Forty were NC subjects and 32 were PC subjects. From each of these groups some are assigned to work on an individual basis and some on a group basis in the experimental phase. The numbers in the four experimental conditions thus created are as follows:

– individual work: 19 NC subjects;
– individual work: 20 PC subjects;

- working in groups: 21 NC subjects participating in groups of 2;
- working in groups: 12 PC subjects participating in groups of 2.

Thus in the experimental phase some subjects work in groups of two, these being children of the same sex and from the same class in school. As previously, they are asked to work together and to try and agree about the village. Two houses are discreetly placed near each of the subjects, to reduce the chances of one child being totally inactive. Subsequently, they are able to reach all the houses. Each item is halted if necessary at the end of 5 minutes.

In the individual conditions the following procedure was instituted. For each of the four items the child continues placing the houses until he states that the village is the same. Without modifying what has been done, the child is then moved to the other side (i.e. to the opposite position) and asked to verify if the village is still correct, or if something should be changed. He begins the next item in this new position and then returns to the old position, and so on. Thus, conditions are created in which intraindividual conflict could arise from the fact that the houses, when placed according to an incorrect strategy, fail to correspond to the same positions when the point of view is modified (see Fig 6.5).

This condition therefore involves a potential conflict between the successive centrations of the same individual while the group condition involves a potential conflict between the simultaneous centrations of two individuals. We can thus contrast an approach explaining cognitive progress in terms of conflicts between observations with our own approach which provides an account in terms of sociocognitive conflict capable of arising in interactions among groups of individuals.

We will not present the results of the experimental phase. It frequently happens that the subjects in the opposing positions propose different villages in turn without reaching agreement. It is therefore impossible to identify a single solution for each group. Consequently let us pass directly to the results of the individual posttests, though not without observing that the procedure of consistently placing subjects of the same level in different viewpoints actually had the desired effect of inducing substantial sociocognitive conflict during the interaction.

Table 6.5 gives the frequency of progress in the two NC and the two PC conditions. As stated earlier, progress for NC subjects means becoming PC or TC in the posttest, while the PC subjects have themselves to become TC to be judged to have progressed.

For all subjects, no matter what their initial level, the results confirm that interindividual conflict resulting from opposite viewpoints, even though between subjects at an identical level, leads to greater progress than the potential intraindividual conflict. The simultaneous opposition of centra-

TABLE 6.5. *Frequency of progress on the posttest*

		Progress	No Progress
Individual,	NC*a*	6	13
Group,	NC*b*	13	8
Individual,	PC*c*	12	8
Group,	PC*d*	10	2

Fisher test, conditions $a + c$ and $b + d$, Z: 1.759, P<0.04; conditions a and b, Z: 1.581, P<0.06.

tions leads to coordinations in a way that is not the case with successive opposition of viewpoints for a single individual. This effect is clear among the NC or lower level subjects, where the difference between the individual and group performance conditions is significant. The results for the PC subjects, whilst in the same direction, do not reach significance. Here we have an effect that we are now accustomed to finding – the group work is most effective during the initial development of a concept: from this initial interdependence, the individual becomes more autonomous.

Differences in social background

Already at several points it has been possible to establish that children from different social backgrounds do not all respond in the same manner to the tests they are given. As a general rule the pretest favours those with a more advantaged social background. Each time, however, it has been shown that at the very least this difference disappears if children from the disadvantaged backgrounds are able to carry out the same task in a group situation. The posttests of the children from these backgrounds then catch up with the pretests of the children from advantaged backgrounds. Let us study the present experiment from the same point of view as this was carried out in two contrasting social environments, in fact, the same ones as those described in the fourth experiment in Chapter 3 (based on coordinations in the cooperative game). As Table 6.6 indicates, a considerable difference is apparent in the pretest between the 59 children from a disadvantaged background and the 66 from the advantaged background retained for this analysis. What would have become of this difference in the posttest if all the children with a disadvantaged social background had been exposed to the group situation? We will again use the extrapolation method, since only some of the NC and PC subjects actually participated in such interactions. Looking at the percentage of NC subjects from a disadvantaged background who became PC or TC and the percentage of PC subjects who became TC in the group performance condition, we can find by extrapolation the percentage of children at various levels in the posttest (see Table 6.6).

Comparisons of the percentages thus extrapolated for children from a

TABLE 6.6. *Percentage of subjects at level I (NC), II (PC), and III (TC)*

	NC	PC	TC
Disadvantaged background, pretest	44	25	31
Disadvantaged background, posttest			
(extrapolation)	14	32	54
Advantaged background, pretest	21	26	53

'poor' environment with the percentage for the children from the advantaged environment on the pretest, indeed indicate that the initial difference disappears. These differences must therefore be based on very little if group work can eliminate them.

Naturally, and as has already been seen, this does not mean that differences between social groups as such disappear. In practice, children from the more advantaged social backgrounds also benefit from this kind of group activity which therefore maintains these differences.

Experiment 4. Decentration of viewpoints

The preceding experiment has illustrated how introduction of different viewpoints into the experimental situation can lead subjects who share the same lower cognitive level to progress as a result of the sociocognitive conflict it makes possible. Can we go any 'further'? This has been achieved in Bologna (by Carugati and De Paolis) starting from the following considerations. In our experiments subjects are confronted with two kinds of difficulty. First, there is the essential feature of disagreement; the breakdown – or the absence – of a consensus where the child might suppose that one would exist, represents a disturbance which leads the subject to search for a regulation which, as we have seen, can be of a 'purely' social kind (compliance, nonconflicting juxtaposition . . .), or better still of a genuinely sociocognitive nature when cognitive regulation is not displaced by social regulation.

But our experimental situations also involve purely cognitive difficulties (Carugati, Mugny *et al.*, 1978) because the items used for the interaction phase can, for the most part, be characterised as complex (and in several experiments starting with the third, only such items were used). What then is the theoretical status of these sociocognitive conflicts? Are they not simply accelerators or 'prostheses', which act on cognitive work that is difficult at an individual level? We have already argued that this question is too unclear and that the cognitive and social poles of sociocognitive conflict are complementary.

However, a novel answer to this question shows that the conflict induced by a contrast of viewpoints can lead to cognitive progress even in individuals for whom the situation presents no difficulties of a purely cognitive nature. Such progress is due therefore simply to induction of social or interindividual conflict. This represents an interesting inversion of the normal learning paradigm. An incorrect model is presented to subjects who can already manage an adequate response to an item which presents no difficulty for them.

The paradigm

The differences between Experiments 2 and 3 lie essentially in the positions of the marks in the experimenter's and the children's villages, and in the positions of the children. In the present experiment, the face-to-face positions of Experiment 3 will be retained but the symmetry in cognitive difficulty of this experiment will be broken by adapting the complex item used in Experiment 2. To clarify the reasoning here let us give an example of an item (Fig. 6.7).

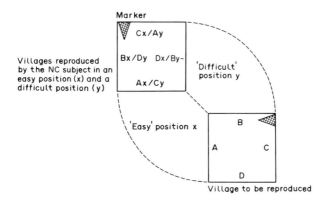

FIG. 6.7 Positions of houses as placed by an NC subject working from a 'difficult' position, and an NC subject working from an 'easy' position.

Consider first the subject in position *y*. For him the difficulty is of the same order as for the normal complex items, particularly those in the individual tests. Suppose that he takes account of the need to modify or transform the apparent positions to conserve intrafigural relations – he therefore encounters a difficulty that is genuinely cognitive.

Consider now the opposite viewpoint of a subject in position *x*. He finds no cognitive problem, since he is faced with a simple item requiring a rotation of 90° to the left, of which all children within the ages considered have been capable.

If there is no cognitive difficulty for this subject (who for convenience we will refer to as the 'easy' subject), are his chances of progress not therefore zero? Not if this child is confronted with another facing him and thus presented with a cognitive difficulty. However, this subject (referred to as 'difficult') must be either an NC or a PC so that he will make an incorrect response for at least one house. For an incorrect placement will – or at least should – pose a problem for the 'easy' child to whom the correct solution is obvious or necessary. Could cognitive progress on the part of the 'easy' subject emerge from such a conflict? Would he not be forced to take into account the other's viewpoint and to elaborate a coordination of viewpoints which would allow him to understand the other's error and indeed even to persuade the 'difficult' subject who is responsible for this sociocognitive conflict?

This then is the principle of the experiment. But are things really as straightforward theoretically as they at first appear? The preceding experiments have shown the complex social dynamics which can arise between children and counteract any beneficial effects of sociocognitive conflict.

A tendency to compliance when an assymmetry is created represents one of the major difficulties, particularly when one member of the interaction is very confident of his own responses. Thus in Experiment 2, the TC subject imposes what is to him the self-evident solution without further explanation. Now, in this new version of the paradigm such self-evidence exists for the 'easy' subject by virtue of the absence of any cognitive difficulty from his position. It is therefore necessary to give the 'dificult' subject a 'chance' to defend his own viewpoint. This will be achieved by introducing social support into the situation.

In the experimental condition which is the most likely to demonstrate this type of sociocognitive conflict, an 'easy' subject will be confronted with two 'difficult' subjects, on the assumption that they will mutually support each other in their initial centrations.

In a second experimental condition a single 'difficult' subject will confront a single 'easy' subject.

More than 100 children were pretested with the usual materials. A particular problem arose due to the fact that only a small number of children were found to be completely nonconserving on both items of the pretest. Subjects finally retained for the easy position included those who managed one item at level I and one item at level II, placing one house correctly and the others according to the usual level I strategy. Progress was defined as success in placing all but one house correctly for each item, or attaining level III by responding correctly to at least one item of the posttest.

Confronting the 'easy' subjects who were all at the same level were NC and PC subjects, divided in equal proportion between the two experimental conditions. As the subjects in each interaction were always drawn from the same class in school, it was not possible to include children of the same sex on each occasion. In point of fact, this was of little consequence in this attempt to extend our paradigm; it was more important that the children in the difficult position should give an incorrect response and this is effectively what happened.

Results

We will not give the results for the difficult subjects; we will only say that they displayed significant progress, which is not surprising if one considers that they interacted with a child who was able to provide the correct response. Table 6.7 indicates the progress of the 'easy' subjects in the first posttest (immediately following the interaction) and in the second posttest 10 days later.

TABLE 6.7. *Frequency of progress on posttests of subjects in easy position**

	Progress	No Progress
Faced with one subject in difficult position	2 (3)	10 (9)
Faced with two subjects in difficult position	5 (6)	2 (1)

*Numbers in parentheses are for second posttest.
Fisher test, first posttest, $P<0.05$; second posttest, $P<0.025$.

The results of these two posttests confirm our expectations. On the complex items in the posttests, which this time did pose real cognitive problems, the 'easy' subjects made progress if during the interaction what was for them the obvious solution had been disputed by two children giving incorrect responses. When they were opposed by a single subject in the difficult position, little progress was observed. In the first, immediate posttest, three out of five cases of progress in the more favourable condition are to level III, two children still being intermediate. In the second posttest, conducted a fortnight later, five out of seven subjects in this condition have become TC whilst in the condition involving only one 'difficult' subject, only one subject among the twelve tested proved capable of such a level of performance, which represents a still more radical differentiation in progress between the experimental conditions.

Analysis of the interactions was attempted, although their number is too small to draw any firm conclusions. It seems, however, that the number of items involving conflict is greater when an 'easy' subject is confronted with two 'difficult' subjects than when he is faced with only one, (Carugati, De Paolis and Mugny, 1979). What is more, when the items produce conflict the 'easy' subject more often decided on the final positions of the houses when he is opposed to two 'difficult' children. Is this not paradoxical? The 'easy' subjects should progress all the more if they defend their self-evident solution more vigorously. But it makes sense that a better coordination of opposing points of view makes the correct solution to a simple item even more self-evident, even more cognitively necessary.

Can this effect be reproduced? Some confirmation is necessary if only because of the small sample sizes. We should explain that there are other possible dynamics in this experimental situation. In the condition which gave rise to most progress, the subjects in the easy position found themselves confronted with two children in a difficult position. It is possible that these two 'difficult' children were not at the same level as we have seen. Now, Experiment 2 taught us that two children placed side by side can progress when one is an NC and the other a PC, and this is sometimes the case in this fourth experiment. Thus the 'easy' children are not only confronted with different centrations, but, in addition, may sometimes observe the progressive elaboration of a correct solution by their partners in the difficult position. This possibility will be excluded in the two variants of this experiment to be presented next.

The first variant

Two variants on this paradigm were carried out with the main aim, not just of replicating the effect, but also of clarifying the dynamics underlying this type of situation.

The main problem with this paradigm is to ensure that an interindividual conflict does occur and that one-sided decisions are not taken by the subject who is more sure of himself, i.e. the one in the easy position. The best way of controlling this tendency is to use the experimenter as disputant. This was studied in the first variant.

A total of 23 subjects (7 NC and 16 PC) are led to interact with the experimenter. The situation presented is nearly the same as in Experiment 4. However, an adult collaborator of the experimenter, occupying the difficult position, responds according to the following principles. Before the 'easy' subject places the houses, the adult forms a village. This village follows a 'logic' which provides the child with no indications of the appropriate transformations. In effect, this solution entails a simple translation of the entire village without taking into account the necessary 90° rotation which children at the age studies can manage. Fig. 6.8 gives an example of the placements made by the adult.

When the adult has reconstructed the village he asks the child's advice, indicating that the positions of the houses can be changed. If the latter modifies the village, the experimenter then asks his collaborator if he agrees. The latter again advances his incorrect solution and asks the child 'Do you agree? Perhaps I made a mistake.' This procedure is repeated each time for the four interaction items.

What are the results? On the first posttest immediately following the inter-

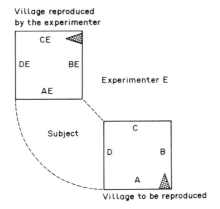

FIG. 6.8   Positions of houses as placed by the experimenter during the first
interaction item.

action phase, it appears that thirteen out of twenty-three subjects progressed.
On the second posttest, about 10 days later, there are now sixteen out of the
twenty-three who have progressed. In addition, out of the thirteen cases of
initial progress, twelve are conserved on the second posttest. Thus the effect
found in Experiment 4 can be reproduced.

What are the dynamics underlying this progress? Experiment 4 has shown
that the subjects who most often resist their 'difficult' partners, that is those
who most consistently uphold their viewpoint, progress more. To verify this
link one may consider the number of houses in the interaction that are
correctly placed; these must have been placed by the child since the adult
always places them incorrectly. Out of the sixteen houses it was necessary to
locate in the course of the four items, subjects who progressed placed them
correctly on average 11.85 times while those who did not progress only
placed them correctly on average 5.9 times, or less than half as frequently.

We rediscover here an effect identified in Experiment 2 on the length conservation paradigm. Subjects who complacently relinquish the decision to
the adult, that is those who respond to the sociocognitive conflict in terms of
a purely relational regulation based on the asymmetry of the partners, have
very little chance of progressing cognitively. It is those who set their viewpoint
against the erroneous one of the adult, despite the latter being in a socially
dominant position, who progress. They were able to integrate the differing
points of view within a single cognitive system and showed themselves able
to solve the cognitive problem posed by the complex items in a manner
superior to their initial abilities. Remember at the same time that during this
interaction they were confronted with what was for them an easy item.

The second variant

Is it possible to obtain the effects of Experiment 4, but with a single child in the difficult situation? This question arises for two reasons. First, the introduction of two 'difficult' children complicates interindividual dynamics that are already difficult to pin down when only two children are present. It is particularly difficult to control the relationship which becomes established between the two children in the difficult position, a relationship liable to vary in ways capable of masking the effect we are looking for; this difficulty arises because Experiment 4 introduces the two children into this position to reinforce their erroneous centrations so as to ensure a particular intensity to the sociocognitive conflict. It should be equally possible to reinforce the weight of a single child in this position.

Recall that in Experiment 4 the 'easy' and 'difficult' partners complete the village together. Such a procedure straight away reduces the possible sociocognitive conflict to disagreements about the placement of only one house, and not about the entire village. Consequently, in this second variation, we first have the entire village constructed by the 'difficult' subject before the 'easy' subject is allowed to intervene. It will be seen that this manipulation is effective.

Indeed, the results show that nine out of eighteen 'easy' children studied in this way (7 NCs and 11 PCs) progressed in the first posttest; in the second posttest this progress is found in eight out of the seventeen subjects that it was possible to retest. Among those progressing, moreover, are six of the nine who progressed on the first posttest. This progress is therefore substantial.

In this variant, are the subjects who progressed again to be found in the groups giving the greater number of correct responses? This is the case: the average number of houses correctly placed (out of sixteen possible) is 12.33 for groups in which the 'easy' subject progressed and 8.89 for those in which this did not occur.

For these interactions between peers the issues are more complex. In effect, with an experimenter, the houses that are correctly placed are by necessity placed by the child in the 'easy' position, since the adult systematically responds incorrectly. This is not necessarily the case in groups of peers. The PC subjects in the difficult position are capable of adequately transforming one dimension. Thus, they can themselves correctly place two of the four houses in each item. For these houses there is therefore no conflict.

On the other hand, we have seen in other experiments that relations between peers should not be studied in terms of compliance as is the case of relations with adults, but in terms of the unilaterality or reciprocity of exchanges. Experiment 2 showed this. If a sociocognitive conflict is to be effective, the different centrations must be expressed without one or the other prevailing too much. Therefore, an index of reciprocity-unilaterality is calculated to account for progress in this second variant.

The percentage of houses correctly placed by the 'easy' subject in each case is calculated. The distribution is then divided into two equal parts according to the following criterion. Those groups which diverge most from a distribution of 50% by the 'easy' subject and 50% by the 'difficult' subject are considered as having a unilateral relation. In practice, these were groups in which the 'easy' subject decided from 0 to 17% of the time (i.e., unilateral dominance by the 'difficult' subject) or 83 to 100% of the time (i.e. unilateral dominance by the 'easy' subject). The remaining groups are considered as having given rise to reciprocal interactions in which both subjects express their different viewpoints. The number of subjects participating in 'unilateral' and 'reciprocal' groups respectively, who do or do not progress on the first posttest, is given in Table 6.8.

TABLE 6.8. *Frequency of progress of subjects in easy position*

	Progress	No Progress
Unilateral groups	2	8
Reciprocal groups	7	1

These results clearly indicate that the source of cognitive progress is related to the confrontation of divergent viewpoints. In the majority of groups in which correct decisions are divided between the two subjects, the 'easy' subject progresses. In contrast in groups where one of the children unilaterally dominates these decisions, very little progress is found.

Conclusions

At this point in the presentation it is apparent that the hypothesis which states that sociocognitive conflict plays an essential role in the progress arising from interactions between peers is confirmed by convergent results. First, it has been seen that the joint performance by children of different cognitive levels can be a source of interindividual conflict and subsequent individual progress. Next, it appears that children at the same cognitive level enter into conflict and subsequently progress if they execute the task together but from different viewpoints. The last experiment and its variations have shown that even with children for whom the test situation poses no cognitive problem (there is no doubt that they can execute the task correctly) sociocognitive conflict can be created by confronting them with other subjects who complete the same task incorrectly because they occupy a different viewpoint which at level I and II produces errors. In these various experiments we have at several points established that conflict does not automatically lead to progress. For this, the interaction must avoid leading to compliance arising from any asymmetries which may exist beyond the specific issue of the task. Thus level III subjects who impose their viewpoint too bluntly create an obstacle to any cognitive collaboration by a level I partner. In the same way in the first variant of the fourth experiment, compliance with the experimenter leads to the same effect. Finally, progress in the second variant can also be traced to the reciprocity of interindividual exchanges that are capable of involving a more genuine coordination of viewpoints.

The same logic underlies the four experiments described so far. These are intended to show that the dynamics of sociocognitive conflict cannot be reduced to 'modelling' effects. At this point the perspective can be inverted to offer an explanation of the modelling effect in terms of sociocognitive conflict.

Experiment 5. The nature of the model and sociocognitive conflict

If one defines as a 'model' the cognitive characteristics of a proposed solution to the problem, then the cognitive approaches which have been differentiated can be considered as constituting models. When children are confronted – as in the interindividual encounters in our situations – with one or more individuals, they are in effect confronted with a cognitive model which is either identical to or different from their own. This is not always overt. Most of the time, others do not make explicit the cognitive operations that underlie their actions. The child must infer these in order to compare them with his own operations. Sometimes, as has been seen, he can coordinate them within a more balanced cognitive system. And yet these models are often incorrect.

In the first length conservation experiment, children judging one rod to be longer than another come to infer equality by coordinating their own centration with the contrasting (and also incorrect) centration of the adult.

What is the nature of the potential models in our interactions and what do they imply regarding any subsequent sociocognitive conflict? This is the question we attempt to answer in the fifth experiment with May Lévy (1981).

Let us first define the various types of model in relation to the child's model of the solution. In order to simplify the discussion, we will consider here only NC (or level I) children who will, furthermore, be the only ones involved in this experiment.

We will describe as a *progressive* model one which, compared to the solution the child is capable of, will be closer to a correct solution. We will talk about a *correct* (progressive) model when the proposed solution coincides completely with the transformation required by the task, and an *intermediate* (progressive) model when the mode of problem resolution is superior to the subject's solution, while not yet achieving the level of the correct solution. Thus, for the nonconserving child, a solution at level II will be an intermediate model while the level III solution will constitute a correct model.

In addition, one could define as *similar* models those based on the same mode of problem resolution as that underlying the child's response. In Experiment 2, it was seen that such a model can involve identical responses and in Experiment 3 that it can also involve different responses when the same viewpoint is not shared.

Finally, it is possible to envisage *regressive* models which offer a solution at a cognitive level inferior to that the child is capable of. Thus in the first variant on Experiment 4, the experimenter carries out only a simple translation of the entire village without taking account of the 90° rotation, of which the children involved are already capable.

Before describing the hypotheses derived from our view of development in terms of the sociocognitive conflicts involved in these various models, we will briefly review other research on cognitive models in intellectual development. Without seeking to be exhaustive, we will identify some trends in relation to which the interpretive strength of the concept of socio-congnitive conflict can be better evaluated.

Almost all investigators who have been involved in this area of research since 1970 include a correct progressive model condition in their experimental designs, often by way of a basic demonstration. The effect of such models is concluded almost unanimously to be strongly positive[1]. There is to our knowledge no study indicating a total failure with subjects involving interactions with a correct model. Indeed, only our Experiment 2 demonstrates such an effect, or rather such an absence of effect. It was found that the subject who was able to provide a correct model imposed his solution abruptly; the NC subject had no part in the situation, no involvement, thus raising the question of whether he was really able to reflect on the problem presented to him at all.[2] Finally, to our knowledge, no systematic regression has been observed in subjects confronted with a correct model. Hence, this type of model appears at first glance to be particularly effective in ensuring cognitive development.

On the other hand, little research has been concerned with the effects of

---

[1] This is what is shown in experiments involving observations of models presented by other children (Murray, 1974; Botvin and Murray, 1975; Cook and Murray, 1975). Likewise, experiments by Beilin (1965), Waghorn and Sullivan (1970, Rosenthal and Zimmerman (1972) and Zimmerman and Lanaro (1974) indicate positive effects of correct models, in these cases provided by adults. Children at a lower level are equally likely to benefit from interaction with another child at a higher level, who gives the correct response (Murray, 1972; Silverman and Stone, 1972; Silverman and Geiringer, 1973; Botvin and Murray, 1975; Miller and Brownell, 1975).

[2] Mackie (1983), who has adopted our paradigm, has obtained similar results.

intermediate models.[1] One researcher (Kuhn, 1972) has proposed that the ideal model should be one at a cognitive level just superior to that of the subject, and not necessarily a correct model which may be at too great a 'cognitive distance'. Allowing the child to observe one of several different models presented by an adult, she shows that the maximum progress actually occurs in subjects confronted with a model at a 'plus-one' level, i.e., just superior to the subject's own initial level of response. The significance of this research resides in the way it shifts the emphasis. Though progress is attributed to the mechanisms of imitation there is nevertheless a very strong emphasis on the constructive and progressive activity of the subject in the interaction. In the preceding research we have found similar effects when NC subjects made progress following confrontation with PC children but not with TC children.

Regarding similar models, there has been little interest. Some experiments (e.g. Kuhn, 1972; Murray, 1974) show that children who observe a model at the same level as their own exhibit insignificant progress.

It is therefore not surprising that regressive models are almost entirely absent in such work, save for one notable exception which we will examine. The effects of these models can however be studied indirectly. Thus when conservers or intermediates serve as models for nonconservers, they can themselves be considered as confronted with a regressive model. However, apart from a few exceptions no notable change is found, neither progress nor, more particularly, regression.

Two researchers located within the behaviourist tradition (Rosenthal and Zimmerman, 1972) invoked the concept of vicarious learning in their study of cognitive development. Thus they advanced the hypothesis of a possible regression by conserving subjects when confronted with a non-conserving model, although their experimental demonstration leaves some lingering doubts (as Silverman and Geiringer, 1973: note). In fact, regression is significant only on the limited items presented by the model, not on the items of generalisation. The subjects may thus have interpreted the task as requiring repetition of the responses presented by the adult model. But no matter what the validity of the experimental demonstration, it is nevertheless the case that the theoretical appeal of vicarious learning has meant that regression has been entertained as a possibility, contrary to most developmental theorists. Similar hypotheses have been advanced within a similar framework in relation to the development of moral concepts (Bandura and McDonald, 1963).

Significant progress is only rarely shown by conserving subjects following an interaction with nonconservers (Murray, 1972). (A result tending in this

[1]Murray (1974) presented nonconserving subjects with an intermediate model, but found no significant progress.

direction is reported by Kuhn, 1972, but the details are insufficient to conclude that there is a significant effect.) It should be noted that the subjects were already initially conservers on almost all the pretest items. Having therefore a status of higher intermediates makes them particularly likely to benefit from any operational exercise presented to them (Strauss and Langer, 1970). Hence the results demonstrate the effects of the exercise on operational generalisation as much as they clarify the actual formation of cognitive processes in a social situation.

What can be concluded from the trends apparent in recent work involving alternative cognitive models? First, amongst the various theoretically possible models, the correct progressive model has been the most frequently studied, which suggests that in all this work interaction is conceived as underpinned by imitation. This also seems to be true of the smaller amount of work postulating progress as a result of confrontation with an intermediate progressive model. If 'in general the most effective intervention is the presentation of a model which induces the child to actively exercise his own mental operations in a way that leads to his apprehension of the contradictions and inadequacies inherent in his mode of solving the problem' and if '. . . observation of a model performing a task in a manner discrepant from (but not inferior to) the child's own conceptualisation of the task, may be sufficient to induce in the child an awareness of alternative conceptions and will perhaps lead to disequilibrium and reorganisation' (Kuhn, 1972: p. 843), it is not clear why it should involve the restriction *'but not inferior to'*; otherwise a mechanism similar to imitation is being postulated even if it is grafted on to the 'spontaneous' development of the child. (see Murray, 1974).

The second conclusion is that *a fortiori* neither a similar model nor, for even stronger reasons, a regressive model are supposed to be effective in cognitive development. The effects studied and the evidence available regarding such models are, as we have seen, minimal.

How then may it be possible to develop a coherent set of hypotheses, based on the concept of sociocognitive conflict which could account for the positive effects of correct models (that are frequently cited in published research), the absence of a positive effect of similar models (circumstantial as we shall see) and also of possible effects of regressive models? These last should in practice be more common in children's experience than their exclusion from the theoretical and experimental preoccupations of researchers in this area implies.

Let us make a few points here. The utility of a model depends on its capacity to engender sociocognitive conflict in the subject whose development one is studying. This capacity is therefore at the same time cognitive (the child must be able to establish an intelligible relation between his own model for solution of the problem and the model underlying the actions of others) and social. It has been seen that a variety of conditions must be met if sociocognitive conflict is to generate the dynamics of development. Only interaction involving reciprocity is effective in that it leads to cognitive regulation of the divergent responses emerging at the psychosocial level, rather than regulation of an exclusively social type.

We should add that in an interaction the child finds himself confronted with successive responses of which only the overall pattern can reveal the other's implicit strategies. The model therefore also effectively includes whatever the child is capable of abstracting from the interaction situation. Recall Experiment 2 in which the TC subject responds in terms of the correct model, but without ever making the reasons for his placements explicit. It is obvious that the NC child, not possessing the cognitive instruments necessary for a correct reconstruction of the village, cannot by himself infer the reasons for the disagreements that emerge. In contrast, the cognitive model underlying the PC subject's responses is not only easier for the NC child to understand, it is also made more explicit by the intermediate subject, who frequently refers to the orientation marker and thus to the necessity of taking into account or conserving the intrafigural relations. Thus, at the same time he makes explicit one or another of the dimensions relevant to an adequate transformation.

The question of models is not simple. The effect of one or another does not only depend on the nature of the cognitive operations involved but also on the nature of the interindividual relations through which they are conveyed.

Regarding the correct progressive model, this should be more effective if it leads to sociocognitive conflict but also if those defending the correct model do so in a way which avoids a straightforward compliance with the solution. Thus an adult who is a good teacher should be able to produce the progress that our TC subjects in Experiment 2 could not. The correct model should have a major advantage apart from inducing sociocognitive conflict; it provides, or can provide, pointers to appropriate change.

But, and this further point can also be derived from our socio-constructivist conception of cognitive development, a correct model is not necessary to cognitive progress. This, of course, is why an intermediate model can lead to progress. But it is with respect to similar and regressive models in particular that the concept of sociocognitive conflict has undeniable significance. Concerning similar models, we have already seen in Experiments 2 and 3 that, depending on the situation, this type of model can have different effects, precisely as a function of the sociocognitive conflict it induces. We have seen that if the similar model produces responses identical to those of the experimental subject, generally the absence of conflict is such that no progress can be expected. The various studies that have failed to show cognitive progress following observation of such a model probably fall within this category. On the other hand, the model that is similar but involves different responses either because it involves opposite centrations (as in the experiments on length conservation) or because it occupies different and contrasting spatial positions, does induce sociocognitive conflict which may, depending on the nature of the solution to which it gives rise, be a source of progress.

Finally, sociocognitive conflict may occur with the presentation of a regressive type of model. This is one of the strengths of our approach and we have seen an illustration of this in the first variant of the preceding experiment.

Let us look at the experimental demonstration of these various observations. The principle of the experiment is as follows. The experimenter will hold the modality of sociocognitive conflict constant across the experimental conditions (an adult presents the models according to a procedure in which most elements are identical for all subjects), while at the same time varying the nature of the alternative model presented to the child. Thus the effects on an NC child will be studied of a correct model (level III), an intermediate model (level II) and of two regressive models.

The experiment

The experiment (conducted by May Lévy) involves seventy-two children aged from 5 years to 6 years 8 months who had all responded in level I terms to the two complex items in the standard pretest. In the experimental phase each subject interacted with an adult collaborator of the experimenter who reconstructed the village after the child in terms of a specific model. Two posttests were then conducted, one immediately following the interaction and another 15 days later.

During the experimental phase the child began each item (there were two items) by constructing his village on the base normally provided. Then the adult collaborator also constructed a village on a base placed beside the subject's, as indicated in Fig. 6.9. Note that the material used is the first one that was devised and is in rectangular form; and that the items are both complex.

Figure 6.9 provides two additional pieces of information. First, it is assumed in the item illustrated that the village is constructed by an NC subject (as all the subjects are). Second, the four models presented by the adult are illustrated:

- In the correct progressive model condition the solution is correct;
- In the intermediate model condition, a level II copy is presented by the adult (a copy chosen so that no house will be correctly placed);

- In the regressive model condition, the copy results from a translation of the entire village so that it does not take into account the 90° rotation which level I children are capable of;
- In what is described as the aberrant model condition, the houses are placed 'any old how': the orientations are not even parallel to the sides of the base. What is more, they are crammed into a corner.

Finally, in a control condition without models the procedure during the experimental phase is the same as in the individual tests. Subjects respond individually by creating copies of the two complex items. Another form of control would have consisted in presenting subjects with a similar model. However, such a model would only have reinforced the subjects' mode of problem solution, and the control would thus have been less strict than that actually adopted. The sociocognitive conflict procedure adopted is as follows in all conditions. The experimenter begins by positioning the houses and commenting on what he is doing: 'You see the red house over there (on the village to be reproduced), I'm putting it here (on the copy board); I'll put the blue one in a corner because it is also in a corner over there, and the white one is in the corner over there, so I'm also going to put it in a corner. What do you think of that; have I got it right? . . .' The formulation is more or less the same and kept constant across the various experimental conditions. Its rationale is to provide no indication of the dimensions used in the reconstruction (left–right, front–back, proximity to the lake, facing the lake, . . .). The experimenter then asks, 'When the man comes out of the lake here (in the village to be copied) does he see the same houses as when he comes out of the lake there (copy)?' The same questions are asked with respect to the subject's own construction as compared to the original village, and in comparing the villages produced by the subject and the experimenter. Each time justifications are requested. Then the experimenter asks the child, 'Do you agree more with this one (subject's construction) or with that one (experimenter's construction)?' . . .

If the child judges his own village to be the more correct, the experimenter defends his in terms of the principles already described, 'Yes, but as you saw, I put the red one here, like over there . . . .'. If on the contrary the subject judges the experimenter's village to be more satisfactory, the experimenter questions his own construction, 'Yes, but I am not entirely certain whether I have placed the red house correctly . . . you know, I can make mistakes too.' These two types of intervention often alternate as a function of changes in the child's responses during the interaction. In brief, then, the experimenter's role is to create sociocognitive conflict (of the same kind whichever of the alternative models happens to be presented), by provoking doubts in the child, making him reflect upon them and making him express an opinion on the adequacy of the various copies of the village that are made. The experimenter ends the procedure when the child appears to be

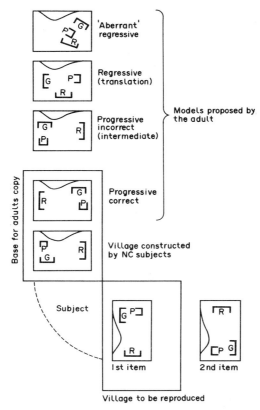

FIG. 6.9 The experimental procedure: the two (complex) items used in the experimental phase and the different level models suggested by the adult for the first item.

stuck (either on a particular choice or through indecision), or when to continue might be distressing, the conflict being fairly strong for the child as it is, given the ceaseless questioning by the adult.

Let us now examine the results obtained with such conflict for the different models. Table 6.9 indicates the levels achieved in the interaction phase.

Note first of all that three of the four experimental conditions differ significantly from the no-model control. The correct model is largely repeated by the subjects, as is the intermediate model. The more interesting result is that the regressive model condition also differs significantly from the control condition while this is not the case for the aberrant model though here also one-third of the subjects produce performances in advance of their pretests.

The first two conditions are unproblematic; subjects respond just like the adult's model, as might be expected. In the case of the two non-progressive models, the subjects present a puzzle which is considered together, as the

TABLE 6.9. *Classification of subjects in the experimental phase*

	NC	PC	TC
No model *a*	12	2	0
Correct model *b*	1	3	10
Intermediate model *c*	2	10	2
Regressive model *d*	8	5	2
'Aberrant' model	10	4	1

Jonckheere's test, conditions *a* and *b*, Z: 4.131, P<0.00003; conditions *a* and *c*, Z: 3.448, P<0.0003; conditions *a* and *d*, Z: 1.694, P<0.05.

two conditions do not differ significantly. The problem is that the adult's model remains constantly before the child's eyes. Is this genuine progress or a compound of the subject's own strategy and the odd responses of the adult that 'accidentally' produces a hybrid village classified in terms of a level that is not really the child's own? Though we are not yet in a position to draw any conclusions, we can state that none of the subjects in these conditions is willing to imitate the adult's model, or certainly not in its entirety. Therefore there was conflict in one form or another. Certainly the same question arises with respect to the progressive model conditions – is it genuine progress or simply compliance? Let us look at the results of the first posttest.

TABLE 6.10. *Classification of subjects in the first posttest*

	NC	PC	TC
No model *a*	11	2	1
Correct model *b*	2	5	7
Intermediate model *c*	6	7	1
Regressive model *d*	5	4	6
'Aberrant' model	13	2	0

Jonckheere's test, conditions *a* and *b*, Z: 3.124, P<0.001; conditions *a* and *c*, Z: 1.485, P<0.07; conditions *a* and *d*, Z: 2.285, P<0.02.

Things become clearer in the posttest. The condition leading to the most progress is that involving a correct model. Following this, and less expected, is the regressive model condition, where we find progress among two-thirds of the subjects, more than a third giving a correct response despite the fact that the model provided no pointers at all that were relevant to a solution more advanced than the child could manage in the pretest: indeed, quite the contrary. This elegantly illustrates the constructivist character of social interaction. The intermediate model condition is itself on the verge of statistical significance. The aberrant model condition produces practically no progress.

Our conjectures regarding the effects of the various models are therefore largely confirmed, even if they are somewhat tempered. Thus the correct model, reinforced by a sociocognitive conflict developed by the adult, provides some success. It is worth noting that the regressive model produces results not significantly different from those of the correct model, while the impact of the intermediate model is significantly less. Why is this so? An explanation in terms of sociocognitive conflict seems plausible. If a subject achieved a level II solution the conflict would end; would he not have conformed to what he might have supposed that the adult expected of him? This could not be the case for the subject confronted with a regressive model, since the disagreement would continue.

The nature of the model however is important in itself since the aberrant model, despite conflict with the adult, produced insignificant progress. The model is, properly speaking, aberrant for the child, as the adult places the houses at complete random. Confronted with such a model, and despite any sociocognitive conflict deriving from the contrast in responses, it is impossible for the child to detect any logic underlying the production of this village. It represents neither a real viewpoint nor an intelligible plan of action. How can one coordinate viewpoints with someone who does not really have one?

The progress observed was largely conserved in the second posttest. Nevertheless, as the effect with the regressive model was a little surprising, the regressive model condition has been replicated, and successfully (Mugny, Lévy and Doise, 1978). Moreover, other results generally confirm the potential for development offered by such models (Lévy, 1981).

Although the effectiveness of a regressive model can no longer be in doubt there remain other questions. The models studied were effective to differing degrees. They were so because of the sociocognitive conflicts induced. But as far as possible the same modality of sociocognitive conflict was sustained by the experimenter's collaborator across the different experimental conditions. The question that now arises concerns the modalities of sociocognitive conflict. With regard to the same regressive model, we will seek to determine how far the actual reproduction of the village constitutes an advantage – or an obstacle – to resolution of sociocognitive conflict via cognitive progress.

Experiment 6. The 'Socratic method' and the significance of the regressive model

One may recall the famous dialogue with Menon described by Plato in which Socrates leads a young slave to deduce the length of the sides of a square, the area of which is double that of a first square. He succeeds, through a series of questions, causing the slave to reason about the various aspects of the problem, and in particular encouraging him to pursue his reasoning, even when he is incorrect. Does not Socrates ask Menon, 'By throwing everything into confusion, by numbing it like a torpedo fish, have we not done wrong?' Evidently not, as the slave arrives at the correct solution. We will, to be sure, dispense with Socrates' *a priorist* hypothesis which claims to demonstrate a theory of reminiscence. We will ignore the fact that Socrates had in mind a model underlying his questions. His questions were based on this and, insofar as it was correct, the sociocognitive conflict procedure (Socrates will, we trust, forgive us . . .) thus developed ends only when the subject (the slave) arrives at the correct response.

Our conception of cognitive development is constructivist rather than *a priorist* and we will study the effects of questioning based not on a correct model, even if it is implicit, but on a regressive model. The issue therefore has three facets:

- First, is a regressive model effective if it is simply presented without introducing any additional sociocognitive conflict? In other words, is its observation alone sufficient?
- Second, is it necessary for this (regressive) model to be executed in the course of the sociocognitive conflict? In other words, is it necessary for the village actually to be reconstructed or is it sufficient to indicate the positions of each house without illustrating the village as a whole. Or, in other terms, is observation necessary?
- Finally, is questioning without a model underlying the sociocognitive conflict sufficient? This certainly would be a significant illustration of the capacity of sociocognitive conflict to introduce progress without even an alternative solution being offered (and here we part company with Socrates' ideas which assume an underlying logic).

The experiment

Fifty-nine subjects were involved, thirty-three from second level infant classes (average age 5 years 8 months), and twenty-six from the first level of primary school (average age 6 years 9 months). All these subjects were at level I on the pretest. They were randomly divided between four experimental conditions, with fourteen in one and fifteen in the others.

In the experimental phase they are, as in Experiment 5, confronted by adult behaviour which varies as follows:

- In the *regressive model* condition the child completes his own village and then the experimenter's adult collaborator completes, in front of the child, a village corresponding to the regressive model (involving the same 'translation' as in the corresponding condition in Experiment 5). The experimenter then simply asks the child what he thinks and whether he wishes to modify anything in his own village or whether he wishes to leave it as it is. This procedure is followed for the two complex items (which are the same in all conditions).

- In the *regressive model plus questioning* condition, the procedure is as in the previous condition, but with the addition of sociocognitive conflict. Let us show in detail how the latter is incorporated into the instructions. This procedure, which is more thorough than that followed in Experiment 5, consists first of an overall reconsideration of the village as a whole: 'You see, I have reconstructed the village too. But isn't the way you've done it a bit strange?' Then, whatever the reply, 'Are you sure that when the man comes out of the lake in yours he will find the same houses in the same places as when he comes out of the lake over there? Don't you think you should change your houses so that the man doesn't get lost?' When the subject has given his opinion the experimenter follows by turning his attention to his own construction: 'And in mine, will the man find the same houses in the same places when he comes out of the lake?' Whatever the subject replies, the experimenter then proceeds with a reconsideration of each of the houses in the village in turn: 'In yours, should the red house really be there where you've put it? Don't you think it would be better to put it like mine, if it is going to be in the right place as it is over there? And the white house, do you think it is right where you have put it? Don't you think it should really be put there like mine to be in the proper place, as it is over there? And what about the multicoloured house, are you sure it is really in the right place? Don't you think you should change it and put it like mine so that it is the same as over there?' Simply by changing the order of the houses, the same questions are then repeated a second time.

The procedure ends with an overall reconsideration of all the houses in the village: 'Well then, are you sure that when the man comes out of the lake in your village he will find the same houses in the same position as when he comes out of the lake over there? Is it still necessary to change anything to stop him getting lost?' The task is repeated if the subject wants to change anything, as it is if he has already changed anything.

- In the *implicit regressive model plus questioning* condition, the questions are the same. However, the experimenter carries out the questioning by merely indicating on his own base the successive locations in which he proposes placing the houses with his finger.

- Finally, in the *questioning without a model* condition, the adult neither places the houses nor indicates the positions with his finger. Questioning follows as closely as possible the same pattern as in the two preceding conditions except that – and this is most important – no positions are indicated. The questions are formulated in the following terms: 'Don't you think you should put it somewhere else?' As in the other conditions, this question is first posed with respect to the entire village, then twice for each house taken individually, and finally again for the village as a whole.

What predictions could be made? Let us first consider the three conditions involving a regressive model. We have seen in the preceding experiments that there is a considerable problem in the fact that sociocognitive conflict can be resolved by compliance rather than cognitive changes. The presentation of such a model could even lead children to display 'regressive' behaviours when the asymmetry in the relation is particularly strong. This research is concerned with examining such compliant responses (at least in terms of the first three conditions).

It is hypothesised that there will be an order among the conditions in the amount of progress engendered. The regressive model without sociocognitive conflict condition should be the least effective in producing progress. A model, which is itself certainly conflicting, is simply offered for the child's inspection. In the absence of any questioning and without indicating to the child what exactly is expected of him, the child should resolve the sociocognitive conflict by adopting 'on the off-chance' the response of an adult who 'ought to know what he is doing'. When a regressive model is presented in the course of sociocognitive conflict and the village is constructed and retained before the child's eyes, progress should be intermediate. Conflict is developed, but the presence of the adult's incorrect village may constitute an obstacle to cognitive progress, the asymmetric relationship being by definition strong. This is the condition whose effects were studied previously. The most favourable condition should be that involving an implicit regressive model. The tendency to compliance is here reduced to a minimum, since the child is provided only with an indication of the positions proposed. The village is not actually present, thus allowing the child more freedom to elaborate a village that is not an open contradiction of the adult's.

'Graduated' progress is therefore expected in these three conditions, in the order described.

For the last condition (questioning without a model) only a general prediction can be advanced. The systematic questioning should provoke sociocognitive conflict sufficient to cause significant progress.

Let us look at the results beginning with the interaction phase. Will we find traces of compliance? This would be revealed in villages finally constructed in terms of the translation underlying the regressive model. Table 6.11 gives the number of subjects who produce such a translation on the two items and those whose best performance allows us to classify them as either NC, PC or TC.

The anticipated ordering of the three conditions involving a regressive model is already apparent in the experimental phase. In t'⁕ condition without questioning, the majority of children adopt the adult's solution to the two items. This is a situation in which the asymmetrical relationship with the adult is made more apparent and it does lead to very considerable com-

TABLE 6.11. *Classification of subjects in the experimental phase*

	Ts*	NC	PC	TC
Regressive model *a*	10	4	1	0
Regressive model plus questioning *b*	1	5	5	4
Implicit regressive model plus questioning *c*	0	0	7	7
Questioning without model	0	2	5	8

*Subjects copying the 'translation' produced by the adult.
Jonckheere's test, conditions *a*, *b* and *c*, Z: 5.171, P<0.00003.

pliance. In the two other conditions the majority of subjects make progress. It is worth noting, furthermore, that in the condition involving a model and questioning the results obtained are very similar to those in the corresponding condition in Experiment 5. When the model is not visually available almost all subjects give progressive responses. It is therefore not surprising to discover that the simplest sociocognitive conflict procedure, which is not even based on an underlying model, is also effective. The child's responses have been systematically challenged, first for the whole village, then for each house and then for the whole village again, and the child will have sought to satisfy the adult via congnitive regulations, and to reabsorb this socio-cognitive conflict.

Before concluding, let us see whether this progress is also expressed in the posttest. The results are given in Table 6.12.

TABLE 6.12. *Classification of subjects in the first posttest*

	NC	PC	TC
Regressive model *a*	12	1	2
Regressive model plus questioning *b*	7	4	4
Implicit regressive model plus questioning *c*	3	3	8
Questioning without model	5	5	5

Jonckheere's test, conditions *a*, *b* and *c*, Z: 3.169, P<0.001.

When the child is tested immediately following the conflictual interaction, the same results are found. Even if progress is, overall, a little less frequent, it remains very considerable. Furthermore, the observed ordering of the three conditions involving a regressive model is conserved, an ordering which is strongly significant. The same is found in the second posttest, and also in a third, although, as might be expected, the differences become rather weaker. Finally, in the condition involving only questioning the progress obtained also shows a robust stability.

The sociocognitive conflict procedures to which the children are exposed are thus remarkably effective. Out of 59 subjects, 32 make progress on the first posttest even though at no point in the experiment is the correct response (or even a partially correct response) given to them. What is more, in 28 cases this progress is conserved in the second posttest and in 25 cases in a third posttest.

However, the tendency to compliance in an asymmetrical relationship with an adult is a considerable obstacle to cognitive progress, at least when the adult presents a model which is not just incorrect but regressive. This experiment shows very clearly that the more explicit the adult makes the placements he proposes as a function of this model, the more apparent the assymetrical relationship becomes. To return to a terminology we have already used, we would say that regulations that are more and more relational and less and less 'cognitive' supplant those regulations of a cognitive order which can alone lead to progress. Not only are such risks produced by adults. It will be recalled that, in the second experiment, TC children provided a correct model without letting the NC child elaborate a cognitive solution; the latter finds itself in an asymmetrical relationship, excluded from constructing the village, which prevents full development of sociocognitive conflict.

There remains a problem. How can questioning alone, without even an implicit model, be a source of cognitive progress? This seems to be one of those trap questions posed by those tempted to reduce the effectiveness of sociocognitive conflict to its purely cognitive aspect. To be sure, a definitive response is not possible. One could, however, sketch out an answer in terms of the systematic denial of the validity of the child's placements in this socio-cognitive conflict procedure. The adult implies that he considers these to be a 'negative' model (in terms of his own responses), that is, a model not to be followed because it is unsatisfactory. Might not the solution for the child, contradicted in this way, be to 'disown' his actions? The child could there-fore be led systematically to invert the right-left and front-back relation-ships, which would in fact result in the correct solution for the complex items. Might this not be the reason why more than half the subjects in this condition complete at least one correct village during the interaction?

If this is the case, then the child's cognitive reflection is not independent of the social conditions which induce it and which, more particularly perhaps, direct it. The child can be led to adopt a different viewpoint but it is still interindividual dynamics that lead him to take a position with respect to his own production. This could be the case even when the child works alone in various successive positions, and also when he is led by the adult to consider simultaneously villages that have been constructed from these various view-points. Moreover, there may exist cultural differences in the degree to which children can be led to coordinate their own successive viewpoints (Mackie, 1980).

Though a child may be working alone, other social dynamics can be involved when he has to take account of certain salient social schemas. This refers to social marking, the subject of the last experiment.

Experiment 7. Social marking

In the preceding chapter the final experiment concerning sociocognitive conflict was the occasion for discussing and illustrating in more detail the central idea in our concept of social marking. We have established that when there was a homology between the structure of the adult-child relations in the experimental situation and those relations involved in the conservation of unequal length sociocognitive conflict gave rise to progress. In the experiment which will now be described (by Diane Rilliet in collaboration with Diane Mackie) such social marking is directly incorporated into the experimental material. To achieve this, the material normally used (the houses in a village, with a swimming pool or lake) are substituted in certain conditions by material that is marked in terms of its social meaning. The swimming pool (the reference point) is replaced by a school mistress's desk and the houses by the desks of pupils. While there exists *a priori* no socially necessary relations in the material normally used, in the new material preferential relations exist based on the relation of the teacher with those being taught. Indeed, one can assume that the front-back relations, for example, will be particularly significant in this relationship. No matter what position the teacher normally adopts, it is one which allows her to dominate the children's positions so that she will be able to see them all without difficulty. Children should carry out transformations that retain the spatial relationships between individuals marked by distinct positions within an asymmetrical social relationship. Such social marking should encourage the appearance of sociocognitive conflict. Let us examine the experimental conditions created to test this hypothesis.

The experiment

In this demonstration only NC children, forty-two in total, were included (namely those who gave level I responses to the two standard complex items in the pretest), those subjects for whom the effects of the experimental variables should be most differentiated. Out of these forty-two children, twenty-six participated in interactions in groups of two, while the other sixteen worked individually in the experimental phase. Each of these conditions, the group and the individual, were split in terms of a second variable. The subjects (in pairs or individually) either worked with the normal material in the experimental phase (swimming pool and houses in a village) or with the socially marked material (school teacher and pupils). Eight groups of two participated in the socially 'marked' interindividual encounter, five groups in the group condition with the standard materials (which can be characterised as not socially marked). Of the sixteen subjects working individually, nine worked during the experimental phase with socially marked material and seven with the standard material.

The procedure was similar to that normally employed. One week or thereabouts after the pretest, the children took part in one or another of the experimental conditions, either individually or collectively, either with or without socially marked materials. A posttest a week later allowed evaluation of the cognitive level attained by the subjects. The forty-two children considered participated in all of these phases of the experiment. Their average age is similar to those in preceding experiments.

The group condition was selected according to the same criteria as in the experiment on social marking of conservation of unequal lengths. Recall that the probability of conflict is very low when interactions are based on such a task. To introduce a conflict in spite of this, the task was socially marked by asking the children to divide bracelets of unequal lengths between the experimenter and themselves. Significant progress then appeared. The principle underlying the group encounters in the present experiment is the same. An interaction was selected (between NC subjects) that should in principle not be conflictual. Experiment 2 in this chapter has given us an example of such a condition. The interaction between two NC subjects, both placed on the same side, produced only a little conflict and consequently little progress. This therefore will be the situation reproduced in the group condition without social marking. In the individual condition without social marking, the children will carry out the same tasks individually. The two other conditions, one group and the other individual, will be altogether equivalent involving the same situations, but different materials.

Let us look at this material. In place of the swimming pool as an index of the village's orientation, a desk (with a teacher) will be used as an indicator of the orientation of the class room. Instead of houses to be located in relation to the swimming pool, there will be small desks (each one with a pupil) which will be placed in the class room 'so that the teacher can see them all in the same places from her position in this class (the experimenter's) as in this class (the child's).' As the teacher's desk is rectangular, in the no-marking conditions it is substituted by a swimming pool of the same form and size. Note that the standard material is used in the individual pretests and posttests.

Plate IV (b) gives an example of one of the two interaction items with the socially marked material.

One important difference should be noted. In contrast to the preceding experiments, one position that is complementary to the place occupied by the teacher's desk cannot be used by the child. This arises because the social marking implied in the 'school class room' material is such that it prevents the child from placing a desk in this complementary position, something that nonconservers are otherwise inclined to do. The social marking therefore gives rise to a straightforward impossibility. To make the conditions with the socially unmarked material equal, it was necessary to make this impossibility general. This was done by putting a band of colour on the two materials, preventing a child from placing a house or desk on this spot. One might expect that this impossibility would introduce purely intrasituational conflicts. But at least the procedure has the advantage of making such an availability equally likely in all conditions. We will thus be concerned with comparisons between the experimental conditions rather than the absolute degree of progress in itself.

The experimental predictions mainly concern the effects of social marking as such, effects which should be reflected in an overall difference between the conditions with and without social marking, the conditions involving such marking being more favourable to the appearance of progress. On the other hand, an order of effectiveness among three of the experimental conditions might be anticipated. The group condition with marking should be the most effective, and the individual condition without marking should be the least likely to favour cognitive development. The individual condition with marking should be intermediate between these two. It is difficult, however, to make a prediction about the effects of social interaction without marking. The results are presented in Table 6.13.

TABLE 6.13. *Posttest classification of subjects*

	NC	PC	TC
Groups, with social marking *a*	3	3	10
Groups, without social marking *b*	5	3	2
Individuals, with social marking *c*	2	4	3
Individuals, without social marking *d*	3	3	1

Jonckheere's test, conditions *a* + *c* and *b* + *d*, Z: 2.154, P<0.02; conditions *a* and *b*, Z: 1.874 P<0.05; conditions *a* and *d*, Z: 1.687, P<0.05; conditions *a*, *c* and *d*, Z: 2.057, P<0.02.

Overall, the effect of social marking as hypothesised is confirmed. Conditions, whether individual or collective, which involve social marking in the materials produce greater benefits in the posttest than conditions based on the usual materials. Nevertheless, this effect is particularly strong when groups interact in relation to socially meaningful material. Indeed, such a condition differs significantly from the individual and the collective without social marking. However, it does not differ significantly from the condition involving individuals working on socially marked materials. The predicted order is well-demonstrated and emphasises that although social marking in itself has an effect, it is particularly favourable to cognitive development when it is associated with group work.

Conclusions

The results of this experiment are certainly not definitive. They open up an important new perspective for research, just as did the final experiment on length conservation[1]. This spatial transformation experiment demonstrates that social elements can be found even in apparently individual situations. Conflict may exist between individuals and lead to cognitive regulation, but it can also exist for an isolated individual when the operations he seeks to apply to a particular situation are contradicted by the existence of various social norms governing this situation. This is certainly a significant form of sociocognitive conflict, even though it may still represent a poor relation in the psychology of development.

[1]Recent research by Paola De Paolis tends to confirm the effects of such social marking (De Paolis et al., 1981).

7

Conclusions

The accumulation of experimental evidence is now such that it is possible and indeed necessary to draw up an assessment, from two points of view. On the one hand we will present of a more complete social-psychological theory of cognitive development, because although the general hypotheses outlined in the second chapter have now been illustrated empirically, it is also the case that the experimentation has in turn enabled a more precise specification of a number of points. On the other hand, we will identify those questions that remain to be answered. The social psychological theory presented here does not pretend to be definitive. It constitutes a step, hopefully a significant one, in developing within science a 'socialised' representation of intelligence. An attempt will be made to evaluate the new opportunities which this conceptualisation offers in terms of areas of research, and at the same time we will try to evaluate the implications regarding the social significance of 'intelligence' as emphasised in the first chapter.

A Social-psychological theory of cognitive development

The social psychological theory that it is now possible to outline can be contrasted with the various other approaches to intelligence which have been considered. First, being social-psychological, this theory contrasts with the epistemological individualism which seems to predominate in cognitive psychology. More important perhaps is the unwillingness to accept the parallelism which naturalistic analyses claim to show between cognitive and social structuring, certainly an elegant way of evading the issue of causality in the development of knowledge. Taking the same approach, the mechanism underlying this dynamic causality will be made more explicit, in contrast to all those who argue for the 'socialisation' of intelligence and assert the social nature of cognitive structures largely without specifying the mechanisms by which intellectual and social dynamics might be associated. Finally, looking at these mechanisms themselves, we would dissociate ourselves from what might be called the 'simple solution' which quite simply postulates mechanisms of imitation. Our theorising can be described as interactionist and constructivist but more accurately it is 'socio-interactionist' and 'socio-constructivist'.

Social interactionism

It is possible to be 'interactionist' at different levels and to different degrees. The question is: interactionism certainly, but between who and what? Or rather, as we have seen, between who and who? Cognitive and developmental psychology have stressed the study of interaction between the subject and his 'physical' rather than human environment. This is still true for both Piagetian theory (the educational repercussions of which have put the accent on the activity of the subject within an 'enriched environment') and for behaviourist approaches, particularly those which consider social stimuli as no different from the 'responses' of the nonhuman environment.

For social psychology, interaction does not simply join a subject and an object; the relation with the object can only be mediated by the relation of the subject to other individuals. We have therefore attempted to generate in the area of cognitive development a shift from 'bipolar psychology (ego-object) to tripolar psychology (ego-alter-object)' (Moscovici and Ricateau, 1972: p. 141).

Social constructivism

Cognitive development is founded on an interaction with others but what kind of interaction? It can be concluded from our experimental work that interaction is not just a source of development simply because it allows processes of imitation to occur. We have considered this point in relation to models. Most recent work still stresses the effectiveness of a correct model, but our experiments have, on the contrary, systematically sought conditions which could exclude any alternative explanation in terms of processes of imitation. This was the case in the experiments involving a similar model, as incorrect as the child's, or a regressive type of model. It is clearly the subject's structuring activity that lays the foundations for cognitive development, an activity that gradually structures – step by step so to speak – increasingly balanced instruments. But what kind of activity and what kind of equilibrium? It is not just the activity of an isolated subject but a 'socialised' activity involving actions and judgements which may differ from individual to individual. Moreover, the coordination of these creates an equilibrium that is itself social in nature, as it integrates and unites the various viewpoints within a social system.

From interdependence to autonomy

The individual, whether child or adult, often finds himself facing cognitive problems alone and attempts to resolve them in a more or less satisfactory manner. Does this mean that such actions can be isolated from the social meanings that they entail?

Looking exclusively at the expression of cognitive competence, the answer would appear to be in the affirmative. If, on the other hand, the question is considered from a developmental point of view, the answer is quite evidently in the negative.

Autonomous expression of cognitive competences is only possible as a result of development based on social interdependence. It has been shown several times that cognitive development – certainly at the level of specific concepts – in its early stages depends to a large extent on the social inter-actions that occur between children. From this interdependence arises a cognitive coelaboration, a coordination of schemata which are otherwise isolated – or of centrations derived from the same schema – which gives rise to cognitive competences allowing the subsequent autonomisation of development. This also accounts for the common difficulty of providing evidence for differences between conditions involving subjects at an inter-mediate level; they have already partially elaborated a new cognitive instrument which they can then more readily perfect no matter what the nature of the ('learning') exercise presented to them. On the other hand, children at a lower level who still have to achieve the elaboration of such instruments are strongly dependent on the interindividual relations to which they may be exposed. Only as a result of these and other conditions to be considered below do they progress. It is important to emphasise this apparent paradox. Autonomisation of development arises from an initial social interdependence, an interdependence which provides the founda-tions for this autonomisation. Here as elsewhere opposites seem to meet.

In addition, each development is based on an earlier development. This is a characteristic of constructivism. Thus there are prerequisites for the occur-rence of development deriving from this interdependence..This brings us back to the old observation that 'one does not learn just anything from just anyone at just any time'. The hypothesis advanced here is that these pre-requisites are themselves based on previous social interactions. Thus cognitive development can be better understood as a spiral of causality in which various preconditions allow the child to participate in more complex interactions, ensuring the elaboration of more complex cognitive instru-ments which in their turn allow participation in further structured interactions.

One consequence of this development from interdependence to autonomy is particularly important. It is only when a new cognitive instrument is being introduced that group work will be superior to individual work, and that the cognitive levels reached during interaction between individuals will be superior to those of isolated individuals. Though such superiority is possible, it is not automatic. In fact, other social psychological processes can interfere and counteract the expression of such a cognitive advance.

Therefore, when looking at individual progress following interaction a cognitive superiority among subjects who have worked in a group should not necessarily be expected. It is only at the point of elaboration of a concept that such superiority can appear. Because of the resulting autonomisation of development, this superiority is not necessarily found at subsequent points in the development of the concept.

It may be noted here that this limiting factor in the superiority of group work may help to explain apparent contradictions in research on group problem solving.

It is possible to represent the progression in development from interdependence to autonomy diagrammatically (Table 7.1), enabling the specification of the twofold hypothesis for various concepts. First it predicts the relation which will exist between individual and interindividual cognitive performances, and second the relation between progress following individual performance and that following interindividual performances. However, the existence of a temporal decalage between these two relations cannot be ruled out. Cognitive coelaboration (at a superior cognitive level) could occur without the individual partners in such interactions showing progress in subsequent individual performances.

TABLE 7.1. *Individual and group progress (+) in relation to specific concepts*

	Individual work	Group work
Prior to elaboration	0	0
During initial elaboration	0	+
After initial elaboration	+	+

It is appropriate here to consider Vygotsky's formulation which we have had occasion to quote earlier: 'An interpersonal process is transformed into an intrapersonal process. Each function appears twice in the cultural development of the child, first at the social level and then at the individual level, first between individuals (interpsychological) and then within the child (intrapsychological).' (Vygotsky, 1978: p. 27).

The authenticity of progress following interindividual work

We now have a clear answer to a major question[1]. The progress recorded

[1] Thanks to the work of A. N. Perret-Clermont.

in the various tasks is genuine. Three factors bear this out. The first is the generalisation of progress to other concepts based on similar operations, proof of an overall restructuring. The second is the stability of progress over time. This is a necessary feature of real developmental change and has constituted an important aspect of our empirical demonstrations. The third bears on the nature of the reasoning expressed by subjects. True operational progress can be inferred from new and original arguments which have not occurred in the interindividual encounter.

A social psychological mechanism: Sociocognitive conflict

The experimental illustrations have clearly shown that interindividual encounters lead to cognitive progress insofar as sociocognitive conflict occurs during the interaction. The social and cognitive poles are inseparable here, because it must clearly be a matter of conflict between social partners about the ways to resolve the task. Such conflict can arise in various interactions.

This is the case for many encounters between individuals without the same response systems. Therefore children at different cognitive levels have a greater chance of disagreeing over specific responses insofar as they (these judgements, actions, etc.) derive from different schemata. However, other genuinely intrasituational characteristics can give rise to conflicts where one might least expect them. In particular, when individuals who are partners in an interaction do not share the same viewpoint and apply the same incorrect type of operation, they can produce divergent responses (see the experiments on reconstruction of a village). Finally, in some cases a divergence of responses can arise in interactions between individuals at the same cognitive level who make different centrations, (experiments on the conservation of length). The effects on the development of the child of models that are cognitively more advanced, in our opinion, constitutes another illustration of the effective impact of sociocognitive conflict.

How does sociocognitive conflict, so defined in terms of differing responses (whether or not based on the same cognitive rules), lead to cognitive development?

One reason is certainly the child's awareness of responses other than its own. As has been seen, social interaction is crucial in the elaboration and indeed the initiation of concept development. This is hardly surprising. One of the characteristics of 'preoperational' thought is ignorance of distinct points of view, or what has sometimes been characterised as egocentrism. In fact, there is occasionally considerable difficulty (given the level of cognitive development relative to a concept) in imagining the possibility of different responses, which makes children stick to their own viewpoints (Aebli, 1967). In a conflicting relation with others, a conflict is created which makes the difference explicit. In other terms, sociocognitive conflict is a source of disequilibrium. It is disequilibrium that is at once both social and cognitive. It is cognitive disequilibrium in that the cognitive system is unable to integrate simultaneously its own responses and those of others within a single coherent whole. It cannot 'account for' others and itself at the same time. It is social disequilibrium since this is not simply cognitive disagreement. It involves relations between individuals for whom this conflict poses a social problem. Without this social problem the child would be unlikely to feel cognitive conflict (one should recall here the difficulty there is in creating in the child a conflict between observations).

The second reason why conflict is effective in stimulating cognitive development is that others can provide relevant clues as to the elaboration of a new cognitive instrument. Also at this level it is not necessary for someone else to provide the correct response, even though this can sometimes facilitate development. It may be sufficient that others provide a centration opposing that of the child who can then progress through combination of these centrations (as in the experiments on length conservation). The situations involving spatial transformations showed that progress can consist in a coordination of viewpoints that is able, via differences in the immediate perceptions of distinct individuals, to reestablish the invariance in intrafigural relationships. Even regressive models, apparently unable to provide the child with anything, can nonetheless indicate the direction to follow when, for example, the nature of the dimensions or transformations relevant to a more adequate completion of the task are made explicit.

A third reason is that sociocognitive conflict increases the probability that the child will be cognitively active, an activity whose importance has been shown often enough by the Genevan School. However, this is not simply action 'on the object', but activity in relation to divergent responses. One arrives thus at perhaps the most fundamental reason.

Cognitive and relational resolutions of sociocognitive conflict

If our sociocognitive conflict procedures provide evidence of considerable effectiveness it is mainly because the problem to which the child is exposed is not merely cognitive, but relational as well. For the child it is not so much a question of resolving a difficult problem as it is of engaging in an interindividual relationship, a relation with others. Certainly conflict can provide an amusing game. In the long term however there develops a need to coordinate the viewpoints within a system which can create agreement amongst the partners. Progress (compared to the initial capacities of the individuals) does not arise by chance from collective interactions. The only way of distinguishing what each person perceives from a different perspective is to include the perspectives within a common space. And the only way of resolving the question of contrasting centrations in judgements on length is the acknowledgement of each centration (each 'difference'), but by coordinating them within a system characterised by conservation of equality.

However, it is not impossible to avoid sociocognitive conflict and this is a considerable obstacle to the appearance of cognitive progress. In fact, conflict can be regulated in several ways. Some are consistent with resolving it in purely social terms. Such is the case when the child complies in an attempt to reduce the interindividual divergence in responses. In this case a social regulation effectively underlies the cognitive regulation. The appeal of this kind of escape is not independent of the relations that are established, and perhaps have already been established, between the partners.

We have seen how conflict between two children can be resolved unilaterally when one has the correct response available and the other is unable to intervene in this asymmetrical relationship. But this issue becomes more obvious when the child is faced with an adult. Indeed, sociocognitive conflict is not merely an opposition of responses; it is a conflict between social agents occupying social positions, the contrast in which can be accentuated by the situation – as for instance in some experimental situations. Thus the child has an asymmetrical relationship with the adult. This asymmetry calls up various behaviours (the child will be more compliant, particularly if he does not clearly perceive the aims of the experimental situation, as occurred with the simple presentation of a regressive model by an adult without commentary – this was imitated by two-thirds of the subjects concerned), and various expectations (the adult knows better than the child), and indeed the recognition of certain differences (according the longer of the bracelets to the adult).

The inhibitory effects on development of this social-psychological tendency to compliance (or perhaps one should say avoidance of conflict in an asymmetrical relationship) can be observed at several levels. Thus it can be identified by making an internal analysis of the data from the experimental phase. It was regularly found that subjects who deferred to others did not progress. However, it is possible to counteract this effect by involving the child in a sociocognitive conflict situation which makes regulation in terms of such compliance difficult. This is the case when the child is systematically challenged without also placing a response model before him, or when two adults advocate two mutually opposing viewpoints which are also incorrect.

Such asymmetries can also be found in the form of failure in interaction which we have called 'individualisation'. In certain group structures (as for example, when children are asked to organise themselves in terms of a centralised or hierarchical structure) or in groups in which functioning is hindered (for example, by preventing the partners from communicating), the outcome of interaction depends essentially on the individual capacities of the partners. In such instances, which are possibly more frequent than one might suppose, the interaction is such that a coordination of viewpoints would not be expected, either because the structure opposes it or because the functioning prevents it. Some reciprocity must exist, allowing the expression of points of view. Without this, sociocognitive coordination of different centrations within more balanced cognitive structures cannot be achieved. Neither putting individuals side by side nor a complete asymmetry between them can lead to progress. Either the individual approaches cannot be coordinated with one another, or one of them fails to be integrated within the social field.

An important outcome results from this analysis of the means of resolving interindividual conflict. Often it is not possible to predict individual cognitive progress following interaction solely on the basis of the group performance. This is sometimes so (in a sociocognitive conflict that is carefully orchestrated by the adult, for example), but not necessarily in interactions giving rise to one-sided decision structures.

Social and cognitive regulations

It was seen in the preceding section that various social regulations (particularly those that are asymmetrical) based upon norms which link the positions of one to another (in the present case, those of the child and the adult) can act against or become substituted for the cognitive regulations characteristic of cognitive development. However, this is not the only possible influence of characteristics specific to a social relationship between children and adults. The existence of asymmetries can in specific situations be necessary for the emergence of cognitive regulations. Some social asymmetries can indeed coincide with (or be homologous with) regulations of a cognitive nature that are also asymmetrical. It has been seen, in relation to conservation of unequal length, that the asymmetric size relation between child and adult led to discovery that inequality is conserved independently of perceptual configurations. It has also been seen, in relation to spatial transformations, that introduction of socially 'marked' material is sufficient to produce significant progress. The teacher–pupil relation involves distinct spatial relations which cannot be as easily ignored as can the spatial relations between houses and a swimming pool. Through such a need, which is based on a social asymmetry, there can emerge a realisation of the need to coordinate viewpoints, leading to cognitive performances at a level superior to those of which the child was initially capable.

The links in terms of homology between social and cognitive structures are, however, numerous. It has been seen how an interindividual asymmetry can coincide with a cognitive relation. But it is also possible to imagine that such an asymmetry could inhibit the development of a concept. Suppose, for example, that in a task for conservation of equal length, the adult asks the child to give him one of the rails saying that, because he is bigger he needs 'more'. In this case the homology involved tends to favour a nonconserving response. One may then modify at will interrelations that give rise to different cognitive dynamics.

We have come a long way from early work of Piaget who viewed relations between peers as a source of development just because of the social equality involved, and adult–child interactions as an obstacle to such development because of the constraint resulting from a fundamental inequality of social status. This was perhaps an idealistic vision, though it sometimes resurfaces with various shifts in educational fashion. Our research has shown that relations between peers can contain traces of asymmetry and that relations with adults can be sources of progress by the very existence of a homology between two kinds of relationship, one social and the other cognitive (relationships of order for example). It would thus be an error to suppose *a priori* that all social interaction favours cognitive growth, or that interaction between peers will be more effective than interaction with adults. The central issue is indeed the nature of these interactions, the contours of which our social psychological theory has defined.

Evaluation and prospects

The preceding pages provide an evaluation of our research on the social development of intelligence. They offer a definition of intelligence which links individual and social dynamics, a relationship which has been clarified and illustrated by the experiments. This social definition of intelligence, this social psychology of cognitive development, should now make it possible to push forward the major debates with which we were concerned in the first chapter. As long as we are content with an 'individualistic' view of development we will lack the conceptual and technical means necessary for the study of a number of important questions. Individual intelligence is but an aspect, an expression of a more complex process that is social in nature. Let us therefore stress some of the consequences of such a view of intelligence for the study of problems with a clear social and practical significance. This will not be so much a matter of definitive conclusions as of new research perspectives that our work opens up.

Sociocultural differences

The consistency of our results regarding the alleged differences between sociocultural groups within the same society clearly illustrates the importance that a genuinely social view of intelligence can assume. Using tasks as varied as those of liquid and number conservation, the cooperative game, and spatial transformation, we have been able to show that an appropriate interaction lasting only a few minutes enables children from less advantaged social backgrounds to attain (at the very least) the levels that children from more advantaged backgrounds can achieve on a pretest. The least one can conclude is that such results are difficult to reconcile with the views of those who attribute different biological inheritances to the members of different social groups.

The social significance of controversies about inequalities between social groups is too great for us to hope to be able to introduce, at a stroke, a decisive argument into this debate on the basis of our research findings. We are nevertheless convinced that these results justify a new approach to the problem. They prove the need to employ a social definition of intelligence in studying the differences between children from different social groups and in particular show that a more specific study should be made of the different social meanings for the members of different social groups that can underlie situations involving solution of a cognitive problem.

Social marking in cognitive development

If there is one particular area of research which is back in fashion it is the study of different aspects of the child's social development. In spite of its ancient vintage, Piaget's (1932) book on moral development remains one of his most cited works. It deals with a very important area of study which lies at the junction of central preoccupations in child psychology and in social psychology.

In the second chapter, we described the way in which the historical origins of basic cognitive operations were identified within the organisation of social identities (Durkheim and Mauss, 1969). Social divisions into age, sex and social classes remain at the basis of those principles of dichotomy which provide a matrix for the organisation of numerous judgements about social reality (Bourdieu, 1979).

A research programme could be organised around the formation and development of these social judgement schemata in children. Various pieces of research provide some first steps in this direction. Differentiation based essentially on size and strength is likely to be established in all young children and the later emergence of sexual differentiation is likely to be built on this:

> It thus seems true that children's stereotypes about masculine power or dominance develop out of stereotypes concerning body size, age and competence. Thus children believe that fathers are bigger than mothers and more intelligent, and finally that they have more power or are in charge of the family. (Kohlberg, 1966: p. 102).

Thus one can explain why:

> the 6 year-old boy is a fully fledged male chauvinist, much more so than his parents, and he is

that way regardless of how he is brought up in a society that fosters role differentiation. (Kohlberg and Ullian, 1974: p. 213).

Certainly this research is not directly concerned with the acquiring of cognitive operations, in the more restricted sense that we have used in this book. However, it is no less important for grasping this social sense of 'the possibilities and impossibilities of relationships and divisions', (Bourdieu, 1979: p. 545), in brief the social classifications that are established in children.

But our main aim remains that of shedding light on the reciprocal causal links between functioning in this 'social sense' and cognitive functioning as such. If it is true, as certain of the passages quoted in the second chapter (by Damon and Waller) would suggest, that all social knowledge presupposes cognitive functioning which can be studied as such, it is equally true that social knowledge is an aspect of social dynamics able to produce progress in the cognitive coordinations performed upon the objects which mediate these dynamics. This is what our experiments on social marking with conservation of liquids, conservation of unequal length and spatial transformation tasks illustrate. Our view of social marking is thus to be found at the junction of different approaches and aspires to clarify the causal intervention of the social in the cognitive, by moving beyond research that is content to study social development alone.

Educational applications

As publication of our research findings proceeds it has found an increasingly favourable reception amongst specialists in the sciences of education. We do not see this interest only as further indication of the social relevance of our approach to cognitive development. We also feel that the location of our research within the context of education and teaching provides an indispensable extension which should help to clarify the view of intelligence on which it is based. Nevertheless, there is an important difference between our experimental research and its possible application in an educational setting.

Experimental research, as indeed its duration alone must indicate, is by necessity a limited and transitory intervention within dynamics which already exist independently of this short-lived experimental situation. It is precisely the constraints and (possibly limited) transformations involved in an experimental situation that should tell us something about the nature of the dynamics studied. The experimental situation is therefore highly controlled to ensure that it will give rise to social interactions that in turn will, at an opportune moment, give rise to cognitive progress. It goes without saying that it is not possible to create an educational intervention that has the same rigour as experimental research. However, our research clearly shows that progress will not arise from just any interaction on just any task. For a child to learn from another child, or from an adult, certain specific conditions must be fulfilled. Even at the risk of provoking the displeasure of advocates of various forms of 'spontaneity' in current educational debates, we feel that the application of our ideas to teaching in school will in no way reduce the importance of the adult's role. The fact is that, in each of our experiments, the situations from which cognitive progress resulted, including even the 'spontaneous' interactions between children, were created by adults. An emphasis on this point is hardly superfluous when it is recognised that new educational methods appealing to the idea of reciprocal teaching by children have been advanced as pretexts for reducing the budgets allocated to education.

Nevertheless, the results of our research argue in favour of a view of education which takes relationships and activities among children seriously and which does not treat cognitive development as exclusively a matter of relations between adults and children.

Research more educationally oriented than our own shows amongst other things the importance that can be assumed by relationships between children within school learning activities. Various experiments (Gartner, Kohler and Riessman, 1971) have demonstrated a 'tutoring effect', namely the personal benefit that a child can derive from teaching that he himself provides for one of his classmates. With the aid of collective drawing, coordinated activities between children from the same disadvantaged background can be intensified and give rise to progress (Cecchini, Dubs and Tonucci, 1972). An 'ungifted' child gives a better performance after teaching another child than after completing a school exercise alone (Allen and Feldman, 1973). Our research has already shed some light on the socio-cognitive processes that may occur in such educational situations. In a current project (by Anne-Nelly Perret-Clermont) a series of investigations is being undertaken which should clarify the conditions under which children are able to acquire more general cognitive and cultural concepts in reciprocal interactions within an educational context.

Longitudinal studies

Our view of cognitive development outlines a progression which moves in successive stages from interdependence to autonomy. At each phase of cognitive development, an already established form of autonomy allows each individual to participate in the benefit from specific social interactions. The research reported in this book only captures one limited aspect of this spiral of development. It must now be developed in other directions. One such direction is indicated by some work (Lomov, 1979) showing how the interactions of adults favour more adequate cognitive performances (see also Laughlin and Jacquard, 1975; Laughlin and Sweeney, 1977). But this research does not yet show how the competences of individuals develop after participating in such interactions.

It is also necessary to undertake longitudinal research, which would begin with a careful analysis of the cognitive and social functioning shown by individuals in various conditions. It would then create the social interactions necessary for these individuals to progress, making a further evaluation before introducing new interactions, and so on. The educational relevance of such a programme of research is obvious. It would force the researcher to devise a range of situations which could act as sources of progress at specific points in cognitive development and within a given cultural context. And the theoretical significance of such longitudinal research would be no less strong. It could in particular reveal the limits that other factors, such as neurobiological development, might impose upon the effects of social interaction.

The importance of experimentation

There is one objection that has often been raised when we have discussed the results of our experiments. These results appear, at the very least, unexpected; it causes great surprise that an interaction of 5 or 10 minutes can so often give rise to stable progress. This surprise no doubt derives from a widely held view of cognitive development which attributes it exclusively to biological maturation, the 'spontaneous' rhythm of which cannot be altered. It is far from our intention to claim that maturation of the neurobiological system plays no important role in cognitive development. Nonetheless, cognitive progress is clearly generated by reorganisation which is socially produced and which does not necessarily need a very extended duration of time.

The task of experimentation is precisely that of creating the conditions of interaction necessary for integrating those organisational schemata already present within the individual, within a more complex structure. When social interaction is experimentally produced at the strategic moment, there should be few grounds for surprise that progress is produced and assimilated by the individual. On the other hand, without experimental intervention, the genesis of such cognitive progress would be difficult and perhaps impossible to identify. One would have to depend upon happy coincidences to observe, at the exact moment, a form of social interaction suitable for stimulating a reorganisation in the cognitive approach of a child endowed with the necessary prerequisites. Instead of waiting for the 'spontaneous appearance' of these actions it surely makes more sense to create them.

It is therefore not in the least obvious that one could identify the social conditions generating cognitive progress without experimentation. Observation of hundreds of experimental interactions capable of creating progress does not make us very optimistic about the possibility of a deeper nonexperimental study of the sociogenesis of cognitive operations. Even interactions which give rise to progress in a posttest do not necessarily reveal this potential for progress as they occur. Thus, if two children stick stubbornly to their respective incorrect responses during an interaction relating to the equal lengths task, they can only progress following the task. The interactions involving spatial transformations often appear to be very poor, without verbal or logical justifications being offered for the placements and alterations in placements of the houses. Only the experimental definition and determination of the structure of these situations allows one to capture these dynamics. If we know which characteristics of social interaction are sources of cognitive progress, it is only because we have produced these characteristics experimentally and not because we have assumed that these characteristics would reveal themselves in a more 'natural' context.

Experimentation in social psychology is often considered as too artificial and insufficiently relevant. This is an unwarranted generalisation. Many such studies in social psychology have cast new light on the fundamental mechanisms linking social and individual dynamics. Our book prides itself in aspiring to this tradition. But it is for our readers to judge.

References

Aebli, H. (1967) Egocentrism (Piaget) not a phase of mental development but 'a substitute solution' for an insoluble task. *Pedagogica Europaea*, **3**, 97–103.

Allen, V. L. and Feldman, R. S. (1973) Learning through tutoring: Low-achieving children as tutors. *Journal of Experimental Education*. **42**, 1–5.

Ardrey, R. (1977) *The hunting hypothesis*. Des Plaines, III.: Bantam Books.

Bandura, A. and McDonald, F. J. (1963) Influence of social reinforcement and the behaviour of models in shaping children's moral judgements. *Journal of Abnormal and Social Psychology*, **67**, 274–281.

Bandura, A. and Walters, R. H. (1963) Social learning and personality development. New York: Holt, Rinehart & Winston.

Beilin, H. (1965) Learning and operational convergence in logical thought. *Journal of Experimental Child Psychology*, **2**, 317–339.

Berry, J. W. (1971) Ecological and cultural factors in spatial perceptual development. *Canadian Journal of Behavioural Science*, **3**, 324–336.

Berry, J. W. (1975) An ecological approach to cross-cultural psychology. *Netherlands Journal of Psychology*, **30**, 51–84.

Botvin, G. J. and Murray, F. B. (1975) The efficacy of peer modelling and social conflict in the acquisition of conservation. *Child Development*, **46**, 796–799.

Bourdieu, P. (1966) L'école conservatrice: L'inégalité sociale devant l'école et devant la culture. *Revue française de Sociologie*, **7**, 325–347.

Bourdieu, P. (1979) *La distinction, critique sociale du judgement*. Paris: Editions de Minuit.

Bourdieu, P. and De Saint-Martin, M. (1975) Les catégories de l'entendement professoral. *Actes de la Recherche en Sciences Sociales*, **3**, 68–93.

Bourdieu, P. and Passeron, J.-C. (1964) *Les héritiers*. Paris: Editions de Minuit.

Bourdieu, P. and Passeron, J.-C. (1970) *La reproduction*. Paris: Editions de Minuit.

Carugati, F., De Paolis, P. and Mugny, G. (1979) A paradigm for the study of social interactions in cognitive development. *Italian Journal of Psychology*, **6**, 147–155.

Carugati, F., Mugny, G. *et al.* (1978) Psicologia sociale dello sviluppo cognitivo: Imitazione di modelli o conflitto socio-cognitivo? *Giornale Italiano di Psicologia*, **5**, 323–352.

Cecchini, M., Dubs, E. and Tonucci, F. (1972) *Teacher training, pedagogical method and intellectual development*. Rome: Instituto di Psicologia (CNR).

Chance, M. and Larsen, R. R. (1976) *The social structure of attention*. London: Wiley.

Charbonneau, C., Robert, M., *et al.* (1976) Observational learning of quantity conservation and Piagetian generalisation tasks. *Developmental Psychology*, **12**, 211–217.

Charbonneau, C. and Robert, M. (1977) Observational learning of quantity conservation in relation to the degree of cognitive conflict. *Psychological Reports*, **41**, 975 986.

Cole, M., Gay, J., Glick, J. A. and Sharp, D. W. (1971) *The cultural context of learning and thinking*. New York: Basic Books.

Cole, M. and Scribner, S. (1974) *Culture and thought*. New York: Wiley.

Cook, H. and Murray, F. B. (1975) *The acquisition of conservation through the observation of conserving models*. Roneo.

Coon, R. C., Lane, I. M. and Lichtman, R. J. (1974) Sufficiency of reward and allocation behaviour: a developmental study. *Human Development*, **17**, 301–313.

Dami, C. (1975) *Stratégies cognitives dans des jeux cooperatifs à deux*. Geneva: Editions Medecine et hygiène.

Damon, W. (1977) *The social world of the child*. San Fransisco: Jossey-Bass.

Dasen, P. R. (1974) The influence of ecology, culture and European contact on cognitive development in Australian Aborigines. In J. W. Berry & P. R. Dasen (Eds.) *Culture and cognition*. London: Methuen.

169

De Paolis, P., Carugati, F., Erba, M. and Mugny, G. (1981) Connotazione sociale e sviluppo cognitivo. *Giornale Italiano di Psicologia*, **8**, 149–165.

Doise, W. (1982) *L'explication en psychologie sociale*. Paris: Presses Universitaires de France.

Doise, W., Dionnet, S. and Mugny, G. (1978) Conflit sociocognitif, marquage social et développement cognitif. *Cahiers de Psychologie*, **21**, 231–245.

Doise, W. and Mugny, G. (1975) Recherches sociogénétiques sur la coordination d'actions interdépendantes. *Revue Suisse de Psychologie*, **34**, 160–174.

Doise, W., Mugny, G. and Perret-Clermont, A-N. (1975) Social interaction and the development of cognitive operations. *European Journal of Social Psychology*, **5**, (3), 367–383.

Doise, W., Rijsman, J. and Van Meel, J. *et al.* (1981) Sociale marketing en cognitieve ontwikkeling. *Pedagogische Studien*, **58**, 241–248.

Donaldson, M. (1978) *Children's minds*. Glasgow: Fontana – Collins.

Durkheim, E. and Mauss, M. (1969) De quelques formes primitives de classifications, contribution à l'étude des représentations collectives. In. M. Mauss *Oeuvres*. Paris: Editions de Minuit.

Eysenck, H. J. (1971) *The IQ argument, race, intelligence and education*. New York: Library Press.

Eysenck, H. J. (1975) *The inequality of man*. London: Temple Smith.

Eysenck, H. J. (1978) Sir Cyril Burt and the inheritance of the IQ. *New Zealand Psychologist*, **7**, 8–10.

Finn, G. P. (1975) *The child's conservation of liquid quantity and its embedding in the social world*. Glasgow: Jordanhill College of Education, Department of Psychology.

Fox, R. (1972) Alliance and constraint: Sexual selection in the evolution of human kinship systems. In B. Campbell (Ed.) *Sexual selection and the descent of man 1871–1971*. London: Heinemann.

Furth, H. G., Baur, M. and Smith, J. E. (1976) Children's conceptions of social institutions: A Piagetian framework. *Human Development*, **19**, 341–347.

Gartner, A., Kohler, M. C. and Riessman, F. (1971) *Children teach children: Learning by teaching*. New York: Harper & Row.

Gersen, R. P. and Damon, W. (1978) Moral understanding and children's conduct. In W. Damon (Ed.) *New directions for child development*. San Francisco: Jossey-Bass.

Glick, J. (1974) Culture and cognition: some theoretical and methodological concerns. In G. D. Spindler (Ed.) *Education and cultural process*. New York: Holt, Rinehart & Winston.

Goldschmid, M. and Bentler, P. M. (1968) *Manual: Concept assessment kit. Conservation*. San Diego: Educational and Industrial Testing Service.

Haroche, C. and Pêcheux, M. (1972) Facteurs socio-économiques et résolution de problèmes. *Bulletin de CERP*, 101–117.

Humphrey, N. K. (1976) The social function of intellect. In P. P. G. Bateson & R. A. Hinde (Eds.) *Growing points in ethology*. Cambridge: Cambridge University Press.

Inhelder, B., Sinclair, H. and Bovet, M. (1974) *Apprentissage et structures de la connaissance*. Paris: Presses Universitaires de France.

Jacquard, A. (1978) *Eloge de la différence*. Paris: Editions de Seuil.

Jahoda, G. (1979) The construction of economic reality by some Glaswegian children. *European Journal of Social Psychology*, **9**, 115–127.

Jahoda, G. (1980) Theoretical and systematic approaches in cross-cultural psychology. In H. C. Triandis & W. W. Lambert (eds.) *Handbook of cross-cultural psychology, Vol. 1*. Boston: Allyn & Bacon.

Jaspars, J. F. M. and De Leeuw, J. A. (1980) Genetic-environmental covariation in human behavioural genetics. In L. J. T. Van Der Kamp, W. F. Langerak, & D. N. M. De Gruijter (Eds.) *Psychometrics for educational debates*. New York: Wiley.

Jensen, A. R. (1969) How much can we boost IQ and scholastic achievement. *Harvard Educational Review*, **39**, 1–123.

Jensen, A. R. (1972) *Genetics and education*. London: Methuen.

Katz, I. (1973a) Alternatives to a personality-deficit interpretation of negro underachievement. In P. Watson (Ed.) *Psychology and race*. Harmondsworth: Penguin Books.

Katz, I. (1973b) Negro performance in interracial situations. In P. Watson (Ed.) *Psychology and race*. Harmondsworth: Penguin Books.

Kelley, H. H. and Thibaut, J. W. (1969) Group problem solving. In G. Lindzey & E. Aronson

(Eds.) *Handbook of social psychology*, Vol. 4. Cambridge, Mass.: Addison Wesley.

Kohlberg, L. (1966) A cognitive-developmental analysis of children's sex-role concepts and attitudes. In E. E. Maccoby (Ed.) *The development of sex differences*. Palo Alto: Stanford University Press.

Kohlberg, L. and Ullian, D. Z. (1974) Stages in the development of psychosexual concepts and attitudes. In R. C. Friedman, R. M. Richart, & R. L. Vande Wiele (Eds.) *Sex differences in behaviour*. New York: Wiley.

Konrad, G., and Szelenyi, I. (1979) *La marche au pouvoir des intellectuels*. Paris: Editions du Seuil.

Kuhn, D. (1972) Mechanisms of change in the development of cognitive structures. *Child Development*, **43**, 833–844.

Lane, I. M. and Coon, R. C. (1972) Reward allocation in preschool children. *Child Development*, **43**, 1382–1389.

Laughlin, P. R. and Jacquard, J. J. (1975) Social facilitation and observational learning of individuals and cooperative pairs. *Journal of Personality and Social Psychology*, **32**, 873–879.

Laughlin, P. R. and Sweeney, J. D. (1977) Individual-to-group and group-to-individual transfer in problem-solving. *Journal of Experimental Psychology, Human Learning and Memory*, **3**, 246–254.

Laurendeau, M. and Pinard, A. (1970) *The development of the concept of space in the child*. New York: International Universities Press.

Leach, C. (1979) *Introduction to statistics*. Chichester: Wiley.

Lefebvre, M. and Pinard, A. (1972) Apprentissage de la conservation des quantités par une méthode de conflict cognitif. *Revue Canadienne des Sciences du Comportement*, **4**, 1–12.

Leontiev, A. N. (1970–1971) Le mécanisme de la coordination des fonctions notirces inter-dépendantes réparties entre divers sujets. *Bulletin de Psychologie*, **24**, 693–696.

Leontiev, A. (1976) *Le développement du psychisme*. Paris: Editions Sociales.

Lerner, M. J. (1974) The moral motive; equity and fairness among children. *Journal of Personality and Social Psychology*, **29**, 539–550.

Leventhal, G. S. and Anderson, D. (1970) Self-interest and the maintenance of equity. *Journal of Personality and Social Psychology*, **15**, 57–62.

Leventhal, G. S., Popp, A. L. and Sawyer, L. (1973) Equity or equality in children's allocation of reward to other persons? *Child Development*, **44**, 753–763.

Lévy, M. (1981) *La nécessité sociale de dépasser une situation conflictuelle générée par la présentation d'un modèle de solution de problème et par le questionnement d'un agent social*. Doctoral Thesis, University of Geneva.

Lomov, B. F. (1979) Mental processes and communication. In L. H. Strickland (Ed.) *Soviet and Western perspectives in social psychology*. Oxford: Pergamon Press.

Longeot, F. (1978) *Les stades opératoires de Piaget et les facteurs de l'intelligence*. Grenoble: Presses Universitaires de Grenoble.

Lukes, S. (1975) *Emile Durkheim, His life and work*. London: Allen Lane, The Penguin Press.

Luria, A. R. (1976) *Cognitive development: its cultural and social foundations*. Cambridge, Mass.: Harvard University Press.

Mackie, D. (1980) A cross-cultural study of intra-individual and inter-individual conflicts of centrations. *European Journal of Social Psychology*, **10**, 313–318.

Mackie, D. (1983) The effect of social interaction on conservation of spatial relations. *Journal of cross-cultural Psychology*, **94**, 131–151.

Madsen, M. C. (1967) Cooperative and competitive motivation of children in three Mexican sub-cultures. *Psychological Reports*, **20**, 1307–1320.

Mead, G. H. (1934) *Mind, self and society*. Chicago: University of Chicago Press.

Mendel, G. (1977) *La chasse structurale*. Paris: Petite Bibliotheque Payot

Miller, S. A. and Brownell, C. A. (1975) Peers, persuasion and Piaget: dyadic interaction between conservers and non-conservers. *Child Development*, **46**, 992–997.

Moessinger, P. (1974) Etude génétique d' échange. *Cahiers de Psychologie*, **17**, 119–123.

Moessinger, P. (1975) Developmental study of fair division and property. *European Journal of Social Psychology*, **5**, 385–394.

Moscovici, S. (1961) *La psychanalyse, son image et son public*. Paris: PUF.

Moscovici, S. (1968) *Essai sur l'histoire humaine de la nature*. Paris: Flammarion.

Moscovici, S. (1976) *Society against nature*. Brighton: Harvester.

Moscovici, S. and Paicheler, G. (1973) Travail, individu et groupe. In S. Moscovici (Ed.) *Introduction à la psychologie sociale*. Vol. 2. Paris: Larousse.

Moscovici, S. and Ricateau, P. (1972) Conformité, minorité et influence sociale. in S. Moscovici (Ed.) *Introduction à la psychologie sociale*. Vol. 1. Paris: Larousse.

Mugny, G. and Doise, W. (1978) Socio-cognitive conflict and structuration of individual and collective performances. *European Journal of Social Psychology*, **8**, 181–192.

Mugny, G. and Doise, W. (1978) Factores sociologicos y psicosociologicos del desarrollo cognitivo. *Anuario de Psicologia*, **18**, 22–40.

Mugny, G. and Doise, W. (1979) Factores sociologicos y psicosociologicos del desarrollo cognitivo: une nueva ilustracion experimental. *Anuario de Psicologia*, **21**, 4–25.

Mugny, G., Doise, W. and Perret-Clermont, A.-N. (1975–76) Conflit de centrations et progrès cognitif. *Bulletin de Psychologie*, **29**, 199–204.

Mugny, G., Giroud, J. C. and Doise, W. (1978–79) Conflit de centrations et progrès cognitif, II: Nouvelles illustrations expérimentales. *Bulletin de Psychologie*, **32**, 979–985.

Mugny, G., Lévy, M. and Doise, W. (1978) Conflit sociocognitif et développement cognitif. *Revue Suisse de Psychologie Pure et Appliquée*. **37**, 22–43.

Mugny, G. and Rilliet, D. Travail individuel ou collectif, et marquage social. In preparation.

Murphy, C. M. and Messer, D. J. (1977) Mothers, infants and pointing: a study of a gesture. In H. R. Schaffer (Ed.) *Studies in mother–infant interaction*. London: Academic Press.

Murray, F. B. (1972) Acquisition of conservation through social interaction. *Developmental Psychology*, **6**, 1–6.

Murray, J. P. (1974) Social learning and cognitive development: Modelling effects on children's understanding of conservation. *British Journal of Psychology*, **65**, 151–160.

Nielsen, R. F. (1951) *Le développement de la sociabilité chez l'enfant*. Neuchâtel: Delachaux & Niestlé.

Perret-Clermont, A.-N. (1980a) *Social interaction and cognitive development in children*. London: Academic Press.

Perret-Clermont, A.-N. (1980b) *Recherche au Tessin: Premiers résultats*. Unpublished University of Geneva Research Report.

Piaget, J. (1932) *The moral judgment of the child*. London: Routledge & Kegan Paul.

Piaget, J. (1950) *The psychology of intelligence*. London: Routledge & Kegan Paul.

Piaget, J. (1952) *Play, dreams and imitation in childhood*. New York: Norton.

Piaget, J. (1965) *Etudes sociologiques*. Geneva: Droz.

Piaget, J. (1966) Nécessité et signification des recherches comparatives en psychologie génétique. *International Journal of Psychology*, **1**, 3–13.

Piaget, J. (1967) *Biologie et connaissance*. Paris: Gallimard.

Piaget, J. (1970) *Psychologie et épistémologie*. Paris: Gonthier.

Piaget, J. (1976) Postscript. *Archives de Psychologie*, **44**, 223–228.

Piaget, J. (1976b) L'individualité en histoire: l'individu et la formation de la raison. In G. Busino (Ed.) *Les sciences sociales avec et apres Jean Piaget*. Geneva: Droz.

Piaget, J. (1976c) Problémes de la psycho-sociologie de l'enfance. In G. Busino (Ed.) *Les sciences sociales avec et après Jean Piaget*. Geneva: Droz.

Piaget, J. (1976d) Logique génétique et sociologie. In G. Busino (Ed.) *Les sciences sociales avec et après Jean Piaget*. Geneva: Droz.

Piaget, J. (1977) *The development of thought: Equilibration of cognitive structures*. New York: Viking Penguin.

Piaget, J. (1980) *Adaptation and intelligence: Organic selection and phenocopy*. Chicago: University of Chicago Press.

Piaget, J. and Inhelder, B. (1952) *The child's conception of space*. London: Routledge & Kegan Paul.

Piaget, J. and Szeminska, A. (1952) *The child's conception of number*. London: Routledge & Kegan Paul.

Piattelli-Palmarini, M. (Ed.) (1980) *Language and learning: the debate between Jean Piaget and Noam Chomsky*. London: Routledge & Kegan Paul.

Pinxten, W. J. L. and Bressers, I. W. M. (1979) Rechtvaardigheid en cognitieve ontwikkeling. Tilberg: Katholieke Hogeschool, Subfaculteit Psychologie.

Rijsman, J. B., Zoetebier, J. H. T., Ginther, A. J. F. and Doise, W. (1980) Sociocognitief conflict en cognitieve ontwikkeling. *Pedagogische Studien*, **57**, 125–133.

Robert, M. and Charbonneau, C. (1977) Extinction of liquid conservation by observation: effects of model's age and presence. *Child Development,* **48,** 648–652.

Robert, M. and Charbonneau, C. (1978) Extinction of liquid conservation by modelling: three indicators of its artificiality. *Child Development,* **49,** 194–200.

Robert, M. and Charbonneau, C. (1979) Effet de l'énoncé d'un problème d'inégalité sur l'aquisition de la conservation par observation. *L'Année Psychologique,* **79,** 393–409.

Rosenthal, T. L. and Zimmerman, B. J. (1972) Modelling by exemplification and interaction in training conservation. *Developmental Psychology,* **6,** 392–401.

Schaffer, H. R. (1977) *Studies in mother–child interaction.* London: Academic Press.

Schaffer, H. R. (1978) Lo sviluppo della competenza interattiva nell' infanzia. In A. Palmonari & P. E. Ricci Bitti (Eds.) *Aspetti cognitivi della socializzazione in eta evolutiva.* Bologna: Il Mulino.

Silverman, I. W. and Geiringer, E. (1973) Dyadic interaction and conservation inducation: A test of Piaget's equilibration model. *Child Development,* **44,** 815–820.

Silverman, I. W. and Stone, J. M. (1972) Modifying cognitive functioning through participation in a problem-solving group. *Journal of Educational Psychology,* **63,** 603–608.

Skinner, B. F. (1957) The Experimental analysis of behavior. *American Scientist,* **45,** 343–371.

Smedslund, J. (1966) Les origines sociales de la décentration. In F. Bresson & H. de Montmollin (Eds.) *Psychologie et épistémologie génétiques, thèmes Piagétiens.* Paris: Dunod.

Stenhouse, D. (1973) *The evolution of intelligence.* London: Allen & Unwin.

Stenhouse, D. (1976–77) Evolutionary, adaptive and ethological considerations in the assessment of intelligence. *Interchange,* **7.**

Strauss, S. and Langer, J. (1970) Operational thought inducement. *Child Development,* **41,** 163–175.

Swerts, A. (1978) De billijkheidstheorie: Literatuurstudie en een experimenteel obderzoek bij kinderen. Leuven: Katholieke Universiteit, Faculteit der psychologie en pedagogische Wetenschappen.

Tarde, G. (1898) *Etudes de psychologie sociale.* Paris: Giard & Brière.

Triplett, N. (1898) The dynamogenic factors in pacemaking and competition. *American Journal of Psychology,* **9,** 507–533.

Van de Voort, W. (1977) Interaktion und kognition. Frankfurt: Fachbereich Gesellschafts-Wissenschaften, Johann Wolfgang GoetheUniversitat.

Vygotsky, L. S. (1962) *Thought and Language.* Cambridge, Mass.: MIT Press.

Vygotsky, L. S. (1978) *Mind in society: the development of higher psychological processes.* Cambridge, Mass.: Harvard University Press.

Waghorn, L. and Sullivan, E. (1970) The exploration of transition rules in conservation of quantity (substance) using film mediated modelling. *Acta Psychologica,* **32,** 65–80.

Waller, M. (1978) *Soziales Lernen und Interaktionskompetenz,* Stuttgart: Klett-Cotta.

Witkin, H. A. (1967) A cognitive-style approach to cross-cultural research. *International Journal of Psychology,* **2,** 233–250.

Witkin, H. A. and Berry, J. (1975) Psychological differentiation in cross- cultural perspective. *Journal of Cross-cultural Psychology,* **6,** 4–87.

Wundt, W. (1907) *Outlines of Psychology.* Leipzig: Wilhelm Engelmann.

Zajonc, R. B. (1965) Social facilitation. *Science,* **149,** 269–274.

Zigler, E. and Butterfield, E. C. (1968) Motivational aspects of changes in IQ test performance of culturally deprived nursery school children. *Child Development,* **39,** 1–14.

Zimmerman, B. J. and Lanaro, P. (1974) Acquiring and retaining conservation of length through modelling and reversibility cues. *Merril-Palmer Quarterly of Behaviour and Development,* **20,** 145–161.

Zoetebier, J. H. T. and Ginther, T. J. F. (1978) *Sociale interactie en cognitive ontwikkeling.* Tilburg: Katholieke Hogeschool, Subfaculteit Psychologie.

Author Index